FIELDWORK FOR
ARCHAEOLOGISTS
AND LOCAL HISTORIANS

Anthony Brown

FIELDWORK FOR ARCHAEOLOGISTS AND LOCAL HISTORIANS

B. T. BATSFORD   LONDON

CATO SILVESTRI

Anchor Brendon Ltd
Tiptree, Essex

Typeset by Keyspools Ltd
and printed in Great Britain by

Anchor Brendon Ltd
Tiptree, Essex

for the publishers
B. T. Batsford Ltd
4 Fitzhardinge Street
London W1H 0AH

Brown, A. E.
    Fieldwork for archaeologists and local historians.
    1. Archaeology—Field work
    I. Title
    930.1′028   CC76

    ISBN 0—7134—4841—5
    ISBN 0—7134—4842—3 Pbk

Contents

Acknowledgements

For permission to reproduce illustrations the author wishes to thank the following people and institutions: Tom Williamson and the Society for the Promotion of Roman Studies (Figs 5, 16); the County Record Office, Huntingdon (Fig 64(b) and (c)); Clive Hart (Figs 39, 45); Andrew Fleming and the Society for Medieval Archaeology (Fig 21); Commander L. M. M. Saunders Watson (Fig 68); the County Record Office, Northampton (Figs 63, 67); University of Cambridge Committee for Aerial Photography (Fig 76); Don Spratt and the Yorkshire Archaeological Society (Fig 41); the Trent and Peak Archaeological Trust (Fig 14); the Royal Commission on the Historical Monuments of England (Figs 27, 34, 37, 43); Colm O'Brien and the Thoroton Society of Nottinghamshire (Fig 51); Professor George Jobey and the Society of Antiquaries of Newcastle upon Tyne (Fig 52); Mike Allen and the Sussex Archaeological Society (Fig 13); Martin Tingle, Vince and Christopher Gaffney (Fig 6); Stephen Shennan (Fig 4); Peter Wade-Martins (Fig 65); Richard Bradley and Steve Ford (Fig 15); James Bond (Fig 30); Paul Barford (Fig 1); Paul Stamper (Fig 38); the Ministry of Defence (Fig 3(a)). For help with drawings the author wishes to express his thanks to Susan Phillips (Figs 7, 66, 72, 75), Peter Taylor (Figs 9, 11, 32, 71) and Ed Dennison (Figs 36, 49); and for other assistance to Chris Taylor and Graham Webster. Most of the unacknowledged figures are the product of field projects carried out under the auspices of the Department of Adult Education of the University of Leicester.

List of illustrations

Introduction

This study concerns basic techniques of archaeological fieldwork (defined as the examination and recording of the surviving remains of past human activity without excavation). This kind of topographical research has had a long and distinguished history in Britain, with roots stretching back as far as William of Worcester in the fifteenth century – long before anyone seriously thought of excavation as a method of extracting information about the past as distinct from the acquisition of valuable or curious objects.

Nevertheless, the current popular image of the archaeologist is still that of the excavator. Newspaper reports of current developments in the subject almost invariably consist of accounts of excavations, and it is quite easy to see why; excavations produce objects, sometimes quite striking ones, and the plans of structures readily comprehensible to the eye. What is more, many modern excavations really are quite spectacular: large-scale, open-plan operations carried out, sometimes over long periods, by full-time specialists with back-up techniques of ever-increasing sophistication to cope with the thousands of finds, environmental material, animal bones and so on. All this has developed relatively rapidly in Britain because of the necessity for rescue archaeology – recovering and recording evidence about the past before it is lost in the face of modern developments, mainly urban and industrial.

In general, the techniques of the fieldworker (who does tend to operate in a more rural environment) have for years remained relatively static. An exception to this, however, is the growth in the use of aerial photography, where modern technology has begun to make its influence felt with the development of machines for the rectification of photographic images and computer-assisted plotting. Ground survey has also begun to feel the impact of new approaches in the form of laser- and computer-assisted mapping techniques. The high cost of such equipment, however, means that it is to be found only in the hands of professional workers paid for out of public funds.

Another feature of the development of archaeology in Britain has been the active involvement of amateur workers at the local level from the beginning; consider the establishment and maintenance of the impressive runs of county archaeological journals for example. The technological advances referred to above should not be allowed to obscure the fact that the ordinary amateur fieldworker can still make a valuable contribution; the main aim of this book is to show how this can be done using extremely simple and inexpensive equipment and making use of what the enthusiast can offer – detailed local knowledge, and a substantial input of time. Indeed, there can quite quickly come a point in anyone's fieldwork when the technology ceases to be useful and the traditional attributes of powers of observation, persistence, shrewdness, patience and enthusiasm are the ones required; we are dealing with an art, not a science.

Local history and archaeology are both aspects of the study of the past and it is natural for them to be linked together; a high proportion of the county journals referred to above are not simply archaeological ones, but contain local historical material as well. An important area in which local historical studies – using both maps and documents – and archaeology can together make a profitable contribution is that of topographical work. This involves not just looking at sites, important though that is, but also placing them in the context of the landscape in which they are found. Indeed, it is now commonplace to say that it is the landscape itself which ought to be the proper subject of study, and this wider study should be used not so much as an end in itself but as a means of finding out about and understanding the people who fashioned the world in which we live. So although we will study the basic matters of recording and interpretation at site level, the student must always remember the benefits of taking a wider approach.

The need for fieldwork is obvious; the discovery, planning, description and analysis of archaeological sites, taking the term in the widest possible sense, is essential if our knowledge of the past is to be advanced. Fieldwork has its own distinctive contribution to make since it is the *only* way to advance certain types of archaeological problem; it also provides the vital information from which judgements about the application of such expensive techniques as excavation can be taken. Even in the medieval and post-medieval periods, for which abundant documentation is available, the techniques of survey and analysis described here have a unique contribution to make which both adds to and acts as an essential corrective to the purely historical sources. For the medieval period, one has only to consider the role of fieldwork in the understanding of the development of settlement patterns; for the post-medieval period an example can be taken from the relatively recent realization of the contribution fieldwork can make to the history of garden design (compare, for example, Strong 1979 with Taylor 1983b).

At a more immediate level, the need to record before destruction is as great as it ever was. New housing estates, factories, mineral extraction developments and roads continue to take their toll of our ancient landscapes, and although the official mechanisms available for the production of a record before destruction caused by the more spectacular agencies are better than they were, say, fifteen years ago, the resources available will never really match the magnitude of the task. Greater still is the need for vigilance in the countryside where small, piecemeal developments in villages and fields can blot out unappreciated evidence of the greatest topographical significance almost before anyone has noticed that it has happened. Such destruction can

sometimes be unwitting and casual, but no less serious for that. For example, it was not until 1978 that the Bronze Age origin of the stone cairns on the Brecon Beacons was appreciated. Most members of the public had no conception of their importance and tended to regard them as the handiwork of recent walkers; they had no compunction in throwing the stones about or removing the cairns and rebuilding them elsewhere (Briggs 1984). At a wider level, the total transformation of the agrarian landscape in the interests of commercial farming can create problems of recording which local authority archaeologists may well find difficult to handle, but which a well-placed local worker might be able to deal with.

Even areas which have been the subject of intensive and well-reported archaeological activity still have much to offer. It is still possible to make striking new discoveries: a brand new round barrow well over 1 m (3 ft) high turned up at Bawsey in Norfolk in 1980, just too late to be included in an important descriptive list of this type of field monument in East Anglia (Wymer 1985); the site of a deserted medieval village adjacent to the important and well-known castle at Stafford was not noticed until 1975; an *oppidum* of 12 ha (30 acres) at Loose in Kent was not recognized for what it was until the late 1960s (Kelly 1971). Sites which have been known about for years can sometimes be looked at anew with profit; at Tilshead in Wiltshire, for example, an earthwork which has appeared on Ordnance maps as a long barrow since the 1930s has now been shown, as a result of careful ground examination, to be part of a Romano-British settlement (Borthwick and Hartgroves 1982). As a further example, one may take the work of the Royal Commission on the Historical Monuments of England, which has been producing inventories of historical monuments on a county basis since 1908. These impressive volumes, with their high standards of recording, description and cartographic presentation, are justly famous, and there is a tendency to regard them as *the* definitive statement about the field archaeology of the areas to which they relate. But this is simply not true. To begin with, there are relatively few of them; only about one-quarter of the country has been covered, mostly in pre-war volumes which concentrated more on architectural remains than on earthworks and had a terminal period date of 1700. More recent volumes have had later terminal dates and much greater concern with field remains and the results of aerial photography; but here again many of the smaller earthworks and some of the larger ones may not have been planned. Of necessity, the documentary work operates at a preliminary level; some wider landscape issues, such as medieval field systems, are only touched upon, and little original fieldwalking is done. These volumes should properly be regarded as the starting point for future original field research.

The study of the British landscape has made great strides in recent years, as a number of important recent studies reveal (Taylor 1983a; Aston 1985; Rackham 1986). The fundamental work is, of course, Professor W. G. Hoskins' *The making of the English landscape*, first published in 1955. These books show that the satisfactory study of the landscape requires many disciplines in addition to archaeology: geology; the analysis of buildings; the study of vegetation in hedgerows and woodlands, and the knowledge of climatic and environmental change in the past. All these things are as relevant to field archaeology as the pottery and flint scatters and earthworks which form the subject of this volume.

1 Preparing for fieldwork

The most important matters which the would-be fieldworker or fieldwork group must decide upon are precisely what their objectives are to be, and where to get experience. To some extent, the answer to the former may come out of the latter. Most of the country is now covered by one of the archaeological units set up in the 1970s as part of the response to the wholesale destruction of archaeological sites then recognized. The primary contact ought to be with one of them (the National Monuments Record can supply addresses; p.147). Most units will embody a sites and monuments record, which in greater or lesser detail contains information about the antiquities of its area. In England and Wales there are just over fifty such records, located more often than not in the County Planning Office but sometimes as part of the museum service or Amenities Department, or even the County Secretary's Department. The local record will be in the care of an officer who better than anyone else ought to know what survey work is in progress in his area and what tasks most need to be done in the immediate future, particularly in relation to development schemes, construction of bypasses, road widening and village infill. He may well be able to include interested people in his own programme and provide on-the-job training, or suggest experienced workers who may be able to help with advice. Most university extra-mural departments and some WEA districts offer courses in fieldwork as part of their programmes (details of these are made available in the newsletter *British Archaeological News*, published regularly by the Council for British Archaeology: address, p.147 Books are a useful starting point, but are no substitute for field experience – looking at neatly drawn-up plans in a publication is instructive, but seeing the same sites on a rainy day, encumbered maybe by undergrowth, fallen trees or barbed wire – may be something of a shock; some sites daunt by their sheer size and apparent complexity.

The day may come, however, when the fieldworker will wish to concern himself not so much with responding to threats but with conducting research on his own. Three broad, interrelated approaches can be identified. The first may involve an attempt to answer a specific question or set of questions about the landscape. For example, the fieldworker may wish to discover whether it is really true that in the third or second millennium BC occupation was almost exclusively on the lighter soils as opposed to the clays in his area; he may wish to test hypotheses put forward on general theoretical grounds for the developing pattern of land use in his region and to see whether these are in fact borne out by fieldwork; or he may wish to examine the pattern of early Anglo-Saxon occupation in relation to the late Roman one. An alternative approach would be to concentrate upon a particular field monument type – for example, by producing plans of the moated sites or deserted villages of an area and relating this work to the relevant documentation, or by assessing the light fieldwork can shed upon the functions and possibly the date of the cross-ridge dykes of a given area of chalk downland. A rather similar line of work might be to examine the field archaeology of a given medieval monastic or lay estate. A third approach is to consider the field archaeology of a block of land and to analyse that, for all periods. This has much to recommend it for the local worker who can use his knowledge of the locality to the fullest extent. Fieldwork which is restricted to a limited chronological range will inevitably take in features which are earlier and later anyway and which ought to be given due weight; the landscape is a developing continuum and should be studied as such. Also, even within one period the various elements in the landscape lock together as part of a single economic and social system and it can be misleading to concentrate on one aspect to the exclusion of the others. Whatever approach is finally chosen, a sensible programme of work has to be arrived at in advance which can be seen to contribute in a useful way to the broader development of the subject. The countryside of Britain is so full of the remains of past activity that almost any descent upon it will come away with something, but for the most fruitful results an objective and a plan designed to realize it are always necessary, although the possibility of revision in the light of experience must always be borne in mind. It is important not to undertake too much, otherwise a fieldwork project can come to resemble so many excavations and remain incomplete and unpublished.

Certain basic initial requirements must be met in the form of a supply of Ordnance Survey maps. The small-scale maps are commonly available, but larger scales have to be obtained from one of the Ordnance Survey agents (details of these are obtainable from the Ordnance Survey itself, p.147). The 1:50,000 Landranger series maps have a few antiquities marked in a generalized way but have too small a scale to show details; they lack the important asset of parish boundaries which the old one-inch (1:63,360) series used to have. But they are useful for finding one's way about; they have contours, given in metres but actually at a vertical interval of 50 feet, which show the general lie of the land; their scale is sufficiently small to enable them to act as broad indicators of variations in the axes of communication at various times in the past, and they are helpful in tracing old roads; they give a good general impression of areas of woodland, moorland, etc. The 1:25,000 series is essential; clear, beautifully produced, they have field boundaries, parish boundaries, the National Grid on a reasonably fine mesh and, most importantly from the point of view of preliminary work, footpaths and bridleways with public rights of way marked in green. The smallest practicable scale for actual field drawing is the 1:10,000 series, replacing the old six-inch series (1:10,560); certain types of archaeological

feature, say, linear earthworks, medieval field systems, stone and pottery scatters, can be plotted directly on to these, but in these instances such maps enlarged photographically or by copying machine to twice their size are better. In the absence of such aids the process can be carried out manually by means of grids of squares drawn at appropriate sizes, but this can be a tedious process, except for small areas (p.49). It is, however, a useful technique, especially for the transference of contours from these maps to plans drawn at larger scales. On the old six-inch maps the contours were drawn at a vertical interval of 25 feet; on the 1:10,000 series the contours are at 10 m ($32\frac{1}{2}$ ft) intervals in mountainous areas but a useful 5 m (16 ft) interval elsewhere. The 1:10,000 series provides a most convenient scale for the broad topographical analysis of landscapes. Twenty-five-inch (1:2,500) maps *can* be used for the direct detailed plotting of earthwork sites but, as will be explained later, really need to be enlarged to twice their size to give a scale of 1:1,250 (maps of this scale exist for urban areas anyway). It is these maps and the enlargements derived from them which provide the initial control of modern field boundaries, buildings, roads and the like which are the essential framework for all archaeological field drawings. Needless to say, all Ordnance maps enable the direction of true north to be worked out easily.

Geological maps, solid and drift, published by the Ordnance Survey for the Institute of Geological Sciences at a scale of 1:50,000 and 1:63,360 are available from Ordnance Survey agents. These maps are of necessity broad in their depiction of geological details; arrangements can be made to visit the British Geological Survey (address, p.147) to secure tracings of the original 1:10,000 or 1:10,560 maps which represent the original survey work. The memoirs which accompany some of the maps are also valuable, as are also on occasion the small number of 1:63,360 and 1:25,000 maps published by the Ordnance Survey for the Soil Survey of England and Wales. This basic kind of geological knowledge is essential; just why settlement came to be located in a certain place and developed as it did will have been the outcome of a vast range of factors, but the geological background will certainly have been one of them. Such matters as the location of spring lines, or the

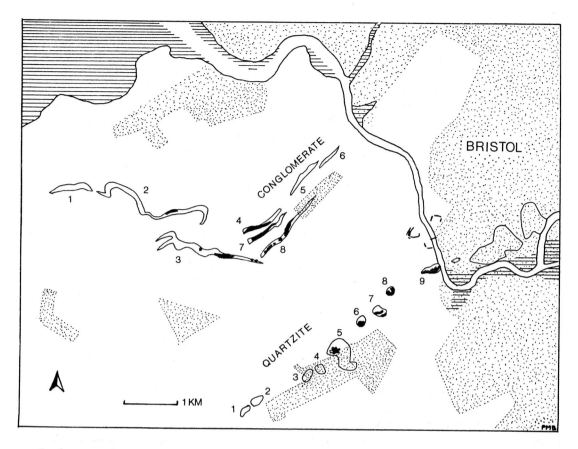

1 *Conglomerate and quartzite exposures to the west of Bristol. Quarried areas are blacked, built-up areas stippled.*

existence of patches of light glacial gravel in otherwise clayey zones, will always have exerted an influence. On occasion an appreciation of geological conditions can be a help in the search for specific kinds of site, or sites of a certain date. There is still abundant scope for the discovery of new Palaeolithic cave sites in geologically appropriate parts of the country; for example, in the Wye valley, in the limestone portion of the Peak District, the limestone falls into two categories, a heavy, hard variety and a softer, coral reef kind; the identification and examination of outcrops of the latter may well be profitable in a search for Palaeolithic shelter sites and the material washed out from them (Hart 1981, 21). Some ancient industrial processes can be related to the appropriate geological deposits in a very direct way. For example, many of the Iron Age and Roman querns found in the Bristol area are known to have been made from quartzitic and conglome-

rate rocks. The exposures of these rocks are limited and identifiable from geological maps (Fig. 1); examination of them suggests that quarrying has indeed taken place in the past, no doubt for building stone but also probably for querns, since what looked like waste flakes and roughouts of quartzite have been found (Barford 1984).

The fieldworker will also have to acquaint himself with recent work by geomorphologists, pollen analysts and other environmental specialists which seeks to explain the changes which have taken place in the natural environment of the country during the last three millennia (Thompson 1980; Jones and Dimbleby 1981; Simmons and Tooley 1981). In places, these have been considerable. Coastal erosion may mean that some sites have been swept away or become drowned, and due allowance for this will have to be made in assessing the significance of the ones left behind. Elsewhere build-up will have separated sites from the sea which was once their raison d'être; the Roman Saxon Shore forts of Lympne in Kent or Burgh Castle in Norfolk are obvious examples. The recovery of old coastlines can explain the location of some sites; concentrations of Mesolithic flints in certain parts of Somerset can now be seen to relate to formerly much more extensive river estuaries (Norman 1982, 16). Similarly work on old coastlines can help in the location of sites. As recent work on the island of Jura in the Inner Hebrides has indicated, sequences of raised beaches not only provide an essential dating mechanism but, since Mesolithic encampments lay along the shoreline, the identification of the beaches was the essential first step in the discovery of the archaeological sites (Searight 1984). An unfinished fortress taken by the Danes in AD 892 has been equated with the earthwork known as Castle Toll at Newenden in Kent, but a more recent appreciation of the true coastline at that time means that this site no longer fits the topographical description given in the *Anglo-Saxon Chronicle* and a new location has to be sought, possibly Rye in Sussex (Kitchen 1984). Elsewhere the development of sand dunes has been shown to have covered a wide range of archaeological features, as at Gwithian in Cornwall.

In the fens of the east of England, detailed palaeobotanical, geological and archaeological work extending over decades has produced a very complicated sequence of development involving a series of marine incursions resulting in the deposition of clays and silts alternating with freshwater peat formation, as well as the creation of sheets of alluvium. In places these deposits cover ancient occupation surfaces. To locate these a survey programme involving the examination of the sides of recut and cleared drainage dykes was instigated, with astonishing results – dykes cutting the Fen Clay deposited c. 2500 BC enabled the underlying Mesolithic and early Neolithic deposits, including flints and postholes, to be reached; perhaps as much as ten square kilometres of very early landscape remains buried. A dyke cutting later alluvium east of Peterborough permitted the discovery of a well-preserved waterlogged late Bronze Age timber structure (Pryor 1983 a and b).

Trees, later cleared by man, once clothed such now waste uplands as Dartmoor, the gritstone East Moor region of the Peak District (the Dark Peak), the Pennines, the Lake District and elsewhere. This not only explains the wealth of mainly Bronze Age monuments to be found in what are now moorland locations but also means that every opportunity should be taken to recover artefacts of earlier, Mesolithic phases in disturbances in the soil – the sides of gullies, erosion patches and opportunities presented by windblows and heath fires should be watched for. The possibility that some valleys once contained lakes held back by moraines of the late Pleistocene should always be borne in mind; such localities would have provided favoured hunting and fishing locations for Mesolithic man, and fieldwork around their presumed edges might produce worthwhile results. The Mesolithic site at Sandbeds, Otley, West Yorkshire is an example of a site in such a location (Yarwood 1981, 36).

Whatever type of survey work is contemplated, material about earlier archaeological discoveries will have to be accumulated and studied. The county Sites and Monuments Record ought at least to provide a summary guide to this; many records are now computerized to aid the retrieval of information and should be expected to provide answers to questions about the existence of field monuments of particular periods and types, or the distribution and nature of sites in particular parishes or Ordnance Survey 1:10,000 sheets. There may also be all sorts of supplementary information – certainly a set of Ordnance Survey record cards, with the back-up plans sometimes produced for inclusion on Ordnance Survey maps; these cards constituted the primary basic record for the area initially and the Sites and Monuments Record was probably built up around them in the first place. There may also be original surveys, records of recent observations, maps with fieldname and geological information, files on a variety of different topics. There should also be references to the older literature somewhere in the system. These references will have to be followed up eventually and the information so accumulated systematically filed. In the absence of finding aids derived from the Sites and Monuments Record, for information about excavation reports, earlier surveys and general accounts of artefact or field monument types published since 1940 the fieldworker will need access to the annual *Archaeological Bulletins* or *Bibliographies* produced by the Council for British Archaeology and also since 1968 to the CBA *British Archaeological Abstracts* series (the two are now, alas, combined). For material published before 1940 and in the absence of a Royal Commission volume, the initial volume of the *Victoria County History* of an area will contain summaries of the current state of archaeological knowledge at the time the volume was produced, with references to the earlier literature, as well as lists of earthworks then recognized and classified according to the scheme put forward by the Earthworks Committee of the Congress of Archaeological Societies. For material published between the appearance of the *VCH* and 1940 there is no alternative but to work through the volumes of the county or local archaeological and historical societies. Collections of other local printed material in county library local history sections can also be rewarding on occasions since minor publications, pamphlets, guides and duplicated reports can contain useful and out-of-the-way information, although a great deal of the material one comes across in these sources is derivative and repetitious. Old newspaper accounts are a valuable contemporary source about old discoveries, but working through runs of old newspapers is tedious and almost an entire research project in its own right.

The older antiquarian literature, county histories and the like, will be a mixed bag. Sometimes this kind of record will constitute the only source of information about a now-vanished site. An oval earthwork known as Stainbarrow Camp in Notgrove parish (Gloucestershire) was marked on Isaac Taylor's map of Gloucestershire, published in 1777, and on Bryant's county map of 1824 as 'scite of Stone Barrow or Turk's Hill camp'. This is the only evidence for this now vanished site (RCHME 1976, 88). Descriptions produced by the late seventeenth- and early eighteenth-century antiquary Ralph Thoresby of an earthwork called by him Gyant's Hill in Armley township on the southern bank of the Aire in West Yorkshire include measurements and references to a 'circular camp' with a 'square below' and a 'rampire' – enough to suggest a motte and bailey or ringwork and bailey castle. The site has been destroyed by a canal and a factory; there is a single medieval documentary reference to it (Moorhouse 1981, 736–7). Unpublished notes by Richard Farringdon make it clear that a cairn, presumably Bronze Age in date, almost certainly existed on

the summit of Snowdon; other, early nineteenth-century, topographical writers imply that in common with other prehistoric mountain-top cairns it had been hollowed out to make a shelter, and was finally removed to build a hut below the summit (Crew 1983). Once their druidical overtones have been cleared away and the idiosyncratic system of measurement deciphered – Farringdon used an original system involving a cubit (about twenty inches) and a bowshot (just over a mile) – the manuscript notes of this late eighteenth-century Welsh clergyman preserved in the National Library of Wales can be seen to possess great value (Kelly 1974). Earlier records can also provide information about now-vanished aspects of well-known sites. At Sodbury Camp (Gloucestershire) the evidence for the further continuation beyond its present termination of a linear bank which exists to the northwest of the hillfort is to be found in a plan published in 1883–4 (RCHME 1976, 103).

Earlier accounts can lead to the rediscovery or re-identification of lost field monuments. At Horning in Norfolk a linear soil mark on an aerial photograph could be correlated with observations made in the early nineteenth century by a local antiquary, Samuel Woodward, whose correspondence survives in the Castle Museum, Norwich; this contained quite detailed references to an earthwork bank cutting off the peninsula between the rivers Bure and Ant on which Horning church stands. The continued but faint existence of this earthwork of unknown date was verified by ground inspection (Rose 1982). A second example concerns Sir Richard Colt Hoare, the celebrated barrow digger and author of *Ancient Wiltshire*, published in 1821. In the section of this devoted to the 'Roman Era' Hoare briefly refers to 'a square circumvallation' with 'many fragments of antique pottery' on the banks of the river Axe in Somerset, at the termination of a Roman road from Salisbury. He marked it on his published map; the site was given the fictitious name of Ad Axium. Much more information about this site could be derived from the unpublished journals of the Rev. John Skinner, preserved in the British Library; he visited the area several times from 1818 onwards, sometimes in the company of Colt Hoare. His accounts include sketches and much more detail, as well as references to extensive encampments on

Bleadon Hill nearby. It was possible to put the accounts of the two men together and locate the remains of the earthwork, still extant, and in places 2 m (6½ ft) high, among a series of modern houses; the 'encampments' on Bleadon Hill are a remarkable group of (probable) Roman fields (Evans and Richards 1984; Iles 1984a, 56).

Earlier accounts can often be usefully reinterpreted. 'An urn, red like coral with an inscription' from Sandy in Bedfordshire, mentioned in John Aubrey's *Monumenta Britannica*, can now be recognized as a vessel of the well-known samian ware (Simco 1984, 7). A curious item in the literature of Herefordshire field archaeology is a cruciform mound with an extreme length of 68 yards (61 m) which existed in Park Wood in the parish of St. Margaret's. This formed the subject of a long letter published in the *Gentleman's Magazine* in 1853; no explanation for it could be offered then and none has since appeared. The recent interpretation of a cruciform earthwork at Banwell in Avon as a rabbit warren may help us to understand the St. Margaret's earthwork (VCH 1908, 164–5; Iles 1984a, 57).

However, not all early accounts are as helpful as these. Many are simply too vague to be matched up with the sites visible today. For example, at Bottisham in Cambridgeshire a series of round barrows investigated some years ago cannot be correlated with any degree of certainty with barrows in the area mentioned in nineteenth-century antiquarian literature (RCHME 1972, 13). Some accounts are confused and a great deal of patience is needed to sort them out. Among the many bronzes dredged from the river Thames at Wallingford in the later nineteenth century were two socketed axes and two socketed knives – the latter referred to as spearheads in several accounts of the period, resulting in confusion with the genuine spearheads also found (Thomas 1984). Sometimes the record is simply bizarre; consider Fig. 2, showing an eighteenth-century plan of what we now understand to be the site of a shrunken medieval village (Nichols 1798). Or it can be downright wrong. A plan drawn in 1932 of the earthworks of the extraordinary formal garden laid out by Sir Thomas Tresham at the end of the sixteenth century at Lyveden in Northamptonshire clearly indicates that the western arm of the large moated enclosure had in fact been dug out

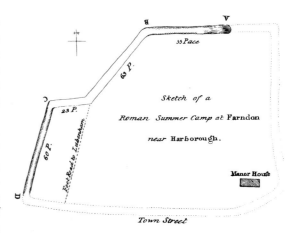

2   *The shrunken village of East Farndon in Northamptonshire, as depicted in 1798. The reality is shown by a recent field survey (right).*

and completed. Yet a fresh field survey showed that this was not the case; this arm had never been properly finished, and confusion probably arose over the remains of a medieval moat set eccentrically to the garden and looking extremely unlike the 1932 plan (Brown and Taylor 1972).

Old records are important, as the following example shows. Long low stone banks, called 'reaves', run for miles over the face of Dartmoor. As a result of recent research they are now known to be the remains of land boundaries of the second millennium BC. Andrew Fleming has shown how, round about the middle years of the nineteenth century, they came to be regarded as trackways; as time went on this view tended to prevail, as a result of repetition and copying, despite sensible observations by a handful of people. Understanding of and interest in these important features had declined to such an extent that archaeologists could until very recently regard a reave as a lynchet or as a medieval feature; yet familiarity with the literature would have shown that they had been correctly identified as prehistoric boundaries as early as the 1820s, as references in Samuel Rowe's *Perambulation of the Antient and Royal Forest of Dartmoor*, published in 1848, make clear (Fleming 1978).

Aerial photographs

These fall into two main groups. To begin with, there are non-archaeological air photographs, mainly verticals taken at various times by such

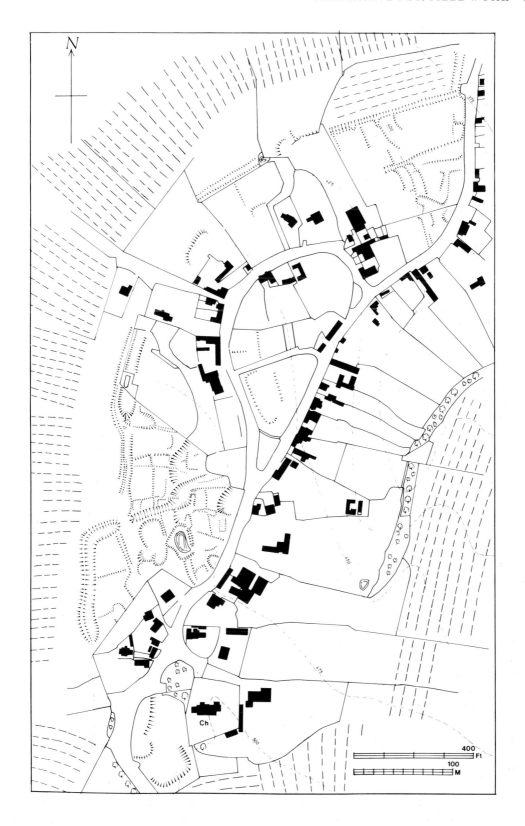

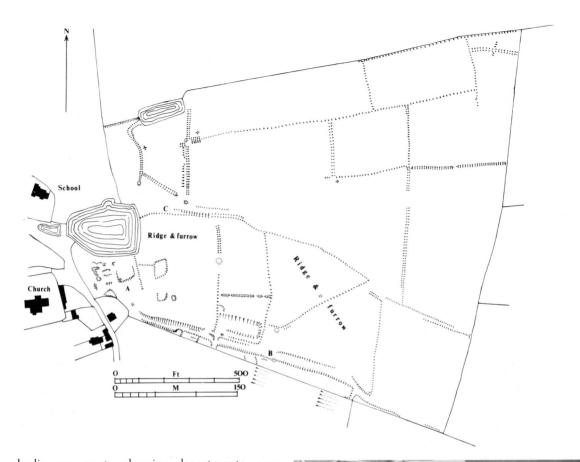

bodies as county planning departments, new town development corporations, and a variety of government departments for their own purposes. Pride of place will go to the country-wide vertical series flown in 1946–7 by the RAF at a scale of 1:10,000. Photographs of this kind may contain useful information about archaeological sites, mainly earthworks, in varying degrees of detail; they can quite often supply a general outline impression of earthworks subsequently destroyed or partly mutilated by agriculture, and on occasion will constitute the only source of information – in Lincolnshire, for example, the site of the lost village of Helethorpe in the parish of Fulnetby, under the plough for many years, was recorded only on the 1946 RAF vertical series (Everson 1983). Because they were intended to cover whole areas, photographs of this kind are particularly useful for general reconnaissance work and in providing blanket coverage of such widespread earthworks as ridge and furrow, saving enormously in time which otherwise would have been spent in ground plotting. But

3   *Part of the village of Clehonger in Hereford and Worcester can be seen in a non-archaeological vertical air photograph taken in 1946. (Crown copyright). A plan of the same area shows the earthworks, mainly of fields, which are scarcely visible on the air photograph. 'A' represents the site of a building; 'B' and 'C' will have been trackways.*

they by no means remove the need for checking and ground survey on a detailed basis, and experiences such as that illustrated in Figs 3(a) and (b) are common, and even where earthworks appear clearly there are quite often certain parts of the site which for one reason or another remain obscure.

Air photographs taken for specifically archaeological purposes, mainly oblique views, have obvious value in discovery and interpretation, as even the most casual glance at the literature will show. Crop marks continue to reveal sites, sometimes of new types, and whole landscapes pretty well invisible on the ground, and careful views of earthwork sites can provide fresh information and aid interpretation. The limitations of the crop-mark evidence are well known – generally speaking such marks are restricted in their formation to the lighter, free-draining soils, and a variety of factors will affect the way they appear on the photograph – depth of soil, the clarity of the atmosphere, the skill of the photographer, his presence at the right place at the right time, relatively minor details of local geology (Wilson 1975 and 1982). So not all areas will receive the benefit of this kind of evidence and even in places which do yield crop marks considerable gaps will occur caused by locally unresponsive fields, built-up areas, roads, woods and the absence of local cover; what is more, some well-known types of site can make a poor showing on crop-mark air photography. There are good photographs of Roman villas in our air photographic archives, but a recent detailed aerial survey of 450 square kilometres (173 square miles) of chalkland in Hampshire and Wiltshire, in which earlier work had led to the discovery of at least 25 Romano-British buildings, produced very little information about them indeed, but abundant soil and crop marks relating to enclosures, pits, ditches and fields dating back to the Neolithic (Palmer, R 1984). In the Popham area of Hampshire none of the known 14 Romano-British buildings could certainly be seen on air photographs (Palmer, R 1983). Short of excavation, only fieldwalking could be expected to provide fresh information about these sites.

An initial problem is to find out where the air photographs which relate to the area under study are to be found. Once more the Sites and Monuments Record should be able to help. It will hold or be able to provide guidance about the location of the early RAF verticals, and maybe any county council photography in existence – quite a few of the larger local authorities have obtained vertical cover for general planning purposes. There will also be a collection of purely archaeological obliques, taken by the local archaeological unit, by private fliers or obtained from other sources; also an indication of what photographs are kept elsewhere. Two sources must in particular be mentioned here. The Air Photographs Unit of the National Monuments Record (part of the Royal Commission on the Historical Monuments of England, address p.147) holds half a million archaeological air photographs and no less than two million non-archaeological ones derived from government photographs accumulated by the former Air Photographic Library of the Department of the Environment; its collection is added to at the rate of 25,000–30,000 prints a year, the results of its own flying and copies derived from fliers elsewhere in the country. These photographs can be consulted by prior arrangement, with the obvious requirement in advance of information about the areas of interest expressed in terms of the National Grid References. The collection of air photographs built up by the Committee for Aerial Photography of the University of Cambridge is another prime source (address, p.147). Again, this is huge (400,000 prints); about one-half of it is archaeological, the larger part of this element consisting of obliques of particular sites or areas. There is a series of indexes incorporating material ordered by type of site, National Grid Reference, or parish or common names; and inquiries can be dealt with in a preliminary way by telephone. The collection can be visited. The National Monuments Record has a duplicate set of indexes. The fact that the Royal Commission on Historic Monuments of Scotland issues catalogues of the archaeological air photographs it has itself taken should also be mentioned.

An obvious comment arising from the above is that of scale – there is a huge amount of air photography around, although good *archaeological* photography will be far from evenly distributed about the country. In the relatively few areas for which a great deal exists, the amount of material to be handled can be daunting indeed — for example, the survey of Hampshire and Wiltshire just mentioned involved looking at 20,000 air photographs. In any large collection of photographs there is bound to be a great deal of repetitious and uninformative material, but everything has to be looked at; there is always the possibility of an oblique crop-mark photograph adding something new to a site, even one that has been known about and photographed for years. The well-known late prehistoric site at Gosbecks near Colchester had been photographed from the air since 1949, yet the Roman fort there did not appear until 1976 (Wilson 1977). All this means that the quantity of aerial photography available must be a consideration in the design of any field survey project.

So is the question of expense. What has been said above indicates that there is really not much of a problem in getting access to air photographs. But the interpretation of them can quite often be a subjective and difficult matter and the same photographs may have to be looked at again and again. If the prints are lodged in a public repository many miles away, this can be a serious problem; and one's own prints are a very desirable asset. All the bodies mentioned above will supply them, but their cost is not a negligible factor in deciding what to do.

Countryside behaviour

Some essential points about the fieldworker and the countryside. Obviously this kind of work involves getting on the land. Finding out exactly who owns what field is not always as straightforward as it might seem, particularly in areas where land ownership is very fragmented, and even door knocking (generally the best way of getting this information), can on occasion produce vain results. But the chore of getting permission is absolutely vital and it is very important that it is handled in the right way, with the farmer understanding precisely what you are up to. To this end it is almost certainly essential to do the whole business yourself, not through third parties, however helpful they may have been in making preliminary soundings or collecting basic information. Sometimes misunderstandings can arise which would never have happened at all had the person actually in charge of the archaeological work been in direct contact with the farmer at an early stage in the proceedings. Always observe the landowner's wishes and keep him informed of what you find; always leave an area as you found it, with all the gates shut as required. In moorland areas appropriate clothing will be needed to take account of sudden changes in the weather; and common-sense safety precautions should be taken in such matters as informing others about your whereabouts in relatively remote areas.

2 Fieldwalking

Fieldwalking is the systematic recovery and recording of artefacts found on the surface of ploughed fields. This deceptively simple statement introduces a technique of great potential and very wide applicability (Hayfield 1980); that is why it is described first. There are only a few archaeological periods for which it does not have something to contribute; and despite times when the archaeological rewards do not seem to be commensurate with the effort involved and possible discomfort endured, fieldwalking stands out as a way of investigating the past which is effective almost anywhere where there are suitable ploughed fields. Aerial photography will only perform well in certain areas where the geology is right, and earthworks will only exist in a reasonable state of preservation in places where past land use has allowed their survival. The huge ploughing-up campaigns during but mostly after the last war have accentuated the destruction of earthworks to an almost unbelievable degree – the chalk downs of the south of England, for example, made famous by the work of such pioneers as Cunnington, Colt Hoare and their surveyor Crocker and which so dominated archaeological writing in the first half of this century, only really still exist in military training areas. In Sussex a survey carried out in the middle 70s showed that 250 of the 660 archaeological sites visited were being destroyed by ploughing (Drewett 1980). This is a tragic loss over the whole country and in reality involves much more than the mere removal of earthwork evidence, but the opportunity offered to the archaeologist to carry out fieldwalking research projects affords a certain degree of compensation.

The plough will bring up odd bits of flint and stone, pottery, building material – of stone or baked clay – traces of certain industrial processes and occasionally small objects of bronze and iron, coins and the like. The distribution of this material on the surface of the fields is not even – there will be, say, concentrations of Roman pottery and tiles here and there which may indicate the presence of sites; these will contrast with a thin scatter of Roman pottery over other parts of the landscape. The distribution of worked flints may well exhibit similar variations in density. It is the task of the fieldwalker not just to obtain a sample of this interesting material by simply picking it up, but to do so in such a way that the distribution of the material recovered can be reconstructed on paper. He must then try to put forward suggestions about the meaning of his observations, taking into account all the evidence available to him – the objects themselves, their distribution pattern, the local geology and topography, other known sites and finds in the study area.

Fieldwalking is probably thought of mainly as a way of finding archaeological sites, and indeed its achievements in doing just this over the last few years have been great. In the Lincolnshire Fens the Car Dyke Research Group, a mainly amateur group working at weekends, examined over 5,000 fields between 1968 and 1975 in the area of the Car Dyke, and added 27 Iron Age, nearly 150 Roman and 15 early Saxon sites to the number already known (Simmons 1975). A Northamptonshire market gardener, working mainly by himself in a small number of Nene Valley parishes, found 44 Iron Age and 88 Roman sites between 1956 and 1971 (Hollowell 1971). When added to the work of other groups and individuals, this has provided new insights into the density of Iron Age and Romano-British occupation in this part of the Midlands, as well as much new information about a scattered but important Roman pottery industry, scarcely suspected before. For a dramatic indication of the effect fieldwalking can have upon the basic problem of site density, compare the distribution of sites in the Nene Valley, shown on the *Ordnance Survey Map of Roman Britain*, third edition, 1956, with the fourth edition of 1978, as has been done by Christopher Taylor (Taylor 1975); the increase in the number known, from 130 to 434, is of the order of 300 per cent. The implications for ideas about the population of this part of Roman Britain, where people lived, and about the success and intensity of Romano-British agriculture, are obvious.

Through the discovery of fresh sites, fieldwalking has the capacity to transform basic ideas about important historical problems. Until recently, most historians thought of the Anglo-Saxon settlement of the Midlands as taking the form of the establishment of nucleated villages, the predecessors of the medieval ones. Careful fieldwalking has shown however that this was not the case, and that early and middle Saxon occupation sites were dispersed over the landscape in a pattern very similar to the Roman one; the formation of villages came later (Foard 1978). However, in north-west Essex fieldwalking has produced a different picture. Here the present-day pattern of occupation, consisting of scattered farms and straggling settlements, can be seen as a result of fieldwalking to be the product of a series of slow changes in the landscape which started in the Roman period or even earlier; early Saxon sites tend to be near Roman ones; early medieval sites near early and middle Saxon ones; later medieval near early medieval sites – a picture broadly of stability in the landscape reaching far back into antiquity (Williamson 1984). In other parts of East Anglia fieldwalking has revealed yet another sequence of development. Because fieldwalking uncovers datable archaeological material it is able to show how occupation can move around the landscape. In central Norfolk Peter Wade Martins has demonstrated how many of the isolated churches in that part of England once had middle Saxon settlements around them; but how eventually in the twelfth and thirteenth centuries settlement shifted, maybe more than once in the case of some parishes, to align itself along the sides of quite substantial greens (Wade Martins 1980). Subsequent changes resulted in the break-up of this pattern. It should be pointed out that none of this information is derived from documents; it is the fieldwalking that has been the sole source of information.

But fieldwalking can do much more than simply locate sites. Hunting camps, farms and industrial sites could not have functioned without access to their share of the available natural resources. Fieldwalking can provide an opportunity of investigating just what that relationship was and what pieces of the landscape were exploited in different ways. For example, it is well known that very many fields which are carefully walked produce a thin scatter of Roman or later pottery. This did not get there by chance and is the result of the carrying of animal manure and other rubbish into the fields and spreading it around, in antiquity. So the recording of this pottery scatter will give an indication of the extent of the arable land which it was found convenient to manure in this way. Similarly, genuinely blank areas are of real interest; these may have been manured in some other manner, perhaps by folding animals on them, or represent pasture or woodland. Arguments based on the geological or topographical background of the pieces of land in question, taken along with the fieldwalking results, may enable suggestions to be made about the way in which different areas were used. The important point is that it is the broad pattern of economic activity in the past, and not just the individual sites operating within it, which is being studied.

Strategy

The fieldwalker or fieldwalking group must devote some time to the definition of objectives. It may be decided to concentrate on the detailed survey of one site or group of sites, or on a single type of site—ploughed medieval villages or moats, for example. Parish surveys have been carried out with success by archaeological groups in the past. Certainly they provide useful information about medieval and later settlement patterns and economic practices, since the parish or township was the unit within which the exploitation of the land was carried out. It has been doubted by some whether their usefulness extends much beyond this, because although Roman and earlier material may well be found, the boundaries need not necessarily have had anything to do with the way the land had been exploited in remoter antiquity. This kind of argument may in many instances have real force, and will become truer the further back in time one goes, but there is a growing realization that some of our parishes, thought of now as mainly ecclesiastical organizations, in fact go back as units of land exploitation a very long way indeed. Also many parishes were quite obviously deliberately set out to take in varying types of land; the long, narrow parishes of parts of Wiltshire, Dorset, Berkshire, Lincolnshire and Northamptonshire, running from river valleys on to the higher land alongside, are obvious examples.

There is a very real need for the detailed fieldwalking of sites defined by crop marks on aerial photographs in an attempt to provide some possible indications of date. The prime requirement here is the accurate transcription of the information on the aerial photographs to the Ordnance map, at a scale of at least 1:2,500. Sketching will not do: experience has shown that the errors in positioning and form are too great (Pryor and Palmer 1980). There are computer programs available for this work, but clearly expensive equipment in the form of a digitizer and a plotter is required, and the average fieldworker will have to familiarize himself with one or other of the well-known but time-consuming manual methods such as the paper strip method or the Mobius network (Wilson 1982, 198–9; Scollar 1975; also Dickinson 1969, 268–72).

Another approach is to consider the changing relationship through time between man and the natural environment in a region or group of sub-regions, defined by means of its geology. Schemes of sampling using randomly chosen squares based on the National Grid have frequently been discussed as possible solutions to this kind of problem, yet have hardly ever been put into practice on any scale in Britain (a few of the squares in Fig. 5 were chosen on a random basis). What have been successfully completed however are a number of projects designed on the lines of Fig. 4. Here the aim was to gain some initial insights into the pattern of human occupation in eastern Hampshire, an area about which little was known. The trend of the geology is north–south, with belts of chalk, clay, greensand and river and valley gravel in alternating zones. Because such a

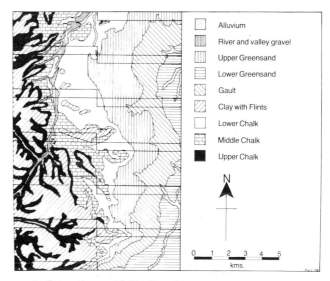

4   Surface geology and fieldwalking design, eastern Hampshire project.

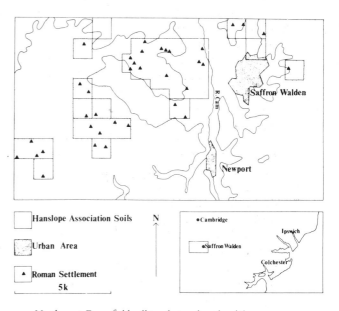

5   North-west Essex fieldwalking design, based on kilometre squares derived from the National Grid, chosen to cover the principal environments of the area.

large area was involved, there was no real chance of walking the whole of it in any meaningful way; so a series of transects 5 km (3 miles) long and 0.5 km (1,350 ft) wide and running east–west across the line of the geology 2.5 km (1½ miles) apart, was walked on a reconnaissance basis. This was sufficient to give relatively quickly a *general* idea of the density of archaeological sites and material at various times in this region and of the overall trends of past land use (Shennan 1985). But to gain fuller information about the different types of site, their relative sizes and differences in the material they produce and hence the possible relationships between them, as well as about the patterns of land use around them, will require the study of contiguous blocks of land. Fig. 5 is an example of this 'block' type of survey, in which 28 square km of the north-west Essex countryside, defined by 1 km Ordnance Survey grid squares so chosen that they covered a range of soil types, were walked with varying degrees of intensity, but sometimes in great detail (Williamson 1984).

Both these surveys were concerned in their different ways with the archaeology of wide tracts of countryside and assumed no knowledge of the existence of any particular kind of site before they were started. Fig. 6 illustrates a different approach. Here a known Roman villa has been chosen as the focal point of a project whose aim is to examine the distribution of other Roman period sites and of land use around it. To this end a circle 2 km (1¼ miles) in radius was drawn around the villa and the land so defined was walked with some intensity; beyond this, transects 500 m (1,350 ft) wide at 500 m intervals have been laid out to sample the downland further away (Gaffney *et al* 1985).

But whatever strategy is chosen must bear some commonsense relationship to the means and time available for carrying it out. Fieldwalking is time-consuming, and due weight must be given to this basic fact. The small area shown in Fig. 7, for example, walked intensively by a group of six to eight people on a tight grid as part of an investigation extending into excavation, took two days. The fieldwalking component of the work

6 *Maddle Farm fieldwalking project, Berkshire; sample design.*

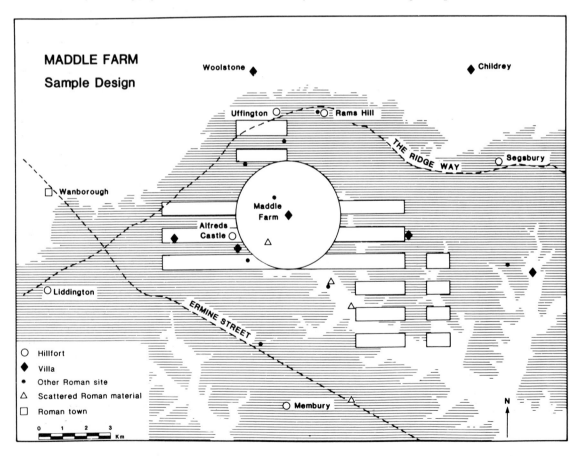

MADDLE FARM
Sample Design

Woolstone
Childrey
Uffington
Rams Hill
THE RIDGE WAY
Segsbury
Wanborough
Maddle
Farm
Alfreds
Castle
Liddington
ERMINE STREET
Membury

○ Hillfort
◆ Villa
• Other Roman site
△ Scattered Roman material
□ Roman town

0 1 2 3
Km

N

which went into the production of Fig. 8, representing the less intensive coverage of 7.2 ha (17¾ acres) by three people, took three days. At Maxey in Cambridgeshire, very intensive work involving the bagging and recording of every find within a 5 m grid over a total area of 3.75 ha (9 acres), took 500 man hours (Crowther 1983). At Churston, Devon, investigation of over 350 ha (875 acres), by one person, consisting of the plotting and bagging of each find individually, took three weeks (Parker Pearson 1981). The fieldwalking of a causewayed camp by a local group, the Haverhill Archaeological Society, took one winter (Charge 1985). These are small areas, though. The eastern Hampshire survey already mentioned involved the relatively unintensive walking of 241 arable fields amounting to 219 ha (540 acres), and was carried out by a team of people employed on a Job Creation Project, as well as local society volunteers and undergraduates, all under a professional supervisor. It took ten months. The north-west Essex work referred to took three winter seasons. A recently published fieldwalking survey by one person of the extra-mural region of the Roman town of Silchester, amounting to the repeated examination of 113 ha (280 acres), took twelve years (Corney 1984).

Similarly, the quantity of finds made and the amount of paperwork generated in record-keeping can be considerable, presenting problems of storage and working space just like those encountered with excavation. At Maxey 4,174 items were recovered. At Churston, there were 2,400 flints. The Silchester extra-mural survey produced 154.25 kg (314 lb) of pottery. In the east Hampshire survey, over 20,000 items of all periods were recovered. This material can require much the same degree of analysis and examination as that derived from an excavation; the basic washing, sorting, counting and identification of the east Hampshire material took nine months full time. All this is to say that a fieldwalking project, which is something that can sometimes *sound* like a relatively easy archaeological option, is not a thing which should be undertaken lightly; there must be an appreciation of the time and effort which will be required. There must also be a *reason* for it which will bear serious examination. No one these days expects an archaeological site to be dug into simply because it is there; so with fieldwal-king, which bears yet another resemblance to excavation in that it involves the physical removal of the material from the place of its discovery.

Initial preparation

The essential basic equipment is simple – a good supply of self-sealing polythene bags, say, 25 × 35 cm (10 × 14 inches) with reserved bands for marking, plus some smaller ones, 10 × 15 cm (4 × 5 inches) for small collections of material or special finds bagged individually; labels to go inside the bags; a clipboard, with record sheets (preferably made out in advance, p.29); pencils, rubbers, a pencil sharpener; ranging rods or other suitable poles or canes; several 30 metre tapes; surveyors' arrows; and a crosshead (p.51). An absolutely fundamental requirement for fieldwalking is a basic working familiarity with the whole range of archaeological material likely to be encountered; not necessarily a very detailed knowledge at this stage but sufficient to be able to recognize the material when it occurs. Visits to museums are only a very preliminary step towards the acquisition of this basic expertise. Every opportunity must be taken to handle the local archaeological material, best of all by helping on excavations, where material is likely to turn up in something like the condition it may have on the surface of a ploughed field. Worked flints and the debris resulting from the manufacture of flint tools can be a difficulty. These are relatively frequent finds in many parts of the country, yet so is the occurrence of countless naturally fractured bits of flint, derived from glacial or gravel deposits, which bear a superficial resemblance to genuine archaeological pieces. There are a number of guides available to help the beginner to distinguish one from the other (British Museum 1968; Pierpoint 1981; Pitts 1980), but there is really no substitute for the practical handling of the material under supervision. Most people, in the writer's experience, soon learn to sort out naturally broken flints from worked ones, but there are always a few who never seem able to master this particular problem.

Tactics

A couple of initial basic points have to be considered. Firstly, unless very detailed work over small areas of the kind carried out at Maxey is contemplated, total recovery of all the artefacts on the surface in normal fieldwalking conditions is practically an impossibility; at Churston, for example, subsequent checking showed that only half the flints on the surface had in fact been picked up, although the local conditions had been favourable for recovery. All that the fieldwalker can do and ought to seek to do therefore is to obtain a *sample* of the material on the surface. This must be done in a systematic and orderly way, in which equal weight is given to all parts of the area under examination, whether a ploughed medieval village or several square kilometres of countryside. There is always a temptation to concentrate upon the pieces of land which produce the most finds, but this feeling must be resisted.

Secondly, there is a growing body of evidence which suggests that normal modern ploughing on reasonably level terrain causes surprisingly little lateral displacement of artefacts in the ploughed soil. At Silchester, for example, detailed grid walking has provided examples of fragments from the same vessel being found in different years within an area of two square metres (Corney 1984). This is because of the practice of reversing the pattern of ploughing from year to year so that material moved to one side (a figure of 25–35 cm (10–14 inches) has been quoted) and slightly forwards on one occasion is pushed back by an equivalent amount the next time the field is ploughed (Crowther 1983). Sloping fields can be a very different matter and will be discussed later (p.36). All this means that material can be picked up close to the place at which it was deposited in antiquity. The strict logic of this is that since precise find spots are important, every find ought to be separately bagged, labelled and its position accurately recorded. This is obviously a practical impossibility for general fieldwalking, and some compromise will always have to be made between the extent of the ground covered and the intensity of the survey.

Most fieldwalking projects involve a progression from initial prospecting to a more detailed examination of selected areas; and tactics are usually discussed under two headings – line walking, more suitable for reconnaissance and general regional work, and grid walking, more applicable to smaller areas requiring intensive

cover, or to individual sites (Steane and Dix 1978, 61–6; Fasham *et al* 1980; Liddle 1985, 7–18).

(a) *Line Walking*. This involves the systematic coverage of a field along a series of parallel lines, marked out by rods a fixed distance apart. Finds can be picked up, say, one to two metres either side of them. The crucial decision is the distance between the lines; the assumption will be that a steady walking pace is used. If reconnaissance is the aim, as was in the case in Fig. 4, then a wide spacing of 25 m has been found useful. This allows most scatters of flints, Roman and medieval pottery to be picked up, but the great disadvantage of all reconnaissance work is that small scatters, particularly of relatively scarce and important material such as some prehistoric and early and middle Saxon pottery, may well be missed. The unit of collection is the line, the lines themselves being marked on a plan of the field and allotted distinguishing numbers; the finds from each line are bagged separately and labelled with the designation of the field – perhaps the Ordnance Survey field number along with the parish name (but see below p.29) and the number of the line. But lines will vary in length with the shape and size of the field and another disadvantage is that they give good recording control in one direction only; the main advantage of this method is relative speed. To improve recording, the lines must be broken down into shorter lengths of at least 100 or 50 metres and the finds from each of these shorter units kept separate. If this procedure is adopted, then line walking can come to differ very little from

(b) *Grid Walking*. Here the area to be walked is divided up into a series of squares; the unit of record here is the square. If an individual site is being examined, squares can be quite small, say 5–10 m. But there is no reason why quite large-scale reconnaissance surveys should not be carried out using a grid as an overall framework, 100 × 100 m, i.e. one hectare ($2\frac{1}{2}$ acres). These are large squares; but in practice they will be broken down into individual transects a hundred metres long with whatever spacing between them is considered appropriate; and the hundred metre transects can be split up into shorter lengths, say, 50 or 25 m if required, the finds from each transect and each transect subdivision being kept separate. The advantage of all this is that a grid already

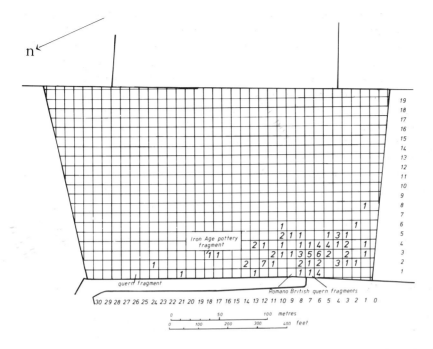

7 *Humberstone Farm in Leicestershire; plot of fieldwalking results. The figures show the number of Roman sherds per 10 metre square. Similar diagrams could have been produced for worked flints and possible Roman building material, for example.*

exists for the British countryside in the form of the Ordnance Survey National Grid and it can be used as a ready-made framework for the field-walking. If this is not done, and an independent system of grids or lines has to be set up, quite often taking a conveniently straight hedge as a base, there may always be the possibility of running into difficulties with the figure and letter combinations which will have to be invented for recording purposes. But the use of the National Grid prevents any possibility of confusion; unique numerical references are readily available for each square of whatever size and the start points of each transect or sub-transect; the find spots of certain individual items, stone axes for example, can be easily and intelligibly recorded; the density of finds per unit area is readily calculated and can be easily presented (Fig. 15); the proportion of the available landscape actually covered by the survey can be easily worked out; and although there are always going to be difficulties owing to the various local factors which have a bearing on recovery rates, comparisons are more easily made with work done in a similar way in other places.

The alternative to using the National Grid is to lay out the lines and squares within the framework of the individual field (as in Figs. 7 and 8). Quite often this is easier to do; but the main advantage this has over the National Grid is the use which can be made for walking purposes of the lines of the crops and this can sometimes be an overriding consideration.

Practicalities

The use of the National Grid as a framework means that the pattern of the fieldwalking can be set out very easily on 1:2,500 maps or enlargements derived from them in advance of the actual fieldwork; bags and labels with the National Grid Reference of the transect and the date can also be prepared in advance. This saves an enormous amount of time and difficulty in field conditions, which might easily turn out to be wet and windy. General line-walking reconnaissance at 25 m intervals can make do with lines marked on maps at 1:10,000, but again enlargements at twice this scale are preferable.

Once in the field, great care must be taken to lay out an initial *base line* aligned exactly along the National Grid (Fig. 9). This can be done by measuring with a tape points at which a suitable National Grid line cuts existing hedges and

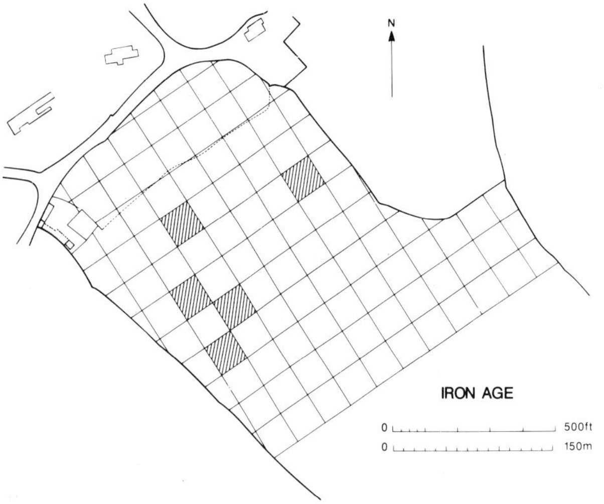
N
IRON AGE
0 500ft
0 150m

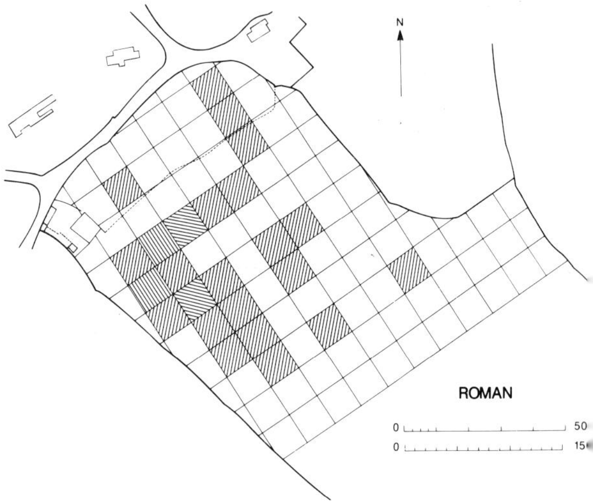
N
ROMAN

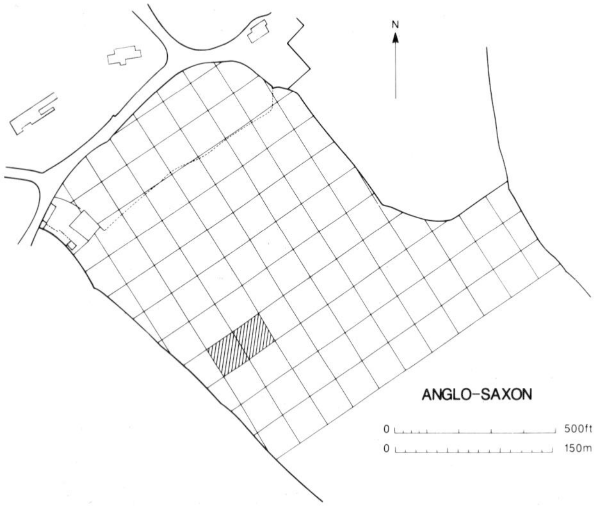
N
ANGLO-SAXON
0 500ft
0 150m

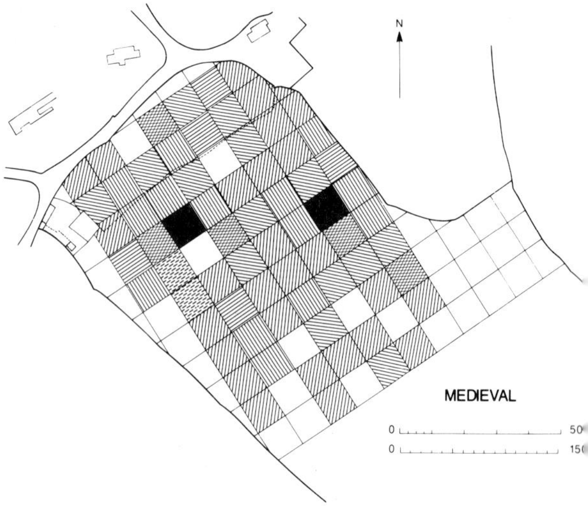
N
MEDIEVAL

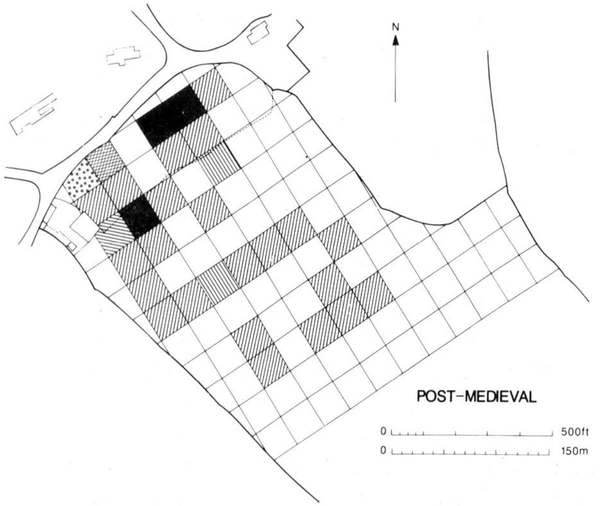
N
POST-MEDIEVAL
0 500ft
0 150m

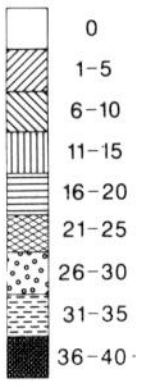
0
1-5
6-10
11-15
16-20
21-25
26-30
31-35
36-40

8 *Grafton Regis in Northamptonshire. The diagrams show variations in the density of pottery of various periods. 30 metre squares were used.*

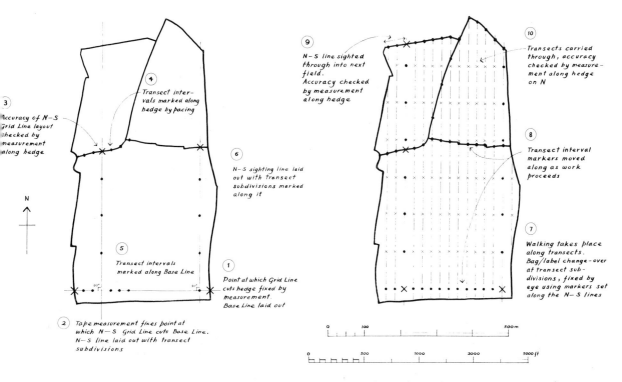

The diagram contains the following labels:

3 — Accuracy of N–S Grid Line layout checked by measurement along hedge

4 — Transect intervals marked along hedge by pacing

6 — N–S sighting line laid out with transect subdivisions marked along it

5 — Transect intervals marked along Base Line

1 — Point at which Grid Line cuts hedge fixed by measurement. Base Line laid out

2 — Tape measurement fixes point at which N—S Grid Line cuts Base Line. N–S line laid out with transect subdivisions

9 — N–S line sighted through into next field. Accuracy checked by measurement along hedge

10 — Transects carried through, accuracy checked by measurement along hedge on N

8 — Transect interval markers moved along as work proceeds

7 — Walking takes place along transects. Bag/label change-over at transect subdivisions, fixed by eye using markers set along the N–S lines

N

9 *A suggested method for setting out fieldwalking transects.*

marking these points with ranging rods; an imaginary line joining these rods will constitute the base line. Using other rods for sighting purposes and 30 m tapes, a rod can be placed along this line at a point at which another National Grid line cuts the base line at right angles. This rod will act as the origin of the grid setting-out operation. From this point, whatever intervals are required for reconnaissance purposes can be physically marked along the base line by means of rods or canes. A number of lines at convenient distances from each other will have to be accurately laid out at right angles to the base line using a crosshead (or any other of the means of achieving a right angle, below, p.50) and the transect subdivision lengths marked along them by rods set up by tape measurement. A second base line, parallel with the first, with the survey intervals similarly set out and marked by rods, can also be laid out now, at a convenient distance from the original one; alternatively, the places at which the lines cut a suitable hedge can be so indicated. But within the framework of visibly marked points along the base lines and the lines at right angles to it, the walking lines and their transect subdivision lengths can be

determined by sighting between ranging rods; and as time goes on and with developing experience, and given favourable conditions, greater reliance can be placed upon pacing and rather fewer tape measurements need be taken.

Pacing is never appropriate for detailed grid surveys. The initial squares can be accurately set out with a crosshead and their corners marked by rods; the sides of these initial squares can be projected by tapes and fresh squares thereby set out. But checks along and at right angles to the original lines will have to be made from time to time to ensure that accuracy is being maintained.

Material can then be collected, placed in the correct polythene bags and the appropriate label placed inside each of them.

The use of the National Grid will of course extend to record-keeping. For surveys of large areas, record sheets representing combinations of hectares can be made out as the cumulative record of their fieldwalking history, on to which information can be fed as work proceeds. The sheet will contain a plan of the squares, with their Grid References and parish name showing the boundaries of the fields they may form part of, with their Ordnance Survey numbers and owners; slight earthworks noted during the work, say lynchets or fragments of medieval cultivation; field boundaries since removed; quarries, ponds; the boundaries of different soil formations, which are often perfectly visible on the plough soil and can be related to the underlying geology; patches of stone and areas of dark soil; past agricultural history; references to other relevant archaeological and historical information such as air photographs, old finds, field names; also the dates on which walking took place and the location and numbering of the transects. In addition to this, entries wil! have to be made directly on to the maps taken into the field about such matters as the date, state of light,

weather, soil and crop conditions and names of the people responsible for the individual transects and the degree to which the subsoil was being brought to the surface, a fact which may affect subsequent interpretation. Material such as recent pottery or large quantities of building material, which it has been decided merely to note the presence of, rather than collect, can be entered up as well.

Factors affecting the efficiency of fieldwalking

Absolutely vital to the success of any piece of fieldwalking is the condition of the ground. Ideally, the ground must not only be ploughed but also pulverized and subjected to a considerable degree of weathering, so that the clods are broken down and the material they contain

10   The effect of a bright, slanting light on the furrows of a ploughed field. Almost half of the surface area of the field is in effect rendered invisible to the fieldwalker because of this.

spread on the surface. Land which has just been ploughed or manured is perfectly useless. There will also be local problems affecting particular parts of a field – pieces of land close to hedges containing trees which will shed their leaves over the surface of the soil are likely on occasion to present difficulties. There are also variations in the way soils weather down. The best time for fieldwalking is when the crops have begun to sprout, but as they develop crops obviously obscure the ground, and the higher the crop the less popular the fieldwalker is likely to be with the farmer. The fieldwalking season generally runs from October to March, but in many parts of the country is getting shorter all the time. Land is now ploughed and sown immediately after harvest and can be obscured by November, particularly if a fast-growing crop such as oilseed rape is being grown. These factors of optimum ground conditions obviously give the local worker a tremendous advantage over anyone else who has to travel some distance in the hope of finding his fields in good condition; this explains why there have been so many good local surveys in the past few years achieved by people connected professionally with the land. Local people can also know more about the complexities of land ownership. To deal with the land agent of a large estate or, say, half a dozen farmers is no problem, but a stranger can have real difficulties in an area of fragmented land ownership and short-term renting out.

The state of the weather is another important variable. Rather dull, uniform lighting is best for fieldwalking. Too bright a sun will cause difficulties with the sharp reflection of light from the soil; a bright slanting light acting against the furrows will create problems of light and shade which will effectively make half the field surface impossible to examine (Fig. 10). Frost will obscure the ground surface as well as making it physically impossible to remove material anyway.

The quality, experience and enthusiasm of the people actually doing the fieldwalking are highly relevant. Inexperience can be compensated for to some extent by prior training and the handling of material; but actual field conditions are sometimes a different matter. Some kinds of pottery can be very hard to distinguish from bits of bark, coal, fragments of ironstone and slate in reason-able field conditions, let alone semi-mud on a frosty day. Fragments of broken stone axes or other stone artefacts are very easily overlooked. As we have seen, a great deal of thought can go into the business of reducing bias and ensuring that coverage is even, but the human factor is itself a distorting element. The greater the number of people involved in a fieldwalking exercise the greater the chance of distortions caused by variations in their knowledge and experience, enthusiasm and boredom. This kind of bias can be weakened by restricting the actual conduct of fieldwalking to one individual, as has been advocated by some; but this is a counsel of perfection. It is natural for groups to want to engage in this kind of activity and they can give obvious advantages in speed and coverage. So precautions have to be taken, such as moving people around from position to position when walking in a fixed order along predetermined lines, and always recording the names of those responsible for any particular piece of walking. Even so, it is possible to have too many people involved in a fieldwalking project, because of the problems of control and of relations with farmers which large numbers will create.

The only real answer to problems of the kind mentioned above is to repeat the walking using the same tactics for as many seasons as possible. This will serve to iron out these variables to some extent, but even so there are always going to be imponderables. Fieldwalking on Elton Common and Gratton Moor in the White Peak district of Derbyshire in 1981–2 produced different patterns of flint concentrations from that observed by different workers in 1968 (Gerrish 1982). Another example is illustrated in Fig. 11, where a crop-mark site walked in identically good field conditions at an interval of about ten years showed a marked fall-off in the pattern of finds. Sometimes differences of this kind can be accounted for by changes in agricultural practice. At Silchester a field immediately outside the walled town on the south-west produced nothing, although walked for eight years. Suddenly pottery began to appear, about 12 kg (26 lb) in the end, including the earliest discovered during the whole project. The reason turned out to be an increase in the depth of ploughing from nine to twelve inches (Corney 1984).

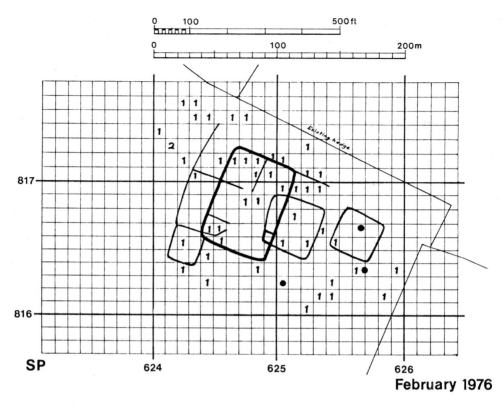

February 1976

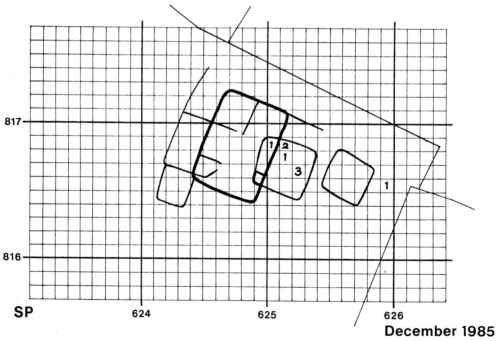

December 1985

11   *Welford in Northamptonshire. The same crop mark walked at an interval of about ten years, in equally good conditions. The crop marks were plotted manually using one of the methods referred to on p25. The figures indicate the number of Roman sherds per 10m square. The dots represent sherds of early-middle Saxon pottery.*

The results

Finds should be washed, marked with their line and/or grid square reference, labelled up and rebagged. A decision will have to be made about the degree of effort to be put into the analysis of all this material. It is an easy matter to draw up standard record sheets by line or square for the purpose of sorting things out into their basic archaeological periods (see, for examples, Liddle 1985; Fasham *et al.* 1980). But fieldwalking has its part to play in establishing the distribution of particular pottery fabric types and any attempt at closer dating within each period will certainly require more than this. There will be problems – the battered condition of some of the sherds will on occasion make identification difficult even to the correct period. Body sherds of Thetford ware can for example resemble Roman grey ware, and – notoriously – Iron Age pottery can be hard to distinguish from Anglo-Saxon. Some shelly pottery fabrics were made in the late Iron Age, Roman, and for much of the medieval period, and small abraded fragments can be hard to pin down within this very broad band. In cases of difficulty, advice will have to be sought, generally from the local excavation unit; and the fieldwalker will have to join the post-excavation pottery network just as the excavator does.

Many collections of flint can be large. This need cause no surprise to anyone familiar with the huge quantities of flints which turn up on some excavations – at two Mesolithic sites at Oakhanger in Hampshire a total of 190,678 pieces of flint was recovered and the weight of flintwork from one of these sites was over a ton (Jacobi 1981). A recent estimate has put the number of lithic artefacts which a single hunter-gatherer group might reasonably be expected to use and discard in their main home occupation areas over a period of a hundred years at sixteen million – and this figure includes tools only, not the huge quantities of flaking debris generated in their manufacture (Foley 1981). Many flint scatters are very mixed and represent the result of activities by a wide variety of groups at different times. Setting aside classifiable diagnostic pieces such as Mesolithic blades, cores and microliths, and Neolithic and Bronze Age arrowheads, the mass of less distinguished items might still be amenable to broad period categorization, as has been attempted, for instance, on the Berkshire Downs on the basis of the overall proportions of flakes and the general quality of the waste pieces (Richards 1978).

Finally, any presentation of the results of fieldwalking must include general maps to show the areas walked in relation to those unwalked, and basic information must be given about the manner in which the walking was done, when it was done, the number of people involved and any identifiable factors likely to have affected the results. The detailed results can be presented in a series of simple tables, but most importantly of all in map form. These maps can show the number of finds of each type within the grid squares by means of simple shading techniques or merely by figures (e.g. Fig. 7); if it is found necessary to show the changing pattern of occupation of an area through time, as in Fig. 8, a series of plans will have to be drawn because of the difficulties of effective and clear multiple shading.

The interpretation of fieldwalking: post-depositional factors

Blanks on maps of areas subjected to fieldwalking *may* represent a genuine absence of finds; but there can be other explanations for them in addition to the variations in the ability to recover material discussed above. Certain local geological factors can have the effect of covering the evidence of early occupation almost entirely. Fields near rivers and streams which have flooded in the past may carry sheets of alluvium which blot out the archaeological layers below; the junction between the alluvium and the ordinary arable is quite often clear and can be sketched on to the record sheets. At Wiverton in the Vale of Belvoir this phenomenon was clearly noted; patches of alluvium could be seen distorting the distribution of the flints (Hills and Liddon 1981). This is a small-scale example, but the cumulative effect of the blanket of alluvium in major river valleys can be very considerable; in the lower Nene Valley around Peterborough, in a sample area of 14,300 ha (35,221 acres), alluvium covers 1,245 ha (3,075 acres), 8·7 per cent of the total area; another sample area around Oundle, 55,738 ha (137,673 acres) has 4,067 ha (10,045 acres) of alluvium cover, 7·3 per cent (Challands 1982). This alluvium prevents effective fieldwalking and does not yield crop marks, but is not archaeologically valueless; it seals old land surfaces and protects sites and earthworks, some of which – round barrows for example – can still be seen protruding above its surface. Sometimes these are low; an example at Orton Meadows near Peterborough was only 0·7 m (28 inches) high but more obvious examples can be quoted. A pair of round barrows in low-lying situations in Henslow Meadow, Aldwincle, Northamptonshire, were once 2·4 and 0·9 m high and a barrow at Earls Barton in the same county 1·5 m high (Jackson 1976 and 1984).

An effect of another sort is the accumulation of colluvial deposits in valley floors at the foot of slopes, the results of slopewash or downslope creep. For the fieldwalker this has two consequences – the masking of material in the valley bottoms and the denudation of soil and objects from the valley sides. The depth of such colluvial deposits can be quite considerable – at Bullock Down near Eastbourne, Sussex, an excavated section showed a depth of deposit of two metres (Drewett 1982, 10–12). At Frocester, Gloucestershire, hillwash from the Cotswold limestone escarpment, amounting to one metre in depth, covered a ditch and a deposit which produced a leaf-shaped arrowhead (Darvill and Timby 1984). At Baston Manor, Hayes, Kent, a Roman bath building noted vaguely in a nineteenth-century source was not relocated by fieldwalking extending over seven years; it took a series of trial pits to find it. The reason was the depth of the remains below the surface, over 1·2 m (4 ft), the result of a wash of loam and pebbles from the hill above (Philp 1973). Colluviation and its impact on archaeological evidence have been most intensively studied in this country on the chalk (Bell 1983), but can occur anywhere. A recent study of the lower Welland valley has found that this process, operating on mainly limestone subsoils, has masked archaeological deposits at the foot of the valley slopes to the tune of over a metre (Pryor and French 1985, 286). The fieldworker should always be on the lookout for indications of the process in operation – evidence for wash at the foot of slopes and lynchet formation in modern fields, for example.

Another post-depositional factor which has to be taken into account is the survival rates of different kinds of pottery in various types of soil, even when the pottery is hard-fired. In North-

12 *The effects of frost. A shattered piece of chalk lies on the surface of a field.*

amptonshire there is a difference between the generally well-preserved Roman pottery from the fields on the ironstone and gravel subsoils of the Nene valley and the Roman pottery from the clays of the north-west, which tends to have lost its surfaces and sharp edges and to be poorly preserved; this is especially true of the finer colour-coated and samian wares, which are often found minus their surface decoration to the point of unrecognizability, giving an impression of poverty which may not be an accurate reflection of reality. But generally speaking, Roman pottery, as is well known, survives very well, as do the hard well-made medieval ones, but the same cannot be said for most prehistoric and Saxon pottery, although surprises can occur. These latter types cannot survive conditions of rain and frost for long very well; Fig. 12 shows what might happen to them. At Marcham Road, Abingdon, Oxfordshire, a quantity of Roman pottery was picked up on the surface but no Iron Age material; yet excavation uncovered only four Roman features and hundreds of Iron Age ones (Hinchliffe 1980). At Cowdery's Down, Hampshire, pottery was actually more common in the excavated late Bronze/Iron Age features than in the Roman or post-medieval ones – yet only Roman or post-medieval pottery was found in the topsoil.

Cultural factors

The relative abundance of Roman and medieval pottery is not entirely a reflection of its better survival properties, however. There was simply more of it in use than in the intervening Saxon period. Excavations on important Saxon sites commonly produce few sherds: Cowdery's Down yielded 146; the Saxon settlement at Maxey, 270; the middle Saxon palace site at Northampton produced 386 (Millett and James 1983; Addyman 1964; Williams *et al.* 1985, 48). This means that quite apart from problems of survival there would be relatively few sherds to find anyway; but these few sherds do not necessarily mean a low population, or a low intensity of land exploitation. Given the interest and importance of the Saxon period, the recovery of this rare but undistinguished-looking material is of great significance to the field archaeologist. Not only is it scarce, but also hard to see; the pieces tend to be black or brownish in colour and frequently small and crumb-like, hard to distinguish from pieces of coke, or certain kinds of stone. So heroic methods have to be adopted to get at it – walking along very close transects, from five metres down to one metre apart, even bent double. This is very time-consuming work and there will therefore be a tendency for this pottery to be found on or near more obvious sites of other periods which also happen to be under investigation. This introduces a bias which may distort the true distribution of the pottery; this can only be rectified by a programme of sampling designed to give fair weight to all parts of the area under investigation.

Another archaeological period with a low degree of fieldwalking visibility is the late Bronze Age. Whereas the amount of earlier flintwork visible on the surface can be considerable, late Bronze Age flints are so poor in quality as to be difficult to distinguish from naturally battered pieces. The pottery tends not to survive very well and the bronzework was carefully looked after at

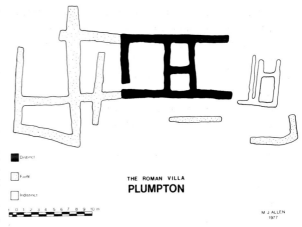

THE ROMAN VILLA
PLUMPTON

M.J.ALLEN
1977

13   *The Roman villa at Plumpton, Sussex. This plan shows the chalk and flint walls visible in the ploughsoil.*

the time and when useless melted down.

In some areas certain archaeological periods were aceramic and so totally invisible to the fieldwalker – in the west midlands and the north of England the centuries following the collapse of the Roman province, for example.

Interpretation

At the end of it all the fieldwalker will have a series of plans containing information about the relative densities of different kinds of artefact on the surface of ploughed fields. Some material will occur in concentrations sufficiently distinct to be regarded as sites, and on occasions the meaning of such concentrations will be reasonably clear. Quite a few Roman villas still in fact exist as plannable earthworks in ploughed land, and even without this betray themselves because of the nature of the finds they produce – building materials of all kinds, dense spreads of pottery. Industrial sites – potteries and tileries, for example – can usually be identified because of the great masses of material they leave behind, some of which, such as wasters and firebars, will provide clear indicators of the kind of activities carried on. Detailed fieldwalking can on occasion produce remarkably full information; at Plumpton in Sussex the plan of a Roman villa could be obtained because the chalk and flint of the walls could be seen in the ploughsoil (Fig. 13); painted plaster, tesserae and flue tiles suggested a reasonable standard of decoration and a heating system;

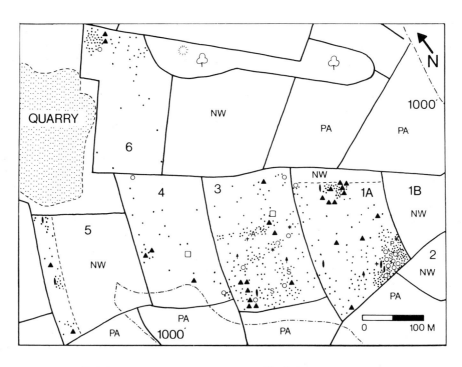

Pot types :

+   POT SHERD
+ 5   GRIMSTON ; FABRIC 5
+ 2   MORTLAKE ; FABRIC 2
+ 3   MORTLAKE ; FABRIC 3
+ 1   FENGATE ; FABRIC 1
+ 4   GROOVED WARE ; FABRIC 4

Knapping debris :

·   FLINT OR CHERT FLAKE
▲   CORE
△   THINNING FLAKE
M   MICROBURIN ?

Tool types :

❚   LEAF-SHAPED ARROWHEAD
O   SCRAPER   ✳ KNIFE
S   WORN-EDGE FLAKE
P   POLISHED FLINT FLAKE
□   MISCELLANEOUS RETOUCHED   FLAKE
⊿   MICROLITH   ↑ BORER
■   USED FLAKE
A   POLISHED STONE AXE FLAKE
A VI / A VII   WITH GROUP NUMBER
❚ ■   BURNT TOOLS
×   BURNT FLAKE

LIMESTONE OUTCROP   PA : PASTURE   NW : NOT WALKED 1983

14   Mount Pleasant, Kenslow, Derbyshire. A plot of finds made during fieldwalking. Note the indication given of the unwalked fields.

pottery indicated occupation in the second and third centuries (Allen 1984). At Noah's Ark Inn, Frilford, Oxfordshire, fieldwalking has provided an outline plan of a small Roman town 30 ha (75 acres) in extent, consisting of five distinct areas of pottery scatters, some of which yielded tile, some not, suggesting differences between buildings of stone and those of timber and thatch. An important discovery from ground survey was an amphitheatre which can in all probability be linked with a temple already known to suggest a religious focus of some importance (Hingley 1982). Fieldwalking may also provide a general indication of the way in which occupation can move about the countryside; Fig. 8 is an example, where the village of Grafton Regis in Northamptonshire shows evidence of occupation from the late pre-Roman period up to the present day, but with varying foci. On a much larger scale, the Silchester extra-mural survey has been able to indicate how the pre-Conquest surface finds lie mainly within the bank and ditch known as the Inner Earthwork, which probably therefore delineated the *oppidum* before the Roman invasion. The *Roman* town of Silchester received its defences towards the end of the second century, but it would be wrong to think of the whole of the town as encompassed within the enceinte; the field-walking has demonstrated how suburbs existed outside the gates and how very considerable expansion of extra-mural settlement took place in the late third and fourth centuries (Corney 1984).

Most rural pottery scatters are not so informative, however, and are usually regarded as farms of one sort or another (but see p.43). Yet even here an adequate fieldwork record will enable statements to be made about the size and form of the scatter, enabling comparisons to be made with other sites; and the material may yield some evidence of date, and the presence or otherwise of fine wares, building materials, coins, etc. may provide other bases on which comparisons may be suggested.

Fieldwalking can also produce information about distinct activity areas within an artefact scatter. Fig. 14 is an example where at Kenslow in Derbyshire detailed record-keeping showed that there were concentrations detectable in a flint scatter covering 500 × 100 m (1,625 × 325 ft). Cores clustered in two places which may have been knapping areas; a group of scrapers and a couple of flakes with worn edges suggested another specialized activity area, and a collection of borers, scrapers and knives elsewhere could have represented domestic occupation. Excavation showed that these areas were not necessarily contemporary (Garton and Beswick 1983). At Biddenham in Bedfordshire it was possible to examine the relationship of flint scatters to ring ditches known from aerial photography. The fieldwalking showed not only that there were ring ditches just outside the concentrations of flint, but also that the flints themselves exhibited significant patterns within the overall distribution, with three locations which produced scrapers, suggesting where the habitation areas were (Woodward 1978). At Bullock Down in Sussex quite detailed suggestions could be made about the layout of Neolithic activities across part of the area examined. Cores were found scattered *around* concentrations of

flakes suggesting that they had been thrown away, whereas the flakes had simply been allowed to fall to the ground. It was therefore the flakes which indicated the actual knapping floors. Concentrations of scrapers and retouched flakes could indicate places where skins had been prepared (Drewett 1982, 48). Collections of burnt flints are noted frequently in fieldwalking projects. These have quite often been taken to indicate cooking – during excavations at South Lodge Camp in Cranborne Chase in Dorset, a mound of them was found, along with a trough, suggesting parallels with the burnt mounds, consisting of heaps of burnt stones, which are widespread in the British Isles (Barrett *et al.* 1981). But burnt flint concentrations can mean other things – the parching of grain and the preparation of filler for pottery making, for example – and many explanations have been sought for heaps of burnt stone, ranging from primitive sauna baths to the use of certain woodworking techniques (Barfield and Hodder 1981).

Still at the level of the individual site, it is pertinent to ask to what extent the plan obtained by carefully plotting the distribution of flints, pottery and the like will relate to the plan obtained by excavation. Some of the surface concentrations will come from archaeological features truncated by the plough. For example, excavations along the line of the Alchester road running south-west from Towcester in Northamptonshire disclosed a series of smithies and other workshops, ranging in date from the late second to the fourth centuries. In some places the structural evidence for the second-century workshops was very slight, having been almost totally ploughed away; it consisted of a few centimetres only of the bases of a small number of post holes. Yet the sites of these presumably humble buildings were marked in the topsoil by concentrations of pottery characteristic of the period (Brown and Woodfield 1983). At Hambledon Hill in Dorset it has been noted that concentrations of finds occur in ploughed topsoil over Neolithic features dug into the subsoil (Mercer 1980). So some groups of finds detected on the surface will represent features recoverable by excavation such as pits and ditches. But the distribution of artefacts on a fieldwalked site will not always simply reflect archaeological features below the surface from which they have been derived, as has been shown in some places where excavation has been carried out from the top of the plough soil downwards. At Maxey there were concentrations of Roman pottery over some gullies, but not over all cut features, while elsewhere dense pottery concentrations had no features below them at all. The explanation offered was that these pottery scatters came from upstanding or level features which were never cut into the surface of the soil when they were in use, such as manure heaps and yards. This means that excavation has to take this topsoil material into account, and not to machine it off, since the only evidence for these non-cut structures will reside in the ploughsoil (Crowther 1983).

The implication of all this is that some sites will exist *only* in the ploughsoil and will exhibit no features when excavated. At Priddy in Somerset three trenches dug into a flint scatter produced only seven stake holes and traces of a post hole; yet there were 1,043 flints and several pieces of pottery (Taylor and Smart 1983). No features could be found associated with any of the flint scatters investigated along the line of the A38 and M5 during rescue work in Devon (Miles 1977). At Tattershall Thorpe, Lincolnshire, there were pits yielding early Neolithic flints, but above these in the ploughsoil were flints of a different type belonging to a later phase of activity with no features to go with them (Healy 1983). Much of British prehistory and early history is therefore held in suspension in our arable land; the argument for the careful walking and recording of artefact scatters is clear.

Moving away from the individual site, fieldwalking, in conjunction with the collection of information from old sources and from excavations, is invaluable in helping to understand distributional problems. For example, surface finds have taken their place alongside excavated examples in the production of a distribution map for the south of England of Mesolithic tools made from pebbles derived from the south-west of the country (Jacobi 1981, 18). The analysis of the different types of flint tools found on all the sites in an intensively walked area can suggest how the sites can be classified into different functional groups. In Upper Wharfedale, for example, Richard Bradley has suggested that the late Neolithic–early Bronze Age sites found by E. T.

Cowling and published by him in book form in 1946 can be divided into four groups: those with arrowheads, including arrowhead cores and blanks; those with tools, mainly scrapers, but little flint waste; those with the by-products of tool manufacture; and others with both scrapers and flint waste. This suggests different activities at different places, but within the same general locality (Bradley 1978, 81). In Somerset, Mesolithic flints from lowland locations tend to be of types to be associated with such activities as preparing skins (scrapers), wood (adzes) and bone and antler (burins). The flints from upland places have higher proportions of microliths and might suggest a greater concern with hunting, say in the summer months. So an integrated approach to the exploitation of whole territories in seasonal cycles is indicated (Norman 1982, 21).

The way in which archaeological material is distributed across the landscape in relation to soils and topography can provide insights into economic and social behaviour. At Welford in Northamptonshire, scatters of Roman pottery occur on the tops of hills overlooking the Avon, at regular intervals. Their distribution in relation to the local topography suggests farms exploiting their immediate surroundings as infield arable, with meadow lower down by the river. At North Stoke in Oxfordshire the flints recovered by fieldwalking conspicuously avoid the cursus and ring ditches known from air photography (Fig. 15), a clear distinction apparently between ritual and domestic and economic activity, although the separation is not great (Bradley and Holgate 1984, 126–7). Fieldwalking will also throw up problems in the relationship between specific geological formations and site distribution which will demand explanation. In the south of England, many Mesolithic concentrations occur on light sandy soils. An explanation advanced for this is that these soils originally carried a dry oak woodland with little understorey vegetation – good, that is, for seeing animals. So this kind of situation tended to be favoured by hunting communities; hence the flint concentrations. But the disadvantage was that this type of woodland was also more susceptible to burning, which tended to produce open ground. In time the ground became degraded, too poor to be of use to Neolithic agriculturists; so it reverted to scrub

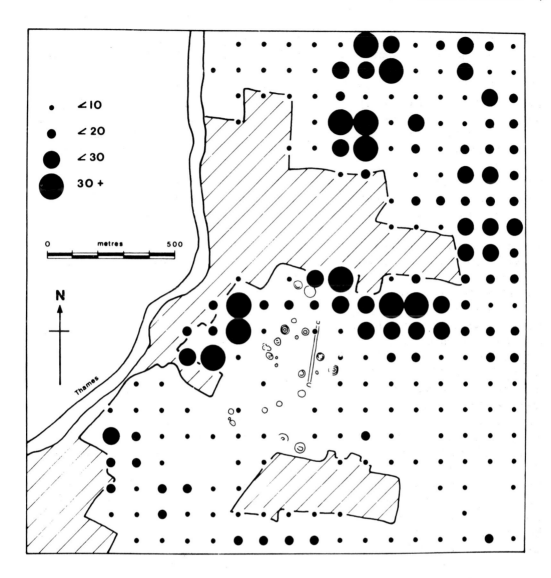

15 *North Stoke in Oxfordshire. The density of worked flints per hectare is illustrated, as a result of a 5 per cent sample of the area. The shaded areas were unwalked.*

and in places was used later on for barrow burials (Shennan 1981). A second example concerns the apparently surprising association noted several times between the heavy acidic formation in the south of England known as clay with flints and scatters of Neolithic flints. In the past the flints, which often include heavy tools suitable for digging and roughing out, led to the suggestion that these at first sight unattractive locations were sought out as a source of raw materials (at Chalton, Hampshire (Cunliffe, 1973); the Frome Valley, Dorset (Bond 1982); in Cranborne Chase (Barrett and Bradley 1981)). But it is now considered that the clay-with-flint areas are the remains of zones once covered with the fertile soil known as loess, long since weathered away; they were therefore more rather than less attractive in the past (Bradley *et al.* 1984). The converse will also apply – areas which consistently produce no finds must be explained. In Bedfordshire an absence of Roman sites has been noted in the Oxford Clay region south-west of Bedford. This is not due to the lack of opportunity to observe sites in the past – in the last century there were many hand-dug brick pits here. The explanation in all probability is the heaviness of the soil and poor drainage.

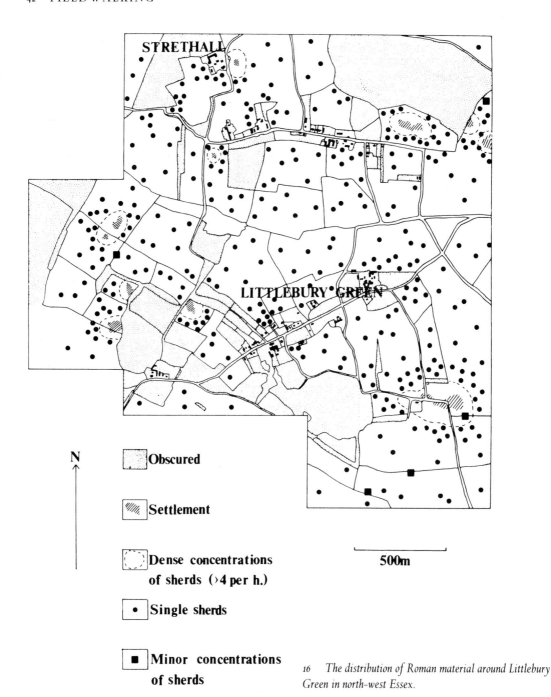

N

▢ **Obscured**

▨ **Settlement**

⬚ **Dense concentrations of sherds (>4 per h.)**

• **Single sherds**

■ **Minor concentrations of sherds**

16 The distribution of Roman material around Littlebury Green in north-west Essex.

Similarly the wet gault clay at the foot of the chalk escarpment near Leighton Buzzard was noted as a blank area by F. G. Gurney, a pioneer fieldwalker in the early years of the century (Simco 1984, 20–21).

The opportunity given by fieldwalking for looking at the landscape as a whole can be stressed again and the matter of manuring scatters discussed once more. There is no doubt that manuring was widely practised in prehistoric and Roman Britain (Fowler 1983, 117). Similarly there are references in medieval manorial accounts to the practice (Wise 1899, 51, 75; Postles 1979). So the reason for much of the background noise consisting of pottery of various periods scattered thinly around will reside in this, although sometimes other explanations have been offered. Similarly this explanation has been put forward for the light flint scatters which are such a feature of plough-land archaeology. The plotting of these manuring scatters can yield information of the greatest value. In north-west Essex the Roman scatter shows just how extensive Roman agriculture was (Fig. 16); it took place in areas subsequently wooded and until very recently considered never to have been under the plough (Williamson 1984). It was not medieval assarts which first brought about the development of the area; the Romano-British farmers had been there first. In the Maddle Farm project, a plot of the manuring scatter enabled suggestions to be made in some detail about how particular areas of land were actually used. Some areas close to the villa (which itself yielded abundant material) yielded few finds and could be interpreted as zones of home pasture; beyond the arable subjected to intensive manuring, as indicated by the pottery scatter, was a dispersed series of small foci of pottery, regarded as the sites of manure heaps, or maybe haystacks, not as settlements, the whole forming an integrated system of land management of great intensity (Gaffney *et al.* 1985).

Finally, although everything which has been said in this chapter has related to the archaeology of *ploughed* land, perhaps the point should be made that advantage should be taken of *any* disturbance of the soil to recover sites and artefacts – such things as bare patches in grass fields, rabbit scrapes, the exposed faces of road cuttings. The celebrated Mesolithic site at Star Carr in Yorkshire was discovered by means of observations along drainage ditches. In towns, public open spaces not only preserve earthworks, but can yield significant artefact scatters if the ground is exposed. The recognition of a flint flake on a path on Hampstead Heath led to the discovery and excavation of a Mesolithic site in 1976 (Selkirk 1978, 24–6). A systematic survey of the bare earth patches and flower beds of the parks of north London produced evidence for extensive scatters of Neolithic flintwork as well as two Roman pottery manufacturing sites (Brown and Sheldon 1969).

3 Recording earthwork sites

A great deal of human activity involves the disturbance of the surface of the earth – digging ditches, heaping up banks, constructing buildings and fortifications, excavating quarries and ponds. After abandonment and decay and in the absence of later alteration or destruction, the places which have been subjected to this kind of disturbance will survive as areas of earthworks. These earthworks – and the term here is taken for convenience to include the grass-covered tumble of former stone structures – were deliberately made. There are other earthworks which, while artificial in the sense that they are the product of human activity, were not necessarily the result of a conscious decision to bring them into being – such as hollow ways, the result of the wearing effect of traffic, or lynchets, caused by the movement downhill of soil loosened by the action of the plough on a slope. Nevertheless, all are witness to past human activity and are very important grist to the archaeological mill.

The purpose behind the techniques of field surveying described here is to record these features by making plans of them – in other words by producing bird's eye views, drawn accurately to scale, according to certain generally understood conventions. Now the very notion of surveying and surveying instruments can act as a damper on enthusiasm and interest. Most people seem to regard surveying as a highly specialized activity understood only by a few professional people in possession of rarefied skills of a mathematical kind and with a peculiar technical language of their own; whereas fieldwalking, which involves finding objects, has a rather greater initial appeal. But the techniques actually required to deal with most archaeological sites are very simple, and their operation a matter of routine. Similarly the equipment needed is very simple. There is a very

pressing archaeological need for accurate field surveys; they are primary records, a source of basic information; and the making of plans in the field can be an enthralling, even exciting business as the realization takes hold that an understanding of a perhaps complex site is becoming a serious possibility.

The real problem in planning an earthwork lies not in the matter of technique or equipment but in deciding just what to measure up and draw and in working out how to represent it on paper. These are matters of judgement and can on occasion be matters of opinion.

Basic principles

Fig. 17 illustrates the basic principles which underlie most of the surveying techniques to be described in this book. For purposes of illustration a very small site has been chosen. A–C represents a *base line*, consisting of two 30 m (100 ft) tapes stretched out across the site. This base line can be represented by a pencil line drawn on a sheet of paper. From the base line on the ground a number of lines (called *offsets*) have been set out one after the other at right angles to the base line to points on the site which are significant for the purposes of making a plan, i.e. where corners occur and where there are changes of direction. Just how these right angles are obtained will be explained later; but perhaps it ought to be pointed out here that there is no strict necessity for these lines to be at right angles to the base line – any convenient angle can be chosen, provided that suitable equipment exists to measure it (Fig. 20). The points from which the offsets were laid out can be scaled off on the drawing at the time they were actually made; and lines, at right angles or otherwise, drawn from the pencil base line from these points can be made to represent the offsets

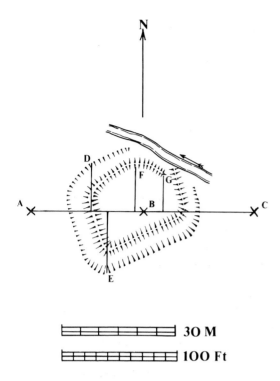

30 M

100 Ft

17 A very small earthwork at Welford in Northamptonshire, surveyed by means of offsets achieved by 'swinging the tape' (p.49).

on the paper. Points of archaeological detail can be measured along the offsets on the ground and the same points measured off to scale on the offsets on the plan. These points on the plan can be joined up, as the survey goes along, to produce a representation to scale of the archaeological site. Note that it is possible to check measurements, say, from B to F or G, to ensure that the plan is accurate and that the measurement on the ground corresponds to the measurement made to scale on the plan. Note also that the drawing of the plan is actually done in the field at the same time that the measurements are taken. It is thus possible to see whether the drawing in fact bears a reasonable resemblance to the site which is under investigation.

Drawing

A major difficulty arises from the fact that earthworks are unlike walls, excavation trenches, fences and even hedges, things which begin and end at easily identifiable places and have readily

measurable dimensions; they are inclined to be amorphous. The tops of well-marked banks and the bottoms of sharp ditches are usually clearly definable points, but even in cases of this kind there may be a problem in saying where the lips of the ditch start exactly and where the slope of the bank really begins, bearing in mind that a plan is drawn on the assumption that these places exist and can be represented on the drawing. Problems such as this will be much greater in the case of slighter earthworks, spread banks and silted-up ditches and the indeterminate bumps and hollows which seem frequently to mark the sites of deserted villages, for example. So what happens is that some judgement has to be made about the dimensions of many earthworks. Consider Fig. 18. This has two drawings, reproduced at the same scale, of a small motte and bailey at Flitwick, Bedfordshire, the first made by an extremely good archaeological field surveyor, B. Wadmore and published in 1920, and the second made 60 years later by a party of extra-mural students. Wadmore omitted the very slight slope which is all that is left of the northern side of the bailey, but apart from that the plans clearly agree about the shape of the earthwork. But the dimensions are not quite the same. This is simply because different people have chosen to regard the various slopes as beginning and ending in different places; but both surveys are correct. Note that there can be no disagreement about the *form* of an earthwork — a square earthwork is not an oval one, one shaped like an elongated sausage is not a rectangle. The basic question of form is almost always perfectly obvious in the field.

Earthworks are represented cartographically by means of *hachures*, a convention which has been in use for centuries. Basically these are tadpole-like marks which indicate slopes; the larger end of which (the head) represents the upper end of the slope and the thin end (the tail) the bottom. Fig. 19 demonstrates this. The length of a hachure should correspond to the width of the earthwork in question, to scale, measured horizontally. Fig. 20 shows how this kind of measurement is in fact made. A–B is a base line and C–D, E–F, G–H and I–J are offsets laid out from it to pick up a bank with a ditch on one side of it. The bank has two sides and a flat top and the ditch two faces and a flat bottom. So each offset has to pick up in turn

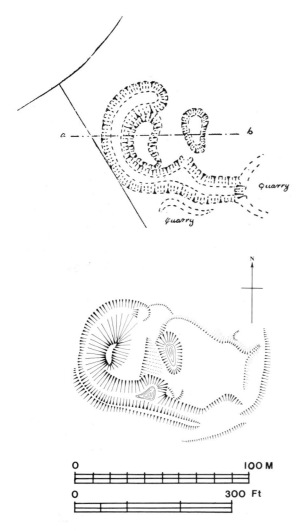

a ———— b

quarry

quarry

N

0   100 M

0   300 Ft

*18   The motte and bailey at Flitwick in Bedfordshire, as
published in 1920 (above), and as surveyed in 1982 (below).*

they turn through angles, fade away, stop abruptly, overlie each other and vary in steepness. All these things have to be indicated on the plan and the necessary measurements taken to enable this to be done. The best way of learning how to do this, apart from practice in the field, is to study carefully a series of good plans, such as those contained in the recent volumes of surveys published by the Royal Commission on the Historical Monuments of England. The fieldworker will also have to familiarize himself with the occasionally specialized language of archaeological field survey. Again, the study of good published plans in the light of their accompanying descriptions is useful. This will bring out such basic usages as the term 'scarp' (a term really derived from the science of fortification and meaning an artificial slope with one face), as opposed to a 'bank' (an upstanding earthwork with two faces), about which there is often some initial confusion.

So far we have dealt only with the problem of representing earthworks in the narrow sense of the term. But in the Highland Zone in particular field survey has to encounter sites composed of other materials – stone walls of various types, spreads of stone, banks with stones protruding at intervals suggesting tumbled grass-covered walls. There is no nationally agreed way of representing these things and the new field surveyor will have to design his own set of conventions and stick to them, making it clear in his published work just what they mean. Again, reference to the work of other field archaeologists will provide useful guidelines (e.g. Fleming and Ralph 1982; Fig. 21).

Scales

A crucial decision is the scale at which the drawing is to be done. It is a mistake to try to plan earthwork sites, particularly large ones, at too large a scale. The site shown on Fig. 33 measures 600 × 500 m (540 × 450 ft), covering 30 ha (75 acres). It was drawn at 1:1,250 and the original field drawing measured 43 × 53 cm (17 × 22 in), a perfectly manageable size for field purposes. Had it been drawn up at 1:500 the drawing would have been a rather less manageable 1·7 × 1·325 m (5 ft 7 in × 4 ft 4 in). It is perfectly possible to record the detail of a large complicated site at a scale of 1:1,250 or 1:1,000. If this proves difficult in certain

the (near) bottom of the bank, its (near) top, (far) top, (far) bottom, then the (near) top of the ditch, (near) bottom, (far) bottom and (far) top. This sounds complicated but in reality can be done very quickly once the basic decision has been made about just where these things are thought to be. This process is repeated as often as necessary to produce the plan; the points which represent the same parts of the feature are joined up by lines as the survey progresses, and hachures placed between these to indicate the direction and strength of the slope.

This is an easy example. The reality is that earthworks are very seldom straight and regular;

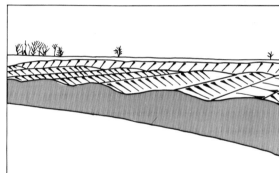

19   Ridge and furrow cut by the Grand Union canal at Great Bowden in Leicestershire, with a headland beyond. The diagram of the same scene (left) illustrates how hachures are used to represent earthworks cartographically.

20   The survey of a bank ditch. A—B is the base line; C—D, E—F, G—H, and I—J are offsets at right angles to this; C—L and I—D are 45° offset lines set out with a crosshead. The shaded portions at the sides represent sections at right angles through the earthwork.

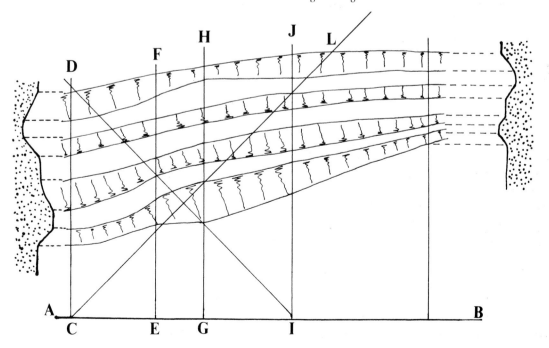

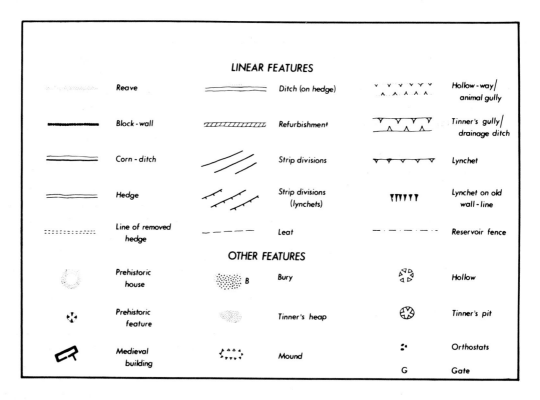

21 Example of a set of conventions in the presentation of survey work on Dartmoor. (Fleming and Ralph 1982)

places particular areas can be drawn at a larger scale and published as insets or as extra drawings as in Fig. 59, where the detail of the seventeenth-century garden, with paths and flower beds, drawn at 1:500, was published as a separate entity. What this boils down to in practice is that for large sites, spreads of medieval earthworks, for example, a scale of 1:1,250 (conveniently twice the standard 1:2,500 Ordnance Survey map scale) or 1:1,000 (currently in use by the Royal Commission on the Historical Monuments of England) is suitable. Smaller earthworks, say moats, mill sites, fishponds, or the complicated detail of larger ones, can be drawn at 1:500. Only very small sites such as individual houses with a great deal of fine detail need be drawn at 1:100.

The decision about scale affects the conduct of the survey in the field. If 1:1,250 or 1:1,000 is chosen, it is impossible to measure anything with a greater degree of accuracy than half a metre. This is because at that scale the thickness of a pencil line will represent that. Similarly at 1:500 it is not really possible to measure below 10 cm. This does not mean to say that inaccuracy is to be tolerated; sometimes there is a tendency to think that estimated, paced or plain guessed measurements within the framework of a base line and, say, a couple of offsets will suffice. This is not so.

Equipment

New surveying equipment is expensive. This goes for instruments of the traditional kind – the level, staff, plane-table and alidade – but it is still more true of the new electronic distance-measuring equipment now on the market. This is quick, accurate and versatile but will involve a layout of several thousand pounds. One of the aims of this book is to convey the idea that good, worthwhile fieldwork can be done by those without access to this kind of equipment but without descending to the level of the pea sticks and visiting card apparently used at one time by a certain eminent archaeologist (Wheeler 1956, 168).

Some essential basic requirements will have to be enumerated at the outset. The surveyor will need one or more drawing boards; these can be made quite easily from good plywood. Plain good-quality cartridge paper will be required; this and anything else will have to be attached to the board by means of drafting tape, not drawing pins. Given the problems of the British climate, transparent drawing film is essential; the drawing can be done on this fixed on top of the drawing paper if rain is anticipated. For drawing on film pencils should be hard (2H or 3H; a sharp HB pencil will do for cartridge paper) and a sharpener and eraser should always be carried; a pencil-like typist's rubber is useful. Also a set of scales will be required, a protractor or at least a 45 degree set square. The fieldworker should also have a notebook or a set of pre-printed or photocopied record sheets with standard headings. Some ranging rods, at least four, will be required. These need not necessarily be the metal or wooden red and white 2 metre ones; broom handles, painted or not, and sharpened at the end will do, or other similar alternatives. Because of their associations with unwanted road and housing development, ranging rods can on occasion arouse suspicion and sometimes hostility, and a less conspicuous alternative is occasionally an advantage. Also some surveyor's arrows or tent pegs will be needed to mark points as the surveying progresses and to fix down the 30 m (100 ft) tapes which will be used; a minimum of three of these will be needed on most sites.

Another fundamental matter is the relationship between archaeological field survey and Ordnance Survey maps. Unless carried out in remote moorland areas, no archaeological plan should be published divorced from its man-made environment of hedges, buildings and roads. Surveying these *de novo* can be a tedious and a time-consuming job, vastly increasing the length of the surveying process. It is therefore sensible to make use of the fact that most man-made features will already have been marked on Ordnance maps. Unless working in one of the relatively few areas for which 1:1,250 maps have been produced, the largest Ordnance Survey scale is 1:2,500, too small for our purposes. So the relevant part of the map has to be abstracted and enlarged by the appropriate amount, mostly × 2, since at 1:500 scale most of the modern detail will probably have to be the subject of original survey anyway. This enlargement can be done photographically, or if this is not possible, manually. Using a set square, this will involve the creation of a grid of squares in

pencil across the face of the map or a tracing taken from it. On a separate sheet a similar grid should be drawn with the sides of the squares twice that of the grid on the map. Such detail as, for example, where field boundaries cut the squares on the original, can be measured, scaled up and transferred to the new, larger grid. The map so produced can be traced, so providing a copy free of grid lines. However produced, the enlargement can be taken into the field fixed to the drawing board and the survey done directly on to it, using as a base line a line joining points marked on the Ordnance map and recognizable on the ground – such things as the sharp (not curved) corners of fields, and the corners of buildings; or alternatively, the ends of the base line can be measured out along hedges and walls, the appropriate points scaled off on the enlarged map and then joined up.

There are certain difficulties in the use of Ordnance maps. In the first place the publication of a drawing based on an Ordnance map is subject to crown copyright; permission must be sought from the Ordnance Survey and a fee paid. This does not apply to maps fifty years old, and so earlier editions are particularly useful. The obvious drawback is that the landscape may well have changed considerably since the older map was made and great care will have to be exercised in deciding whether the points which look useful as the terminal points of base lines on the ground are in fact the same points on the map. This is sometimes harder to do than it sounds. If an error is made then clearly the whole survey will be wrong.

Surveying procedure

(a) *Swinging the tape.* There is no reason why a little site such as that shown on Fig. 17 should not be surveyed entirely by the very basic method of *swinging the tape.* As already described, a base line is laid out across the site, using a 30 metre tape. One of the surveyors takes another tape and holds the zero end over archaeological detail which it is wished to plot in. Another surveyor stands against the base line and swings the second tape against it until the shortest distance between the base tape and the point of interest is obtained, measured horizontally, as all tape survey measurements must be. The second surveyor can then read off the point on the base tape at which this is found, and the shortest distance reading itself. He can call his measurement out to a third person responsible for the drawing (in a fixed order – measurement along the base line first, measurement away from the base line along the offset second) or, if he is doing the drawing himself, plot them directly on to the paper. This very basic method involves no instruments but has the disadvantage that it only really works over very short distances, say up to 15 m (50 ft) on unencumbered ground. Accuracy tends to decline sharply the further from the base tape one goes; the swinging tape is always liable to engage on tufts of grass and suchlike minor protuberances and to develop kinks. But it is a technique which is always useful, even on surveys of large sites in which instruments are being used, to fill in points of detail which are a short distance from any of the lines laid out during the survey.

(b) *3–4–5*. A traditional way of obtaining a right angle is the *3–4–5 method*. In this case a point is chosen on the base tape from which it is desired the right-angled offset should proceed. This is marked by a surveyor's arrow and another point on the base line 4 metres (or a reasonable multiple thereof) from it similarly marked. A second tape should then have its zero end fixed at the first point and the 8 metre mark (or the appropriate multiple – i.e. twice the distance measured out along the base tape) held at the second point. The 3 metre (or equivalent) point on the second tape should then be taken and the tape stretched out on the correct side of the base line until taut. The 3 metre mark on this tape should then line up with the initial point on the base line to produce a right angle, and this offset line can be marked out with ranging rods. If a ranging rod is placed at the point from which the right angle leaves the base line, then this line can be projected to the other side of the base line and be used for survey there. Again this is a method best used for the creation of offsets intended to run for relatively short distances; it is actually quite hard to get a good right angle this way. There is a certain cumbrousness about the method and it is not useful for fixing a line at right angles to the base line *from* a point of interest; its main purpose is to set out offsets from the base line itself and it is not always easy to so arrange matters that these go exactly to the most

useful places. However, short offsets can be obtained by swinging the tape from significant points to the main offsets thus set out as well as to the original base line and it is possible to get complete surveys done in this way.

(c) *Optical Square*. A useful instrument for getting offsets at right angles to a base line over short distances from a significant point is the *optical square* (Fig. 22). Essentially this little instrument consists of a metal pillbox with an eye aperture and a hole opposite this. It is therefore possible for someone standing on a base line marked out by a tape and ranging rods to align the instrument along the base line. The instrument also contains a mirror set at right angles to this line of sight and an opening in the side of the instrument opposite the mirror. So the image actually seen through the eye aperture is a split one, half representing what is straight ahead, in this case the ranging rod and the base line, the other half what is at right angles to this. The optical square can therefore be used to set out offset lines at right angles to a base line from a predetermined point upon it – the square is held over this point and someone with a ranging rod moves to right and left on the desired side of the base line until the person with the optical square can see that the vertical images of the base-line ranging rods and the rod set to one side coincide. The optical square is particularly

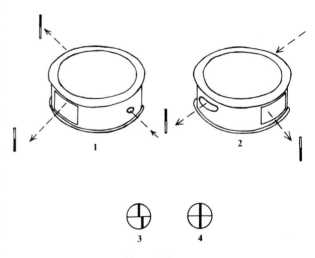

22   *The optical square. (1) and (2) show the instrument in use; (3) and (4) show the view through the aperture before and after the images of the ranging rods have been matched up.*

useful for one-man surveys. In this case the point on the site to be measured in from a base line is marked by a ranging rod. The surveyor then walks along the base line with the optical square aligned with the ranging rods set along it until he sees the image of the rod placed on the archaeological feature coinciding with that of the base-line rods. A tape from the point to be surveyed to the base line at the place at which the coincidental images were visible will be at right angles to the base line.

(*d*) *Crosshead.* A more flexible instrument is the *crosshead.* Nowadays a crosshead bought from a firm of instrument-makers would be an expensive optical instrument. But a simple home-made version can be produced which will do a perfectly good archaeological job with considerable accuracy; Fig. 23 illustrates a couple of examples. The instrument consists of a head with a series of slits in it (or a board with nails, a cheaper version) at 45 degrees to each other. Its method of operation can be illustrated by means of a simple site, Fig. 24. The base line is laid out in the ordinary way and the various pieces of the site close to the start of it drawn in directly from the base line where cut by it, or by swinging the tape. The crosshead is then set up anywhere on the base line convenient for the initial part of the survey; it does not have to be at any fixed distance, say 10, 15

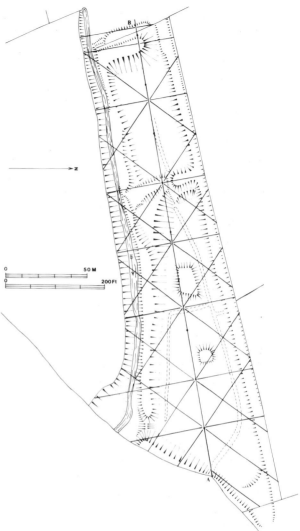

24 *A portion of the Priory fishpond complex at Harrold in Bedfordshire, showing the base line A—B and the radial lines set out with a crosshead. Details not cut by these or the base line were surveyed by means of simple offsets. 30 metre lengths along the base line are indicated by dots.*

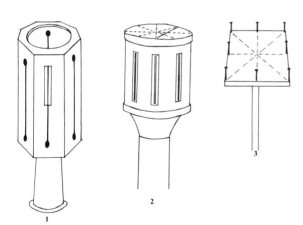

23 *A variety of crossheads. The first is a professionally made instrument, now hard to obtain. The second was home made on a lathe; the broken lines indicate lines of sight, and the continuous line shows the error of misalignment easily made with this design. The third is home made, board-and-nails 'bird-table' type.*

or 20 metres from the origin of the base line, as some people at first tend to think. It is then sighted along the base line using the base-line ranging rods and a pair of opposing slits; this must be got right and it is advisable to repeat the operation twice, on both sides of the crosshead, to make sure. Once correctly set up, lines of sight from opposing slits of the crosshead, the position of which must be marked on the plan, will therefore be at 45 or 90 degrees to the base line, and six of them are possible, three a side. So a system of radiating lines can be laid out one after the other from the place at which the crosshead is fixed. These will cut archaeological detail which can be plotted in directly; anything not measured in this way can be plotted by swinging the tape if it is not too far from one of the radial lines. In this way the first part of the site can be covered with a network of lines yielding measured points which can be joined up on the plan as the survey proceeds. The crosshead can then be moved further along the base line and the process repeated. Despite its simplicity a well-made crosshead is quite an accurate instrument and throws of 60 m (200 ft) can be obtained using an instrument with narrow slits. But the further the radial lines are from the base line the further apart they move from each other; swinging the tape becomes less reliable as a way of filling in the gaps. Now there is no reason why the crosshead should spend all its time on the base line. It can be removed, its place taken by a ranging rod, and taken to any convenient point on one of the radial lines and sighted back to the base line. A fresh set of radial lines can then be laid out which will in places cut lines already laid out and which will have produced measured information on the plan. So from time to time the same points can be measured in twice on the plan and a check automatically obtained on the accuracy of the survey.

Larger sites, or sites with problems of intervisibility caused by tall hedges or buildings, may require more than one base line. Fig. 25 is an example of this, where a large site with prominent earthworks could not be dealt with effectively from a single base line laid across it. The solution adopted here was to lay out two further base lines at right angles to the first – lines indistinguishable from offsets, in effect. But particular care was taken to make sure by means of checked measurements using 45 degree offsets from the new lines back to the original base line that they were correctly set out. An alternative way of dealing with the matter of more than one base line is to lay out the base lines required to cover the site within the framework of the fields occupied by it. Each field or group of fields can be surveyed separately and the whole survey finally put together using an enlarged Ordnance Survey map.

(e) *The Plane-table*. An instrument commonly thought of as useful for archaeological field survey is the *plane-table*. As its name implies, this is merely a drawing-board which has a simple device on one side to enable it to be fixed to a tripod. It has to be used with an alidade, which at its simplest is a ruler with collapsible sighting vanes at both ends; complicated alidades with telescopic sights marked up for tacheometry and with various levelling devices are also available. There are also other accessories which can be used such as plumbing forks and the box compass. The methods of survey known as intersection and traversing will not be described here (for these see Fryer 1961). But there is a simple method of using the plane-table which is found convenient by some archaeologists, known as radiation. In this case the plane-table, suitably covered with paper and film, is set up in a place from which most of the site can be conveniently seen and measured; a point is marked on it to correspond with the point on the ground below the table from which measurements to points on the site are to be made (an exact method of achieving the correspondence is to use a plumbing fork). The table is levelled up using a spirit level or more simply by placing a pencil on it and moving the table about until the pencil ceases to roll off. A helper can now stand at one of the places on the site which has to be measured in, holding a ranging rod. The surveyor then places the alidade against the point marked on his table (the point can be marked by a pin and the alidade held against that) and sights it at the ranging rod. Using the edge of the alidade, a pencil line can be drawn on the plane-table to correspond with the line of sight directed at the ranging rod. A tape fixed to the ground by means of an arrow below the table can be laid out in the direction of the rod and the distance of the rod from the point below the table scaled off on the drawn line; this fixes that particular point on the survey. While the tape is on the ground minor offsets can be taken from points near at hand and plotted directly on the table in relation to the drawn line. The ranging rod can then be moved to another part of the site, the process repeated and the points on the plane-table plan joined up as the survey goes along. The process produces accurate plans, and some people find that drawing on a table is convenient. But the plane-table itself

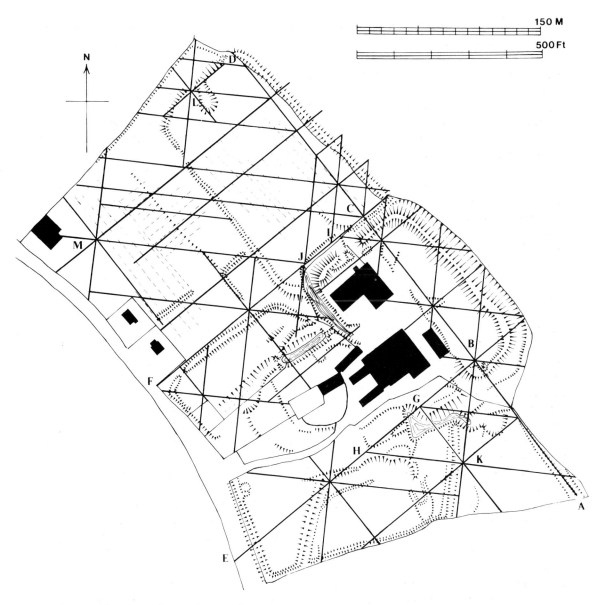

150 M

500 Ft

is a rather cumbersome thing to carry about and there is a tendency for it to blow about in the wind.

(f) The Compass. So far nothing has been said about the provision of north points on archaeological plans. As far as possible all plans should be published with north at the top, for consistency and intelligibility in relation to the parallel written description. Unless the survey has been drawn directly on to an enlarged Ordnance Survey map the field plan has to have information placed on it which will enable its orientation in relation to north to be fixed. This can be done in

25 *Lavendon Castle in Buckinghamshire: a complicated site, showing the main survey lines used, employing an accurate crosshead. ABCD is the base line. B—E and C—F are long offsets designed to get at detail to the south-west of the bailey; check lines have been set out from these at G, H, I and J back to the base line. Note how the crosshead has been moved from both the base line and the main offsets to, for example, L, M and K, to take in features some distance from the principal lines; the long lines north-west of the bailey were set out to enable the ridge and furrow to be measured in.*

two ways. One method involves using a compass to take a bearing along one of the base lines and recording this on the drawing; in practice two readings should be taken in both directions for checking purposes. The difference between the two readings should be 180 degrees. This will enable a line to be drawn on the survey which will show the direction of magnetic north. The position of true north can be calculated using the standard information given on 1:25,000 Ordnance Survey maps. An alternative and perhaps easier method is to work out the direction of north from the way in which the Ordnance Survey north–south grid lines cut the hedges, fences, etc. in the area of the site. Since the boundaries of the plan will be the same as those on the Ordnance map, the direction of north can easily be transferred to the archaeological drawing.

The compass can be used as a surveying instrument in its own right. Raymond Farrar has described a simple system for earthwork survey which is particularly suitable for one-man work in that it cuts out a great deal of the time-consuming walking about which can be such a tedious feature of this activity (Farrar 1980). No base line need be laid out since the compass carries its own base line around with it – the angles obtained by reading the compass are always related to the same point, magnetic north. For a detailed description of the method the reader is referred to Raymond Farrar's pamphlet, but in essence it is this. A point is chosen on the ground from which the survey is to begin. This is marked on the paper. A ranging rod is set up at the next point on the ground which it is desired to measure in. A compass reading taken from the start point to the new point will give the bearing of the latter from the former. A line can be drawn on the plan from the start point to represent the angle of the bearing of the new point; magnetic north can be taken to coincide with the top of the sheet of drawing paper used – the survey can perhaps best be done on transparent film over graph paper, which provides plenty of lines from which bearing angles can be measured. A horizontal tape measurement from the start point to the new point will give the distance of one from the other; this can be scaled off on the plan. The surveyor can then repeat the process as much as he likes from the original point, or move to one of the new ones and survey

in fresh points using the same method, joining up the appropriate points on the paper as he goes along.

A variation of this method which has been used by the writer on small, compact sites has been to stand with the compass in the middle of the site (or better still place it on a tripod). A point can be marked on the plan to represent this and, unless graph paper is being used, a line can be drawn passing through this point to mark the direction of magnetic north. Bearings can be taken to any point on the site from the fixed point in the centre and lines drawn on the plan to represent these, at the correct angles to the line representing the direction of magnetic north. A tape can be used simultaneously to record distances between the central point and the places to which bearings have been taken, and these distances can be scaled off on the drawing. There is of course no difficulty in drawing a line to represent the direction of true north with surveys done in either of these ways.

Heights

The measurement of height sometimes seems to be a difficulty. These must be vertical measurements. There are small hand-held clinometers and height meters available which can be used for this work, or an accurate measurement can be obtained by holding a ranging rod vertically at the foot of a scarp, with a tape held against the rod; another rod or tape can be stretched out horizontally from the top of the scarp to meet the rod, and the distance from the point at which this happens to the ground read off. But after a while it is possible to judge by eye the heights of earthworks, particularly relatively low ones, with sufficient accuracy for the purposes of field survey. Deep ditches and high ramparts can be measured accurately enough by using the method recommended many years ago by Dr Williams Freeman (1915, 331). This involves working out the height of one's eye from the ground; and then proceeding up the earthwork, noting points equivalent to one's eye level during the process.

Measured profiles are really required relatively infrequently. There are instances, though, when it is worth producing one – for example, to demonstrate just how powerful a set of defences were, what the profile of a well-preserved barrow is like, or how carefully the terraced path of a post-medieval garden was designed; sometimes the relationship between the natural topography and the earthworks has a special importance and can be usefully illustrated by a section. However, even if a high bank or deep ditch is encountered, the chances are that when a measured profile is taken and reproduced at the same scale as the rest of the drawing, the differences in height between the various parts of the section line will appear to be insignificant compared with the impression given on the ground.

If a measured profile is not provided – and this will be the case in the majority of instances – the relative steepness of slopes can be suggested by variations in the thickness and density of the

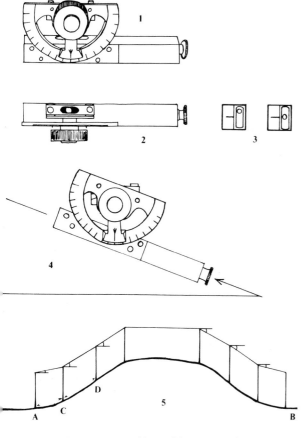

26   *The Abney level. (1) and (2) are views of the instrument; (3) shows the spirit level bubble and the sighting bar; (4) shows the instrument in use, demonstrating how the angle in relation to the horizontal is obtained; (5) indicates how the section measurement is set out and carried forward.*

hachuring. If natural slopes are shown by hachuring the hachures must be differentiated from the ones representing the artificial slopes, perhaps by giving them hollow heads. The contours of the local topography can be added to the archaeological plan by copying them from the 1:10,000 or 1:25,000 Ordnance Survey map (e.g. Fig. 37).

If a measured profile is required, a suitable instrument is the *Abney level* (Fig. 26). This consists of a tube with an eyepiece at one end. Attached to the tube is a fixed protractor-like scale of degrees and a movable knob to which is attached a spirit level and an arm which moves against the degree scale. A view through the eyepiece along the tube shows an image split vertically into two; the left side of the tube has a small indicator bar set horizontally and the right side has the bubble of the spirit-level moving up and down inside its tube. The use of the level involves the following procedure. As a preliminary, a ranging rod is driven into the ground and the top of it marked with a piece of surgical tape or something similar at the eye level of the observer. At the site, a line is marked out with ranging rods to correspond with the line over which a profile is required (Fig. 26(5), A–B). The terminal points of this line must be marked on the site plan. The surveyor places a ranging rod at the first point on the ground along the marked line which is considered useful for the purpose of enabling the profile to be drawn (C on Fig. 26(5)). He next stands at the start of the marked-out line and points the tube of the Abney level at this ranging rod so that the sighting bar coincides with the mark made at the top of it. He then adjusts the knob at the side of the level to bring the spirit level bubble opposite the bar. This will at the same time move the indicator on the side of the instrument along the protractor scale; the level can then be taken down and the angle between the eye-level indicator at the top of the ranging rod and the horizontal noted down. The distance can also be noted between the start of the line of survey and the first point to which a reading has been taken, measured along the ground and not horizontally (this is one of the very few occasions on which this is done in field survey; (A–C in Fig. 26(5)). The surveyor then moves the ranging rod to the next useful or significant point along the section line (e.g. where there is a change in the profile) and stands at the point to which the last reading was taken. He repeats the process of measuring the angle and distance along the ground; and goes on doing this until the whole line has been dealt with, noting the angles, distances and whether the angles show that the profile is tending upwards or downwards. This information can then be drawn out to scale, preferably on squared paper, which makes the reproduction of lines representing the angles in relation to the horizontal an easy matter This rather stilted drawing can then be smoothed out, perhaps at the same time as the squared-paper drawing is traced off on to the finished drawing of the whole site.

The Abney level is relatively cheap and easy to use, but is not so accurate as the level proper. This instrument, which must be used in conjunction with a Sopwith staff, is expensive, relatively cumbersome to use but extremely accurate. Its workings will not be described here (there is a good account in Coles 1972, 93–108). In addition, however, to its function as an instrument useful in obtaining accurate profiles, the level is essential in the matter of contouring (see below) and as a way of measuring horizontal distances by means of the technique known as tacheometry (Fryer 1961, 30–31). This has its uses in field archaeology in measuring areas of ancient field systems, when the distances to be covered can be considerable.

The level is also of use in the solution of the kind of problem illustrated in Fig. 24. Many fishponds have mounds in them, usually interpreted as islands on which wildfowl could breed; one of these ponds had two. In order to test whether the usual explanation could be right in this case, a level was used to compare the heights of the mounds with the scarps marking the edges of the pond, the dam and the outflow channel. This showed that when the pond was full the mounds did indeed project above the water, by 10 cm.

The base line

The best place for this to be sited is across the middle of a site, with an even spread of earthworks on both sides. But wherever it is placed and whatever survey method is used, the terminal points must always be securely marked, and if possible their ranging rods left in for the duration

of the survey. These are the primary fixed points on which ultimately all sighting depends. Moving tapes along the base line as the survey proceeds can sometimes be a source of error. Obviously the base line will have to be measured out as the survey goes along in units of 30 m (100 ft); it is useful to mark the terminal points of these individual lengths with small circles on the drawn representation of the base line, to distinguish them from other working markings. But it is possible when the tape is being moved forward from one 30 m length to another to re-lay it the wrong way round. Clearly the zero end must always point towards the end of the base line from which the survey started, but sometimes the 30 m end can be made to do this, a source of grave error for any surveying carried out subsequently. Checking back in the way indicated will pick the errors up eventually, but much time can be wasted in the interval and in the process of putting things right.

The aim of the above paragraphs has been to indicate a range of very straightforward techniques using simple, inexpensive equipment. What the field surveyor basically needs is some way of measuring distances and a way of measuring angles in relation to a fixed line; these techniques are not mutually exclusive but can be used in combination with each other.

Note taking and writing up

While the survey is in progress the fieldworker must make notes from which a written description of the site can be prepared; pre-prepared record sheets are a useful aid in this. This is an aspect of field survey which is frequently neglected. Good notes *must* be made while the survey is in progress; it is simply no good hoping to write the details up from memory afterwards and the site may not still be there in its original form for checking in three months' time. Such basic facts as the heights of scarps, depths and profiles of ditches (V- or U-shaped, flat-bottomed), the widths and characteristics of banks (flat- or round-topped, how constructed), are required; sketch sections may be helpful in particular instances; the relationship of one feature to another (e.g. cut by, overlaid, or on the same alignment as another one), or its state of preservation and the reasons for this (say destroyed by a modern farm track, or old quarry, or clearly partially overlaid by modern farm buildings) must be recorded. With very small sites such as Fig. 17 it may well be possible to write these things on the field drawing itself as the work goes ahead, against each particular feature; but for most sites this will not do, and a more formalized system is required. For years excavators have been familiar with the business of allotting numbers to each feature or layer encountered during their work, and field surveyors could easily adopt the same mode. A record sheet could be made out for each surveyed site, giving its parish name and its own name (if any), the National Grid Reference, basic ownership details, the scale, name of the surveyor and date; but also the sheet could contain a series of numbers corresponding to numbers marked against features on the field drawing and allotted as the survey proceeds. The necessary remarks could be made against the relevant number on the record sheet.

When all this has been done and the field drawing and notes completed, the process of preparing the final drawing and written description can begin. If the field drawings have got dirty or if the site has been drawn in the field in sections, a pencil tracing of the whole plan, complete with surrounding topographical features, will have to be made. This will show the guidelines for the hachures, enough hachures to give an adequate idea of the nature of the earthworks and in particular the reference numbers of the various features. If the original field drawing is in good order this tracing will not be necessary. The north point must be added, the name and grid reference of the site, the scale, the date of the survey and the name of the person who did it. This and the field notes are archive documents, as important in their way as any original drawings of a section on an excavation. The written description of the site must be done now and not left until a later date when the details will have faded from the memory; certain points not necessarily ascertainable when the fieldwork was done such as the details of the local geology must be sorted out. This description will amount to an *interpretation* of the site based on the accumulated and hopefully objective evidence enshrined in the field notes and drawing. Thus

reasons will have to be given, or at least clearly implied, for saying in the write-up that a shallow linear depression with a gently rounded bottom is a hollow way and not just a broadish ditch; it must be indicated that the statement that a series of low sub-rectangular mounds represents the sites of houses is a suggestion made on the basis of probability, experience and just possibly excavated evidence somewhere, and not an absolute certainty. The fact is that some quite well-preserved earthworks turn out on excavation to be a poor guide to what lies beneath. At Middleton Stoney in Oxfordshire, a large motte turned out to be simply destruction rubble around a square stone keep (Rahtz and Rowley 1984). At Richards Castle, Hereford and Worcester, a rather similar situation was found in that the huge height of the motte was discovered to be quite substantially due to the levelled-off lower part of a massive octagonal tower (Curnow and Thompson 1969).

Finally the definitive inked tracing of the survey can be made, using drawing film. The guidelines showing the tops and bottoms of the scarps are not drawn, but hachures are inserted between them to show the form and character of the earthworks. Almost anyone can produce competent hachures given practice and a little effort; the very best hachuring requires a degree of skill and talent not often found. North points, topographical detail, scale bars in feet and metres and contours should be added, as well as such lettering as is required to name features and to relate specific parts to the written description. A drawing such as this is a finished product, but thought should be given to making it a more pleasant and exciting thing to look at by adding a border, a title or even some decoration, perhaps appropriate heraldic shields (Fig. 27). There is no reason why an archaeological drawing should not be an attractive object, provided the decoration is not carried too far and as long as the person doing the drawing has the necessary skills. If they are not there, stick to the plain but serviceable.

On seeing earthworks

Obviously the methods of surveying just described will not work unless the earthworks are recognized and understood by the fieldworker. In the case of big earthworks such as those shown in

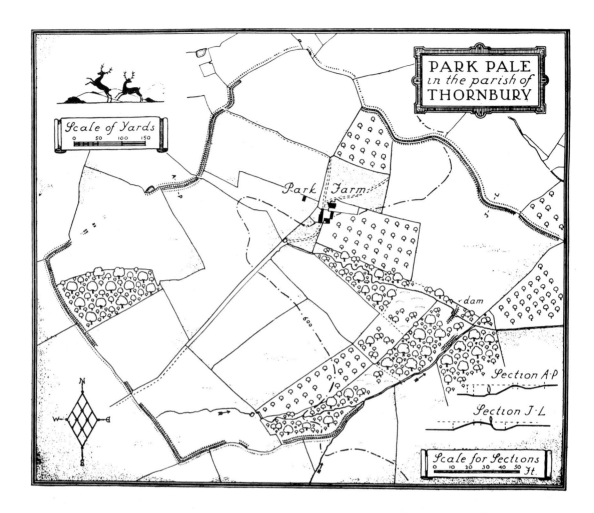

PARK PALE
in the parish of
THORNBURY

Scale of Yards
0   50   100   150

Park Farm

dam

Section A·P

Section J·L

Scale for Sections
0   10   20   30   40   50   ft.

N
W ——— E
S

27   *Park Pale, Thornbury, Hereford and Worcester. Taken from an RCHM volume of the 1930s, this illustrates how it is possible to combine accuracy of fieldwork with attractive presentation.*

Fig. 25, or the ponds in Fig. 24, there is little difficulty; but many earthworks are relatively slight. The beginner is quite often in some difficulty to see them at all, let alone being able to visualize what shapes these slight irregularities have and how they are to be represented on the drawing. The answer is as usual experience under supervision. This is an important matter because, as will be explained later, many sites have preserved in odd corners traces of the landscape on which they were set − low ridge and furrow, often very battered, for example. The recording of this is absolutely vital, but it is easy to miss such faint traces. Just as there are people who are by

nature good at fieldwalking, so there are those who are naturally able at the business of seeing earthworks, although some people will always find it a difficult task.

However, in addition to experience and natural talent, it is important to be aware of the conditions that make the chances of seeing and understanding low earthworks easier. No one would dream of doing serious earthwork study on moorland in summer, when bracken is high; the height of grass can be a serious problem anywhere. The early spring months are the best, with low grass and the chance of slanting light to throw low scarps into visual clarity. Melting snow can transform one's appreciation of the landscape; Fig. 28 is an example where the snow enables the low ridge and furrow to be seen more easily. Similarly changes in the nature of the vegetation can be significant; Fig. 29 shows how

28 Flattened ridge and furrow revealed by melting snow at Kibworth, Leicestershire.

29 Kibworth, Leicestershire. The ridge and furrow here has been almost flattened by modern ploughng. The alternating light and dark bands show how variations in the colour of the grass and other vegetation still enabled the earthworks to be seen, although the effect was transitory and was obliterated as the grass developed.

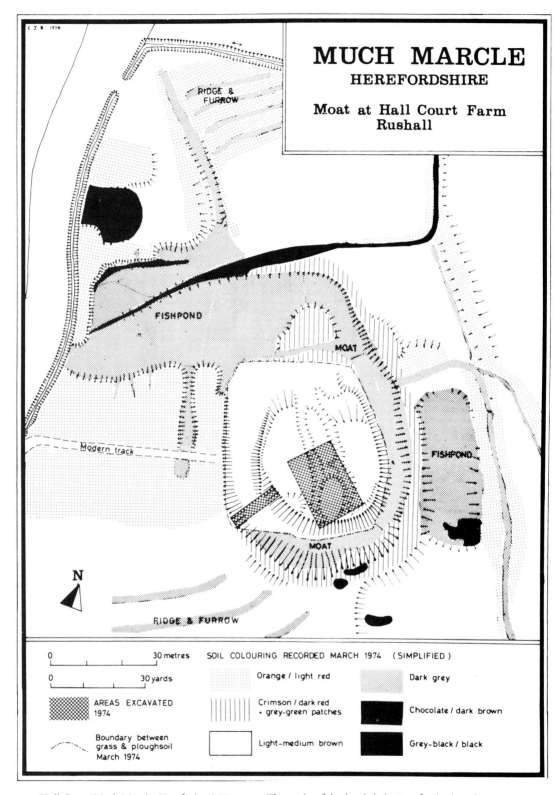

30   *Hall Court, Much Marcle, Hereford and Worcester. The results of the detailed plotting of soil colour changes.*

even slight changes in the colour and quality of grass can betray the faint traces of poorly preserved ridge and furrow.

Earthworks which have been ploughed can be a particular problem because of the way they merge with the surrounding landscape. Lighting is crucial, as are sometimes variations in the colour and nature of the soil and the presence or otherwise of stones. Plough ridges frequently betray themselves by their colour differentiation. A spectacular example of the effects of ploughing could be seen at Hall Court, Much Marcle, Hereford and Worcester where the area around a rather insignificant moated site was revealed in winter after ploughing to contain two fishponds, a perimeter bank, a complex system of leats, building platforms and a possible mill site, all marked by colour changes in the soil and not really visible before (Fig. 30; Bond 1978).

Contouring

Everything therefore depends on the acuteness of vision and understanding of the fieldworker; the whole business is a matter of subjective judgement and interpretation, as is the drawing of sections on an excavation. The only absolutely 'scientific' and objective method of field survey is contouring (for the technique see Coles 1972, 110–14). This can be done fairly simply but may be exceedingly time-consuming; it involves the use of the level and staff and the creation of a grid across the site, level readings being taken at the intersections and the positioning of the contour lines determined by interpolation. There are occasions when a contour plan might seem to be preferable to a hachured one, as for example in showing the precise shape of a mound, something difficult to do with hachures. But such occasions will be relatively few. Generally speaking, contour surveys of earthworks are hard to interpret, less informative and sometimes downright misleading compared with hachured ones. Compare the drawings in Fig. 31. The contour survey omits much of the detail of the hachured example, notably the ridge and furrow which is an important feature of this particular site.

Surveys of large areas at small scales and of built-up areas

The fieldworker will frequently find himself

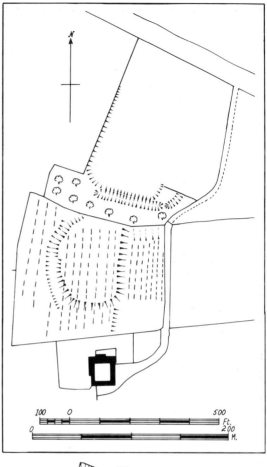

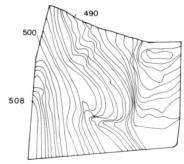

31   *John of Gaunt's Castle at Daventry in Northamptonshire; plan produced by conventional tape survey. There is probably a sequence here; the moated site, badly damaged by a nineteenth-century brickworks, survives only in the thin strip of woodland across the middle of the drawing. This may have replaced the D-shaped earthwork to the south of it; this in turn had been over-ploughed with ridge and furrow. Below is a contour plan of the southernmost field with contours at a vertical interval of one metre. Although the outlines of the earthwork can be made out, the details are obscure, and phasing would be harder to suggest.*

engaged in the survey of archaeological features which run for considerable distances – long dyke systems, Roman or other ancient roads, medieval park pales, leats and embankments belonging to industrial complexes. In these cases the formal set piece survey at 1:1,250 or 1:1,000 is inappropriate. These features can be plotted by tape or sometimes by pacing directly on to 1:10,000 Ordnance Survey maps using suitable conventions, or better still on to maps of this type enlarged to twice their size. Quite frequently a thick line can be used to denote a bank, a thin line to one side of it the outer edge of a ditch (Fig. 50; but here this convention has in fact been used in reverse). But if possible hachures should still be used – these give greater precision and avoid misunderstandings (Fig. 27). From time to time sections can be taken with the Abney level and their locations measured in. For final publication a redrawn version of the field drawing done on an Ordnance Survey base will be perfectly satisfactory, on the lines of the distinguished precedents set by Sir Cyril Fox in his famous Offa's Dyke survey (Fox 1955) or I. D. Margary's work on Roman roads in Sussex (Margary 1948).

For ridge and furrow dashed lines representing the direction and the often curved shape of the plough ridges (not every ridge, impossible at a small scale) should be sufficient (Fig. 40). In the field the low banks representing the headlands should be looked for; these mark the boundaries between the furlongs, are generally bigger than the plough ridges, and may be the only earthworks left. Plough ridges will have run at right angles to them, although not necessarily on both sides of the same headland. In this kind of survey an appreciation of the details of the microtopography is important; such things as the fall of the ground, breaks of slope and the existence of quite small valleys had a determining influence upon the way in which the land drained and conditioned the layout of the furlongs. The remains of old trackways exemplified archaeologically by hollow ways and terraces can also be picked up, as well as the ditch systems which sometimes formed elaborate drainage schemes.

It may be thought that the plotting of landscape features in the field directly on to maps had little part to play in built-up areas, but this is not really true. The analysis of the plans of towns and villages demands an understanding of the underlying topography at a detailed level, and the Ordnance map may not give the complete answer; so sketching the behaviour of the landscape on 1:2,500 maps is an essential part of the process. Fig. 32 is a working drawing of Towcester in Northamptonshire prepared in this way, really in an attempt to work out the line of the defences of this much-fortified town by looking for scarps and changes of slope in back gardens. The opportunity was also taken to plot the location of finds of Roman material from early printed sources and by discussion with local people. These show a marked tendency to follow the lines of known Roman roads. Since there are many finds along the general line of the modern road to Brackley, it can be suggested that this had a Roman basis, leading possibly to a large site at King's Sutton; and the observation by the nineteenth-century antiquary Sir Henry Dryden of large quantities of Roman material turning up in the area of the railway station in the 1860s suggests that yet another road, leading this time to Duston near Northampton, ran along dry ground on the northern side of the River Tove. It cannot be claimed that the results of this kind of survey are particularly conclusive always, but they do throw up possibilities which could be taken into account in planning excavations.

Photographs

Of course photographic records should be made of earthwork sites to show their general form and condition; but there are certain difficulties. Quite frequently it is impossible to get a wide enough view of a site to make a meaningful photograph; and lighting can be crucial in enabling detail to be shown. Careful records should be made whenever a site is photographed – many photographs of earthworks have a sameness about them and if the prints are not produced soon after the photographs have been taken it may be hard to distinguish one site from another. A scale, human or otherwise, should always be included in the picture.

Air photographs, particularly oblique ones, are another essential adjunct to field survey and can be taken into the field in a suitable transparent plastic holder. These will help to make obscure

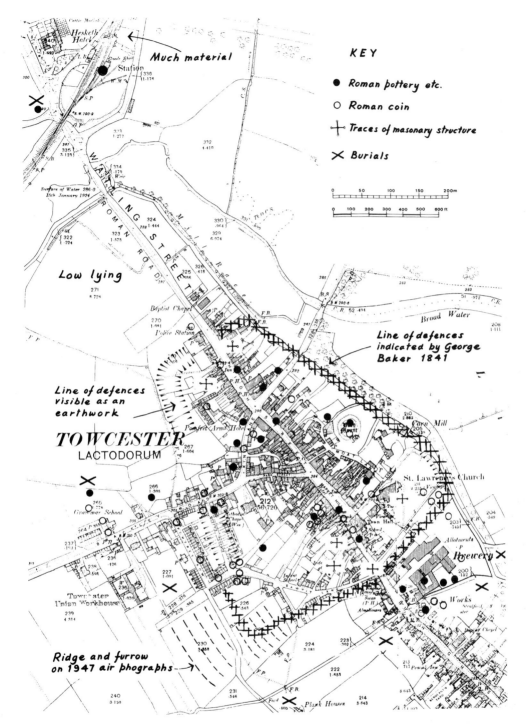

KEY

● Roman pottery etc.

○ Roman coin

✛ Traces of masonary structure

✗ Burials

Much material

Low lying

Line of defences indicated by George Baker 1841

Line of defences visible as an earthwork

TOWCESTER
LACTODORUM

Ridge and furrow on 1947 air phographs →

32   Sketch plan, on an OS base, of Towcester in Northamptonshire. Note how the line of the defences sketched by Baker in the nineteenth century seems to be at variance with the ridge and furrow, which is no longer extant but recorded on old air photographs. Note also how the medieval burgage plots in the south-west part of the town stop short along the line of Sawpit Lane, suggesting perhaps that the Anglo-Saxon burh or early medieval defences took a different line here from the Roman ones. Both these points could only be resolved by excavation. (With acknowledgements to the Ordnance Survey)

features more intelligible on the ground and will on occasions reveal details which might otherwise go quite unnoticed. The most-studied deserted medieval village remains in the country are those at Wharram Percy (North Yorkshire), yet a complete understanding of these *as earthworks* was not obtained until a set of oblique air photographs taken in 1979 indicated significant details of the early medieval layout not appreciated before (Hurst 1984).

4 The interpretation of earthworks

So far we have dealt with the actual mechanics of earthwork surveying, together with the kind of immediate interpretative judgements which have to be made in order to get the survey done – such basic matters as the making of decisions about the form and behaviour of the various elements of the area under examination, how to show these on the drawing, and what their dimensions are. But this is just a start, and the process of interpretation has obviously to be carried further than this. At its most basic, interpretation will involve saying what a site actually is in archaeological terms and assigning it to its correct period or periods. Quite often fieldwork can do more, and will enable an attempt to be made to trace the development of a site or a particular piece of ground through time. But individual sites did not and do not exist in a vacuum, and the process of interpretation can be extended still more to take in the development of substantial pieces of the landscape using the same techniques of analysis. Because this is a separate section it should not be thought that this part of the interpretative process is somehow separate from the recording; they must go on together at the same time, although in the nature of things a final view may take some time to achieve, particularly if other source material, maps and documents for example, has to be looked at. Chapters 5 and 6 will discuss these things.

It is not the intention of a book of this size to provide full descriptive lists of all the major field monument types likely to be encountered in England and Wales. Appendix Two is intended to give a brief guide to sources which will help in the identification of sites, in the main through the provision of illustrations.

The identification of many well-preserved or clearly defined earthworks is in reality quite straightforward – no one could doubt for example that Fig. 18 is a motte and bailey or that

Fig. 43 represents a prehistoric hill fort. But matters are not always so simple. There are regional differences in field monument types which have to be taken into account, depending on a wide range of factors – cultural, the kinds of building materials available, the different economic possibilities created by the local geology and topography, for example. A fieldworker used to the landscapes and sites characteristic of the Midlands may well find himself initially at sea if he moves to Cornwall or Cumbria. Very often a whole range of factors has to be taken into account in deciding just what a set of earthworks represents, in addition to the basic matters of differences in shape and siting which at the purely formal level differentiate one type of monument from another. The context of a site in relation to other landscape features, say roads or extant settlements, or to other archaeological sites is highly relevant. Much will depend upon the detailed analysis of the earthworks, since the same site or area can have had a very long, not necessarily continuous, history in terms of human activity; the purpose to which a site is finally put may be far different from its original function.

There is the problem that certain common earthwork forms, banks and ditches enclosing substantial areas, for instance (p.151–2), could have been put up at widely varying dates for a variety of purposes; the fieldworker must always be aware of the range of possibilities. South-west of the Roman town of Verulamium (St Albans) is the well-known series of earthwork enclosures at Prae Wood. Sir Mortimer Wheeler was clearly aware of the complexity of these earthworks and knew that they had developed over a period of time, but thought of them as representing one kind of site, the late Iron Age predecessor of the Roman town. But a recent very detailed field survey, taking into account the form, alignment and in particular the interrelationships of all elements in the system of banks and ditches, has permitted a more refined separation into a number of phases. As a result, a large enclosure with a ditch on the outside regarded by Wheeler as part of the early Roman system can now be thought of as something very much later, the medieval wood bank which enclosed Prae Wood itself (Hunn 1980). In this case it was close attention to detail which enabled this identification to be made; in other instances it will be documentary evidence. Wood banks like the one at Prae Wood, with external ditches, are very commonly met with (Rackham 1976, 115–17), but these simple earthworks can very easily be confused with other similar features. Another very common element in the medieval landscape was the deer park – there were 108 in Sussex and 102 in Essex, for example (Cantor 1983). A high proportion of them had earthen banks around the perimeter to carry wooden fences or pales to keep the deer in, this time with a ditch on the inside. But the fieldworker will come across quite a few deer park pales which now have no visible ditch; what will really make certain their identification and their separation from, say, wood banks is the documentary evidence about them.

But there are always going to be anomalies which complicate matters. A documented park pale at King's Somborne (Hampshire) is 3·7 m (12 ft) high with a ditch on the *outside* (Crawford 1960, 194). The existence of giants like this makes it easier to understand how a few genuinely defensive banks could be misinterpreted as pales. Despite the absence of documentation, which should really have prevented the error, the striking late prehistoric earthworks at Stanwick in Yorkshire, with defensive ditches 6 m (19½ ft) wide and ramparts 4·56 (14·8 ft) high, were for a time thought to be a medieval park (Wheeler 1954). More often, however, the misinterpretation of these commonplace medieval earthworks worked the other way and they were sometimes thought of as fortifications, but in the instances to be quoted below preconceptions were probably responsible for the misidentifications. Until recently it was believed that an earthwork defence ran around the Roman town of Silchester, outside the stone-walled enclosure, representing a very early Roman defensive line. Recent fieldwork has shown that there are indeed ancient earthworks along

part of the line on the south-west, probably late prehistoric in date, but elsewhere this circuit is an illusion. On the north a park boundary, mistaken as defensive in character, was probably one of the reasons for belief in this defensive system in the first place (Fulford 1984).

Nineteenth-century county historians wished to regard prehistory as a version of the military history familiar to them from the writings of classical authors. This led them to assume some ordinary linear earthworks connected with agriculture were defensive banks around forts. In Gloucestershire the 'British camp' in Black Grove at Bagendon consists in fact of a series of strip lynchets; Saintbury 'Camp' or 'Castle' is a set of medieval or later boundaries and settlement earthworks; a perfectly ordinary boundary bank, too low ever to have been of any defensive value, was misinterpreted as a rampart at Cold Ashton (RCHME 1976, 6, 99, 34).

More or less circular mounds (p.148–9) can have a variety of origins. Some of these will be prehistoric round barrows but, as reference to quite recent Ordnance Survey maps will indicate, other things can be confused with them. Small mottes without baileys were frequently regarded as barrows; yet their profile is generally different, steeper and flat-topped, and there is usually a deep defensive ditch. Their location close to churches and farms is typical. These misidentifications can be persistent; it was not until an excavation in 1975 that a mound at Driffield, Humberside, was seen to be a Norman motte and not the barrow it had been considered to be since the early years of this century (Eddy 1983). Records of old, misdated excavations sometimes help to maintain the confusion. A large mound at Kibworth Harcourt in Leicestershire was dug into in 1863 by Sir Henry Dryden; a contemporary newspaper account speaks of the discovery of Roman (but perhaps medieval?) pottery. The notion that this mound might in origin have been a barrow derives from this and still lingers on in the literature (Howell 1983, 7–9), yet its steep profile and deep ditch must mean that it is a small motte; it lies within the known area of the manorial demesne. Windmill mounds, formerly very common, present another possible source of difficulty. They are also flat-topped and sometimes ditched but are usually smaller than mottes, having no defensive purpose; their distinctive feature can be a cross-shaped depression in the centre, where the beams on which the mill structure was set were fixed. Such mounds required access, and in open field areas where ridge and furrow is still preserved it is often possible to see how this was achieved by means of tracks and headlands. Another earthwork type which has to be distinguished is the mound, not necessarily round, made for ornamental purposes in connection with elaborate landscape gardens from the sixteenth century onwards. Here its relationship to other elements of the landscape design is usually a good indicator. Large oval mounds by rivers might be the sites of artificially raised platforms for the operation of medieval fisheries, involving not just fishing and the maintenance of nets but also smoking and drying; documents exist to substantiate this and characteristic finds such as net sinkers and pottery fish smokers can be made (White 1984). Even such everyday things as the mounds of earth resulting from the cleaning of ponds have been confused with burial mounds (Brown 1972a); and some mounds turn out to have completely unpredictable origins. A Cambridgeshire mound, the scheduled ancient monument upon which the Emmanuel Knoll tree formerly stood at Godmanchester, proved to be nothing more than the result of nineteenth-century ditching around the tree, although a genuine Roman barrow had once existed 50 m (166 ft) away (Green 1973). Another scheduled barrow, located at the junction of Tumulus Place and Tumulus Avenue at Walker in Northumberland and regarded as a burial mound since at least the eighteenth century, was revealed on excavation to have the Roman Military Way running underneath it; its contents,

33   Burton Lazars in Leicestershire. The main complex of earthworks represents a medieval leper hospital, with its boundary (H and M), fishponds (K) and associated enclosures containing ridge and furrow (A and C). There are also settlement earthworks and hollow ways (N, O, P); I is a post-medieval garden; L is one of a series of relatively late quarries in a line running north-east to south-west.

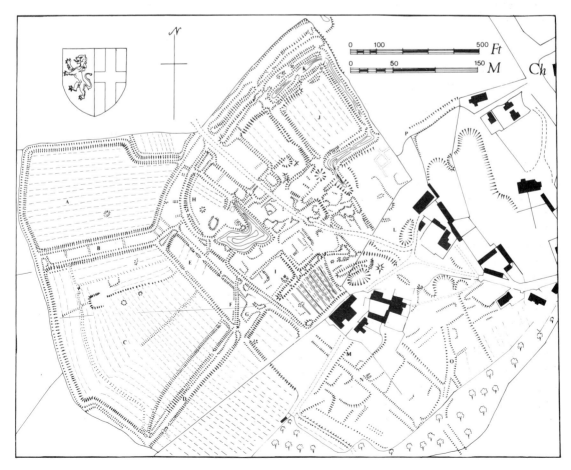

burnt wood and earth and bits of fired clay, suggested the dumping of waste material from some early industrial process (Jobey 1965). In a rather similar way the mound known as Foxburrow in Bedfordshire appeared to be the result of the accumulation of debris from pottery manufacture in the Roman period (Simco 1984, 40).

A certain difficulty continues to be caused by mounds built as rabbit warrens (p.148). Typically these mounds are neatly made structures, rectangular, with gently rounded tops, often set askew the contours, presumably to facilitate drainage. As pillow mounds they have attracted a certain literature and have sometimes been confused with long barrows. They are frequently found in groups on what was once rough ground or in 'manorial' contexts; they can sometimes attain considerable lengths – at Rockingham castle is a pair 100 m (333 ft) long (Brown and Taylor 1974). Such warrens can sometimes be square or round, as at Gretton in Northamptonshire, where there is a group in a typical medieval location close to the site of the manor house (RCHME 1979a, 58). A pair of mounds across the neck of a promontory at Sharpenhoe in Bedfordshire suggested the defences of a promontory fort but turned out on excavation to belong to a rabbit warren (Dix 1983).

Medieval moated sites (p.150) constitute a common field monument type; the most recent estimate of the number present in the country is 5,300 (Aberg 1978). Essentially a moated site consisted of an island usually occupied by a building surrounded by a ditch which was intended to hold water. But there were many enclosures bounded by water-filled ditches constructed in medieval England which were not intended to hold buildings. At Burton Lazars in Leicestershire the complicated earthworks of a leper house include a moated enclosure which contained earlier ridge and furrow, still well preserved; there was never a building within the moat, which probably enclosed simply an orchard or something similar (Fig. 33, J). At Barton Seagrave in Northamptonshire are two moated sites; one of these, to judge from the disturbed surface of the island, held the manor house of the manor of Barton Hanred; the other, linked to it by a narrow channel, contained no space for a building but instead an island with three small rectangular depressions in it, probably fish breeding tanks, the

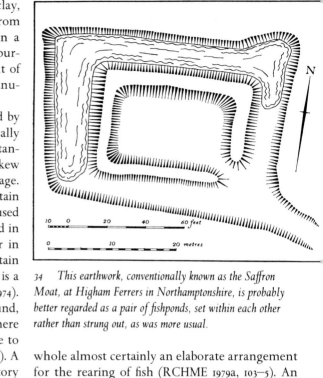

34   This earthwork, conventionally known as the Saffron Moat, at Higham Ferrers in Northamptonshire, is probably better regarded as a pair of fishponds, set within each other rather than strung out, as was more usual.

whole almost certainly an elaborate arrangement for the rearing of fish (RCHME 1979a, 103–5). An earthwork at Higham Ferrers in the same county, traditionally regarded as a moat, is also probably a fishpond (Fig. 34); the central island has been dug away to form a small rectangular pond, cleverly set within a larger one (RCHME 1975a, 56). At Lavendon Abbey in Buckinghamshire a three-sided water-filled enclosure marked as a moat on the Ordnance Survey maps has a flat interior but never held buildings; however, its topographical position indicates that it must have acted as a reservoir to collect and hold water, which was then taken by a complicated series of leats to feed the monastic fishponds lower down the slope. Another type of earthwork commonly thought of as a moat is the abandoned garden of sixteenth- or seventeenth-century date, as in Fig. 59, where a water garden formed part of an elaborate layout known to have been in existence in 1669 (Brown and Taylor 1978); it is marked as a moat on the Ordnance map. In instances like this the confusion with true moated sites is made easier to understand because gardens and fishponds are features which quite often formed part of manorial earthwork complexes. In other instances stock watering ponds, usually post-medieval, have been regarded as moats (Thompson 1955); so have abandoned hollow ways of deserted or shrunken villages, and perfectly natural features such as oxbow lakes close to streams, as at Edith Weston in Leicestershire (Brown 1975, 7–8).

The earthworks of medieval settlements (p.151) usually have an underlying regularity, but as Fig. 51 indicates they at first sight present an appearance of great complexity, with hollow ways, plot boundaries and minor disturbances of various kinds; the earthworks of fishponds, moated manorial sites, even monasteries and castles can go with them. In some circumstances the hummocky ground produced by quarrying can look similar. Not all hollow trackways are ancient or to do with village sites, however. At Chester on the Water, Irchester, Northamptonshire, there is documentary evidence for a settlement in the medieval period, along with some undistinguished earthworks next to the farm. The most prominent feature is a long depression running east–west across the site, and this has in the past been taken to be a hollow way associated with the hamlet. Yet there are no property boundary banks in any relationship with it; to the west the hollow way turns into an embankment overlying ridge and furrow which makes for a sharp, relatively recent opening in the defensive bank of the Roman town of Irchester. In fact the hollow way is not medieval at all but a small cutting for an ironstone railway, and the axis of the hamlet of Chester on the Water ran north–south at right angles to it, along a trackway running to the River Nene (Brown 1978).

As always, work on the upland moors will produce its own distinctive range of problems. Small outcrops of rock, quite recent spoil heaps, quarry waste tips or piles of stone left behind by boundary wall builders can look like prehistoric cairns. Genuine cairns, when heavily robbed, can resemble another field monument type, the enclosed cremation cemetery, a circular area enclosed with a rubble bank. Cairns are often carefully formed and can have visible kerbs; these characteristics help to mark them off from yet another monument type, the small cairns which can occur in groups running into hundreds and which seem to be the result of the clearance of stone into heaps for agricultural purposes; often they are associated with the earthwork remains of

early field systems and with house sites (Jobey 1981; Fowler 1983, 147–50). The house sites themselves can look like the platforms which used to be made to carry hearths for charcoal burning; in this case abundant charcoal fragments will help to sort out one from the other (RCAHMW 1976, 72). They can also look like the platforms of stones which were formerly made to keep heaps of peat dry, and which could be round, although more usually rectangular.

Natural features can quite easily be mistaken for field monuments. Mounds of glacial origin have been taken for burial mounds. At Pilleth in Powys a couple of mounds in the valley of the Lugg are marked on Ordnance Survey maps as antiquities and regarded as the burial places of the English killed in Owen Glendower's victory of 1402 (Williams 1905, 311–12). Yet their form and location indicates that they are really glacial moraines. In certain hilly areas such as the Cotswolds it is possible to get a situation in which bands of hard and soft geological deposits alternate; differential weathering will erode the soft deposits, leaving the harder rocks remaining to form scarps which look very much like ramparts. Elsewhere protruding strips of limestone pavement can resemble tumbled walls or ancient roads; and its dissolution by water action can create irregular depressions in the ground surface which look like earthworks. Such irregularities near Gib Hill in Derbyshire give the impression of a circular earthwork with a flattened external bank and have led to the suggestion that there was a protohenge here, the predecessor of the famous Arbor Low nearby, but the earthworks were almost certainly entirely natural (Radley 1968). Another problem is caused by the behaviour of lias clay on steep slopes. When wet this is notoriously unstable and will tend to slip downhill, producing bulges which can look remarkably like earthwork terraces or lynchets. Such earth movement will also distort earthworks which happen already to be there, or make difficult the understanding of ones which are later formed on top of the natural slippage. Downhill movement caused by solifluction in arctic conditions can produce similar difficulties. Stripes seen in sandy ploughed fields and on heaths, consisting of alternating bands of stones and finer material running down slopes, are also the product of arctic circumstances; they are sinuous and discontinuous, but at first sight resemble ridge and furrow. Another legacy of the ice age is the pingo, the result of the forcing upwards and subsequent melting of large cones of ice; they leave behind sometimes perfectly circular depressions with earth banks around them which look like hut circles, pond barrows or bomb craters.

To make matters worse from the field archaeologist's standpoint, occasionally instances are met with in which perfectly natural features were used by man for his own purposes with minimum alteration of their form. A pair of circular mounds excavated near Cambridge in 1973 on the assumption that they were barrows turned out to be quite natural in origin – yet Bronze Age burials had been inserted in them (Martin 1975).

Some earthworks are in fact virtually impossible to assign precisely to a period, although their general type and sometimes their function may be clear. In the absence of a relationship with other datable features or of documentary evidence, linear banks and ditches can have a very wide potential date range. In Hampshire the date of a series of linear earthworks known as the Froxfield dykes is quite unknown, although they are usually thought of as Anglo-Saxon (Hinton 1981). A recent survey of the Bolster Bank, an earthwork 3.3 km long which cuts off St Agnes Head in northern Cornwall, indicated that it was too big to be regarded as a cliff castle, but was quite unable to suggest a date range any closer than the first millennium BC to the end of the first millennium AD (Johnson 1980). Defensive enclosures, a basic earthwork type, can present similar difficulties. At Castle Hill, Godstone, Surrey, a prominent earthwork cut off the end of a spur, forming a defensive promontory position; excavation was able to demonstrate just how strong the defences were. Yet there was no datable material, and the excavators were unable to show that it was in fact a medieval site, although it was traditionally known as a castle; it could equally well have been a prehistoric promontory fort (O'Connell and Poulton 1983). The earthwork at Newenden, Kent, which has been put forward as the remains of a *burh* taken by the Danes in AD 892 before it had been completed, looks in plan just like a denuded prehistoric hill fort (Davison 1972).

Form alone can be deceptive; one cannot always assume that the obvious or generally accepted interpretation of an earthwork is the right one. Many rectangular enclosures considered to be Roman forts have – on closer inspection or as a result of further, more extensive work – turned out to be something else. A pair of rectangular earthworks in Northumberland, at Hartburn and Apperley Dene, were thought with some justice to be Roman fortlets, the latter especially so because of its proximity to Dere Street; the great eighteenth-century antiquary John Horsley certainly regarded it as a fort, and excavations in the 1950s, which produced Roman pottery of second- and fourth-century date, seemed to confirm this. But field survey since then has shown that many native farms of the second to the fourth century in this area were in fact rectangular, and this site along with others has had to be reconsidered (Greene 1978). A small square earthwork enclosure overlooking the sea at Eggardon, Dorset, was thought to be a Roman signal station, yet turned out on excavation not to be so; there were several quarries within the enclosure and some mounds considered to be spoil heaps – yet when excavated the largest proved to be a Bronze Age round barrow containing some later inhumations, possibly Anglo-Saxon (Putnam 1982). At Rhuddlan (Clwyd) a substantial bank and ditch, recognized since the eighteenth century and generally regarded as the defences of the Norman borough founded by Robert of Rhuddlan in 1073, was shown by excavation to belong to the *burh* established by Edward the Elder in AD 921 (Manley 1984). At Middleton Stoney the earthworks of the eastern bailey appeared to be contemporary with the medieval castle, but in fact were discovered by excavation to be Saxon (Rahtz and Rowley 1984).

The possibility of the transformation of a site or feature into something else must also be considered. Such changes may not always be obvious from surface inspection. North of Chichester is an extensive series of banks and ditches which, on the evidence of excavated sections and parallels with similar dated systems elsewhere, as at Colchester, can be regarded as late Iron Age in date. But sections close to the eastern end of the system indicated that part of the bank and ditch there belonged to the late medieval period, something quite unexpected; the probable explanation is that this part of the late prehistoric earthwork was re-dug to form the boundary of the park of Halnaker (Bedwin and Orton 1984). In Cornwall an earthwork at Lanivet, which looked like a Class 1 henge monument, with single entrance and inner ditch, seems to have been remodelled in perhaps the thirteenth century as a *plain an gwarry*, a place where religious plays were performed; the earthwork was given a fresh profile, the ditch re-cut and another entrance added (Thomas 1964). Mottes were quite frequently converted into garden features; this fate befell Clifford's Tower in York, Marlborough in Wiltshire and the small example in Bedfordshire shown in Fig. 18. When this happened significant visible alterations could sometimes take place; at Marlborough the motte was given a spiral walkway around it. At Clifford's Hill in Northamptonshire a huge motte now 14 m (46 ft) high, perhaps not used for any length of time because of the slippage of the material of which it was made, had a bowling green set on it in the seventeenth century; an unknown amount was shorn off the top in the process. Clay pipes can be found (RCHME 1979a, 87–8). Medieval waterworks were frequently put to other pur-

poses by later owners. Moats could sometimes be converted into gardens; at Bindon Abbey (Dorset) the moat surrounding the house built by Sir Thomas Poynings after the Dissolution could well have been based upon the monastic fishponds (Keen 1983). On a larger scale, prehistoric hill forts have been used as the basis for castles. At the Herefordshire Beacon, Malvern, the Iron Age defences are intact but a small ringwork has been inserted at the top of the hill (RCHME 1932, 55–7). At Barwick-in-Elmet and Almondbury (West Yorkshire), the earlier defences are obscured to a greater degree by the medieval ones (Keighley 1981, 116). That this kind of thing happened might lead one to expect that other castle earthworks might entirely conceal earlier, prehistoric phases of which as yet nothing is known.

The subsequent treatment of a site vitally affects its intelligibility to the fieldworker. Ploughing can of course virtually obliterate sites. The great henge at Durrington Walls in Wiltshire shows up on air photographs as a combination of soil and crop marks, but the earthwork remains do not accurately reflect the true nature of the site thus revealed. The outer bank exists as a

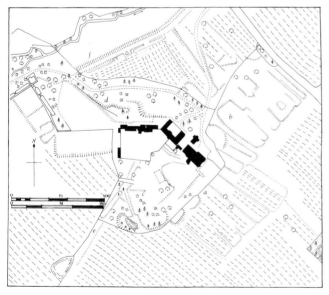

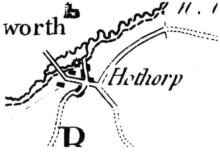

35   The site of the deserted village of Hothorpe in Northamptonshire, now occupied by a country house. Note how the earthworks at b and around the house itself are denuded and battered compared with those at a, where ridge and furrow is still preserved. Hothorpe village can be seen on the Eyre map of Northamptonshire, surveyed in the mid-eighteenth century but not published until later. The street system of the village (north-west and south-west of b, and at d and e) can be identified as earthworks using the eighteenth-century map; f represents earthworks associated with the mill, shown on the map by a conventional symbol.

spread feature on the north and west, but on the south the earthwork to be seen is really a lynchet, in part following the course of the ditch but elsewhere bearing only a general relationship to the monument, for instance cutting directly across the bank close to the south-eastern entrance (RCHME 1979b, 15–17). At Thorpe Lubenham in Northamptonshire, a large enclosure attached to the east of a scheduled moated site has only recently been recognized because over-ploughing with ridge and furrow has caused its outline to be obscured.

In the case of village remains, where a settlement has slowly fallen into decay the earthworks may be well preserved and intelligible, but when organized clearance has happened, say in the process of imparkment, deliberate flattening will have been involved and they will be much less easy to see. Fig. 35 illustrates this, where there is a difference between the state of preservation of the earthworks around and to the north-east of the house where they were systematically levelled in the nineteenth century and those to the south-east where this process did not take place. Subsequent industrial activity, particularly quarrying, can lead to obvious difficulties; extensive quarrying caused doubt to be cast upon the existence of a large fortified site on Churchdown Hill in Gloucestershire, which had been suggested in the earlier nineteenth century. As a result of observations carried out when a pipeline was put through in 1972, and other finds, the site can now legitimately be regarded as a genuine Iron Age hill fort (Hurst 1977).

Also archaeological sites and features remain part of the landscape and sometimes continue as functioning elements in it; because of this their true significance can on occasion be overlooked. At Fawsley in Northamptonshire a round-topped bank over a metre high acts as a parish and farm boundary and carries a hedge. The bank can be equated with a dyke said to be an old one in a land grant of AD 944 but its status as an antiquity was only recognized relatively recently (Brown et al. 1977), probably because the hedge had masked it. In the same way the ditch of a moated site can still function as the boundary of paddocks and small fields near working farms; and modern field boundaries can perpetuate the divisions between ancient fields. Indeed, many quite ordinary fea-

tures of the British landscape, not normally thought of as antiquities at all, are immensely old, roads and boundaries in particular; many existing property divisions in towns and villages marked today by walls and hedges of no great age, which may or may not have banks below them, are ancient and as significant in what they have to tell us about the evolution of the landscape as the earthworks of the neighbouring shrunken or deserted settlement. A classic example is the Bronze Age farm at Shearplace Hill in Dorset. Here the earthworks of the settlement were integrated with trackways. The main north–south double lynchet-way joined an ancient east–west track which ran among a set of Celtic fields; but it also went on to join a line of existing field boundaries, which continued into a parish boundary on the same alignment (Rahtz 1962).

The relationship between sites and the natural topography is important. Topography can of course determine the choice and form of a site in the first place – the relationship between hilltops and defended enclosures is obvious; medieval moated sites must always have been sited with an eye to a good water supply. The relationship between round barrows and skylines and false crests has been commented on since the days of Stukeley; the manner in which a prominent ridge has been deliberately chosen as a location for barrow cemeteries is vividly illustrated by the huge concentration of barrows on the Dorset ridgeway. But there are more subtle ways in which the topography can influence the form of a site. At Bolnhurst in Bedfordshire are the much-damaged remains of a large earthwork enclosure; pottery found during fieldwalking suggests an Iron Age date (Fig. 36). The actual shape of the site is odd in that there is a marked re-entrant on the northern side. The reason for this is that a stream once flowed from the re-entrant, its course scarcely visible in the landscape today – it can be seen on early air photographs and followed by minor changes in the contour.

An appreciation of topography is essential to understand the functioning of the many medieval earthworks connected with the management of water. Simple dams across valleys and the insertion of leats in valley bottoms to conduct water to moats and fishponds are readily understood, but

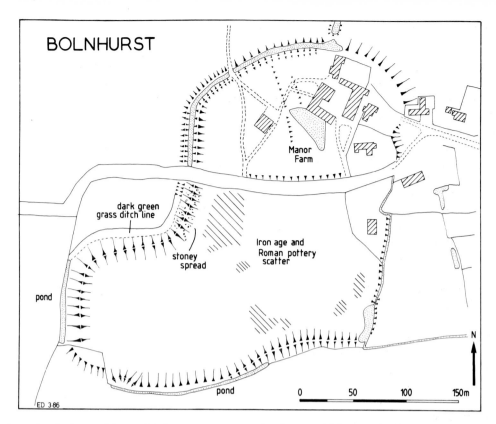

BOLNHURST

dark green
grass ditch line

stoney
spread

Manor
Farm

Iron age and
Roman pottery
scatter

pond

pond

N

0   50   100   150m

ED 3.86

*36   An earthwork of unusual form at Bolnhurst,
Bedfordshire. The slight depression to the west of Manor
Farm indicates an arm of the medieval moated site cut out of
the prehistoric earthwork.*

some patience and a good deal of surveying time
are required to piece together the workings of
certain of the more complicated examples of
water management, as at Harrington, Northamptonshire (Fig. 37). Note how the course of the
main valley stream has been diverted around the
whole set of ponds to form a relief channel along
their western sides; how a gap enabled water to be
taken from the stream into pond *c* and thence
into *b via* an opening in the dam between the two
ponds, while unwanted water from *c* could be
conducted into the relief channel by means of an
opening in the north-west corner. Water from *b*
could be led into *a* using a channel in its north-
east corner. Water could be led back from *a* into a
tiny pond cleverly set into the dam between *a* and
b, perhaps a breeding tank. There was an outlet in
the north-west corner of *a*. Two more water
sources were used, coming in from the east. It was
the southernmost of these which determined the
siting of the dam between ponds *c* and *b*, since the
arrangement of the sluices shows that water from

this leat could be switched from one pond to the
other or taken straight into pond *a*. There was a
hollow way running down from the site of the
manor house which crossed the large dam along
the northern edge of pond *a* (now breached) and
went to the neighbouring village, Arthingworth
(RCHME 1979a, 77–8).

Sometimes, however, it is the disconformity
between the topography and the field archaeology which is the important observation. Many
sets of Celtic fields can be seen to be arranged in
great blocks observing relatively straight align-
ments, the axes of which pay no attention to
variations in local topography (Fowler 1983, 102;
Bowen 1975, 106). The implication of authority,
control and planning is clear.

The importance of looking at earthwork sites
in relation to other sites should also be stressed. In
south-east Dorset work on both long and round
barrows has shown how carefully these monuments were sited to be seen to good effect from
certain directions. But they were also carefully
placed in relation to each other. The Winterborne
Monkton long barrow points exactly towards the
end of the long mound which runs the length of
Maiden Castle; there are nine other long mounds
within 9½ km (6 miles) of this. Similarly round

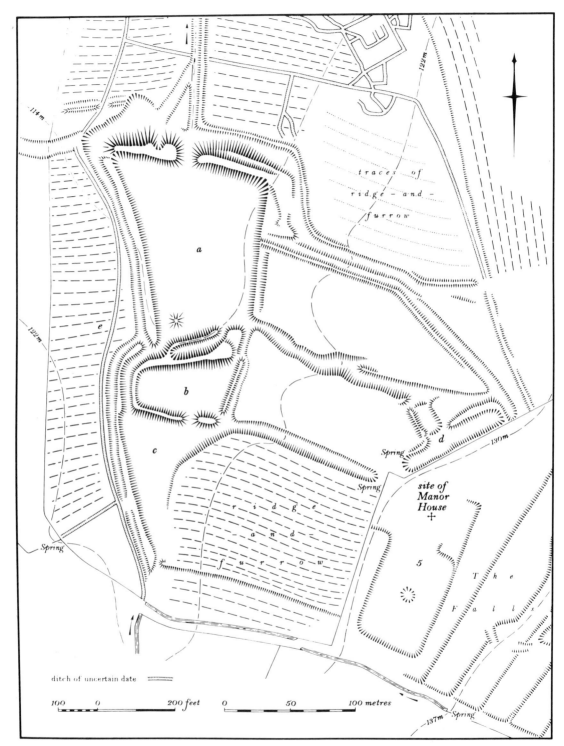

traces of
ridge - and -
furrow

Spring
Spring

site of
Manor
House
✝

ridge
and
furrow

Spring

5

The
Falls

ditch of uncertain date

100   0   200 feet   0   50   100 metres

Spring

37   *The fishponds at Harrington in Northamptonshire.*

barrows are carefully placed to be near long ones; **the 233 barrows** considered to belong to the Dorset Ridgeway Group are contained between two of the very long mounds known as bank barrows. A handful of smallish enclosures can be interpreted as of ritual or funerary significance because of their connection with barrow cemeteries (RCHME 1970a, 420–9). Cross-ridge dykes are a common feature of upland field archaeology but are in themselves very hard to date; their association with areas of Iron Age occupation, as at Knowle Hill, Dorset, implies a prehistoric origin for many (RCHME 1970a, 509). In Wiltshire a study of the cross-ridge dykes along the ridge between the rivers Ebble and Nadder suggests that the bivallate dykes (i.e. those with two banks with a ditch between) which ran across at particularly

38   *The earthwork castles at Farnham in Hampshire.*

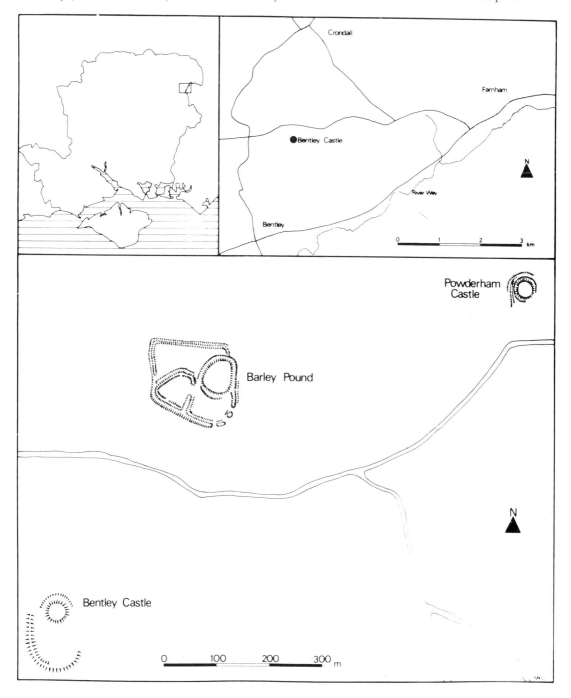

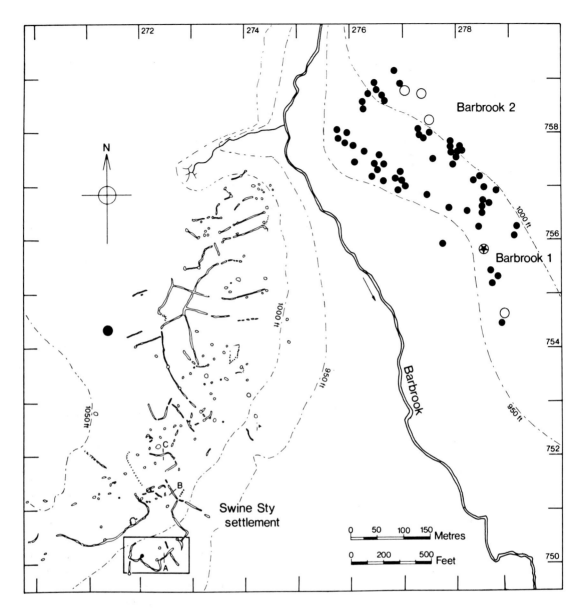

The Bronze Age landscape
of Big Moor

● Cairn

○ Ring bank

✪ Stone circle

39   The prehistoric landscape of Big Moor, Derbyshire.

narrow points, served to divide the ridge up into territories of roughly equivalent size (Fowler 1964). Fig. 38 shows a group of three earthwork castles west of Farnham. Obviously these earthworks can only be understood in relation to each other; the explanation is that the two simpler ones consist-

ing basically of smallish mottes and baileys were siege castles built by the Bishop of Winchester, Henry de Blois, in his attempt to win back his castle of Udelea, taken from him by Brian Fitzcount in 1147 (Stamper 1984).

From this kind of argument it is a short step to recognizing how important it is to see individual sites in the widest possible context. In favourable

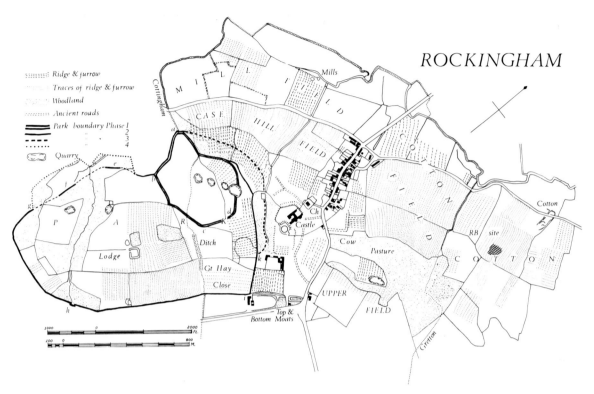

ROCKINGHAM

40   Rockingham in Northamptonshire. This plan of the parish shows, amongst other things, the arable (represented by ridge and furrow), the meadows (the blank areas close to the river) and some of the rough grazing available. The plan also shows the lordship of Cotton (actually in Gretton parish) with its earthworks and Roman site, discovered by fieldwalking, and also the park of Rockingham, much of which lay in Cottingham parish, and its phases (compare Fig. 68).

circumstances it is possible to recover extensive areas of ancient landscape and to work out how they were organized. Fig. 39 shows an area of rough moorland on the gritstone of north Derbyshire (Hart 1981, 63); distinct zoning is evident in this Bronze Age landscape, with habitations and fields to the west of the Barbrook, burial and ritual sites to the east. Exactly the same kind of exercise can be carried out with medieval earthworks. Fig. 40 is a representation of the earthworks of Rockingham parish. This not only brings out the location of the economic resources of the village – fields, meadow land, rough grazing, mills – but also the relationship between the castle and its park, together with a village whose wide street and regular appearance indi-

cates a planned market centre set out as an adjunct to the royal castle.

The combination of studying earthworks in relation to both natural topography *and* other sites can profitably be illustrated with regard to the investigation of the Cleave Dyke in north Yorkshire (Fig. 41). This dyke consists of a series of linear banks and ditches which run for 9 km (5.6 miles) along the line of the western part of the Hambleton Hills. Attached to its eastern side are other similar dykes, running at right angles to it, towards the heads of tributary valleys of the river Rye. Field survey by Don Spratt has shown how one of the latter dykes cuts a round barrow; others were clearly aligned on barrows which were probably therefore already in existence when the dykes were laid out. There was an original gap in the main Cleave Dyke in the area of the hill fort of Boltby Fort, suggesting that fort and dyke were in contemporary use; excavations in the fort produced a little pottery of the first millennium BC. Some of the subsidiary dykes were cut by and therefore earlier than the road known as Hambleton Street; documentary evidence shows that the road was in existence by the early thirteenth century, but it was probably a good deal older. An appreciation of the overall pattern of the earthwork in relation to the topography suggests that both north–south and east–west dykes were in use together as part of a system of territorial apportionment related to the allocation of rights in upland summer pasture for settlements located on the lower ground on both sides of the Hambleton Hills; the dykes had no defensive purpose. The earlier upland barrows on the watershed probably had had a similar function as territorial markers. The construction of the Cleave Dyke can be thought of therefore as a logical development of the early and middle Bronze Age method of land division (Spratt 1982a).

The possibility of significant relationships between earthworks and buildings must not be overlooked. Clearly there is little point in separating the examination of a moated site from that of a house and outbuildings still inside it; or looking at, say, the earthwork remains of the estates of the abbey of Evesham and neglecting the still-standing barns and dovecotes (Bond 1973). At the grandest level an understanding of just how the waterworks around such places as Kenilworth and Caerphilly castles actually worked to provide water-filled ditches and lakes for defensive and pleasurable purposes will add an essential dimension to an appreciation of the original appearance and function of these well-known sites. At Stowe Nine Churches in Northamptonshire an earthwork survey shows that a track must have run at some time below what is now the chancel of the church; at a later date it was diverted to run around the churchyard as a terrace, then to resume its original course once more (Fig. 42). The realization that this had been the sequence of events enabled a reconstruction of the original very small late Saxon church to be attempted; and once the original course of the road had been reconstructed and allowance made for later garden build-up near the manor house, it could be seen just how striking the siting of the original church had been, on top of a prominent knoll, with very wide views. This gives added force to the fact that preserved inside the church and incorporated in its fabric are several carved stones which must on stylistic grounds pre-date the surviving late Anglo-Saxon tower; this and accounts of the lives of seventh-century saints associated with Stowe indicate a very ancient holy place (Brown *et*

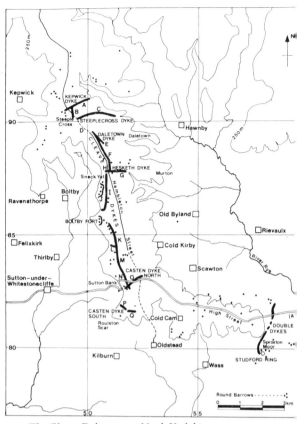

41   *The Cleave Dyke system, North Yorkshire.*

al. 1981). Nearby at Fawsley are the now collapsing ruins of the attractive building known as the Dower House. Architectural investigation shows that this was a two-phase structure of sixteenth-century date, initially a small brick hunting lodge with a tower which could serve as a stand to enable the hunt to be viewed, soon afterwards enlarged to form a small dwelling house. But around this ruinous building are the low earthworks of a rectangular enclosure. These earthworks interrupt the course of a pair of substantial parallel banks and ditches and obviously post-date them. These facts can be interpreted in the following way. The large banks represent the northern and southern sides of the deer parks in Fawsley and Badby parishes belonging respectively to the Knightley family, which obtained the manor of Fawsley in the fifteenth century and were noted depopulators, and the abbots of Evesham, who had a moated grange at Badby used for purposes of recreation. In 1542, after the Dissolution, the Knightleys acquired Badby. The

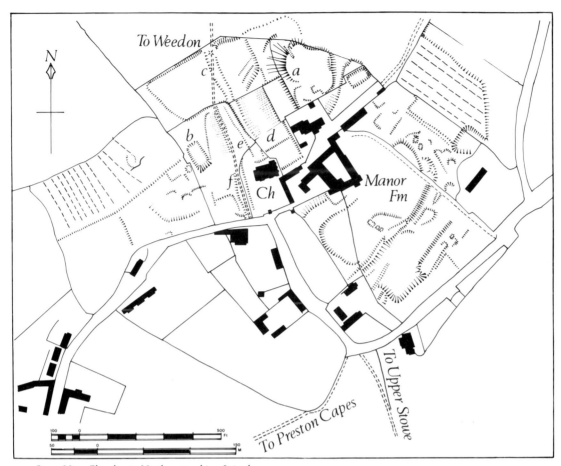

42   *Stowe Nine Churches in Northamptonshire. It is clear that the track c, continued by e, originally ran below the chancel of the church, and that the terrace f represents a later diversion. a is a rather damaged but presumably early medieval fortified site; b is a typical small fishpond; d are post-medieval garden terraces.*

Dower House was therefore a hunting box carefully set at the point where the two old parks met, and the fact that both the pales were obliterated by it shows that it was intended to serve the large park formed by the amalgamation of the two earlier ones and owned by this wealthy, ambitious and influential family; it must therefore post-date 1542. In the same county at Horton are numerous earthworks and scattered buildings which once formed part of an elaborate park and garden design of eighteenth-century date (RCHME 1979a, 69). Among the buildings is a rather gaunt gateway now standing free, but earthwork survey shows around it the pits which once held trees designed to partly mask it from

view and which indicate that the original appearance of the building was different.

Occasions will arise in fieldwork when it will be fairly clear that a complicated set of earthworks represents several phases of development, yet the survey alone will be unable to unravel them. It is very unlikely that the two sets of ramparts belonging to the hill fort shown in Fig 43 were put up at the same time, yet the plan does not really enable a decision to be made about which is earlier. But at other times opportunities will present themselves which will enable this to be done. Sequences manifest themselves in several ways. Fig. 44 is a plan of the earthworks of the latest of the series of windmills belonging to the parish of Naseby in Northamptonshire. The mill mound sits within a small enclosure *a*; but this enclosure contains the battered traces of ridge and furrow on the same alignment as that to the west. This means that the mound has been placed on top of part of one of the furlongs of the open

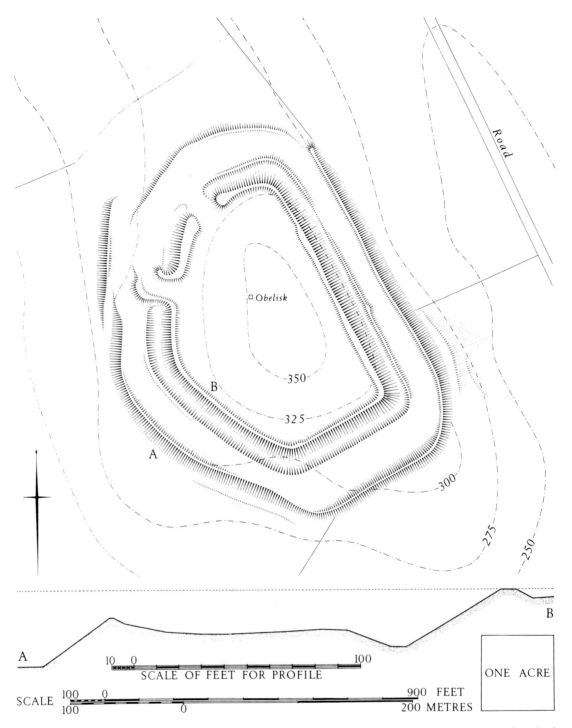

43 *Weatherby Castle hill fort, Milborne St Andrew, Dorset.*

fields, shortening some of the plough ridges and leading to the creation of a new headland at *b*. But this headland does not extend to the west; the implication is that the remaining plough ridges in this part of the furlong continued to be ploughed for their full length, as before. But the access ramp *c* which sits on top of them belongs to a time when they ceased to be ploughed altogether and perhaps relates to the period after the enclosure of the fields of Naseby in 1820, to which belonged the hedges of the paddock in which the mound sits. This earthwork happens to be a late, nineteenth-century example, but the principle of looking for sequences and the establishment of chronological depth by recognizing the superimposition of one earthwork upon another applies to the whole range of field archaeology. The famous henge monument at Arbor Low in Derbyshire has had a round barrow placed on top of it; in a similar way the Conquer Barrow at West Stafford in Dorset sits upon the bank of the Mount Pleasant henge (RCHME 1970a, 504–5). Two Dorset long barrows have had round ones placed on them (RCHME 1970a, 421); similarly the large oval mound known as Gib Hill in Derbyshire (Radley 1968). In Northumberland, in areas undisturbed by modern ploughing, quite remarkable sequences of archaeological features relating not just to individual sites but to whole landscapes have been established ranging backwards in time from post-medieval farmsteads, medieval shielings and ridge and furrow with below them scooped settlements, enclosed settlements with field walls,

unenclosed settlements and cultivation terraces and vast areas of narrow rig; sequences which must stretch back into prehistory (Topping 1983). The same kind of arguments will apply to relatively recent industrial remains. At Dolaucothi, Dyfed, is a remarkable set of earthwork water leats, tanks and opencast workings associated with the extraction of gold and usually regarded in the main as of Roman date; the Carreg Pumsaint, the 'Five Saints Stone', now standing on a low mound but earlier lying flat, is often pointed out as a relic of the hand-crushing of quartz by the Roman miners. Nearby is a conical mound normally regarded as a medieval motte. Yet its ditch is filled up with debris from a processing area exemplified archaeologically by a series of tanks, channels and possible working surfaces; these must therefore be late, but will pre-date, say, the early eighteenth century, when historical references to these workings could reasonably be expected (there is none). If the sequence established by field survey is correct and if the motte is indeed that and not a large spoil tip, which can only be settled by

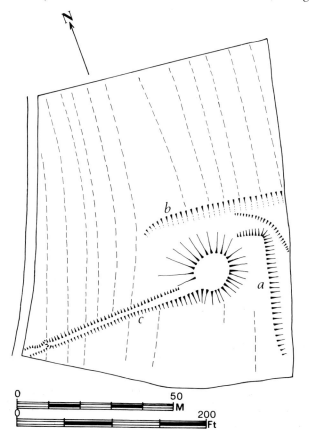

44   *The earthworks of a windmill at Naseby, Northamptonshire.*

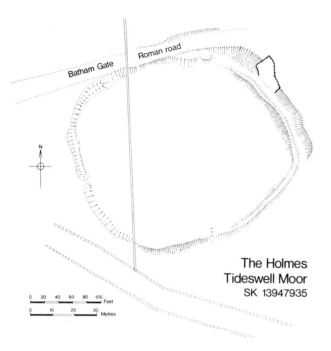

The Holmes
Tideswell Moor
SK 13947935

45   *Earthwork at Tideswell Moor, Derbyshire.*

excavation, then the possibility must be entertained that at least some of the Dolaucothi earthworks are medieval or later; the famous stone might even be a mortar stone deriving from a post-Roman trip-hammer (Austin and Burnham 1984).

Elsewhere a sequence can be established because one feature clearly cuts or interrupts another. In the eighteenth century Stukeley noted how the Roman road from Old Sarum to Badbury Rings, the Ackling Dyke, cut away a portion of one of the Bronze Age disc barrows on Oakley Down in Dorset. The chronological implications of this are perhaps hardly a revelation, but elsewhere the behaviour of Roman roads provides a very valuable relative sequence. On Tideswell Moor in Derbyshire, Batham Gate, the road from Buxton to Brough-on-Noe, cuts the rampart of an undated oval earthwork enclosure, which must therefore be pre-Roman (Hart 1981, 77; Fig. 45).

At Burton Lazars in Leicestershire (Fig. 33) the scarp at *m* clearly blocks the hollow way *n*, throwing it out of use. This scarp represents the final boundary around this leper establishment; its creation led to the diversion of the hollow way from its original north–west–south–east course to a new one running north–south. The same kind

of observations can be made in relation to medieval field systems and associated earthworks. The plough ridges at *e* are obviously cut by the banks and ditches on either side of them and are relics of an early phase of ploughing; later, the direction of ploughing was changed through 90° to give *c*; later still the ditch *f* cut through the later plough ridges, implying that they had been laid down to grass. Fig. 46 is a plan of part of a very long series of earthworks north of the village of Odell in Bedfordshire. Clearly a hollow way can be seen running north–south through this part of the site. The earthworks on the eastern side *a* are confused and disturbed by modern dumping, but those on the western side can be construed to produce a coherent sequence. The plough ridges north of *c* are short and irregular, unlike the block to the west of them. The probability is that once this ridge and furrow extended over the whole of the block of land between Hobbs Green spinney and the hedge to the south, where there is a headland. Houses, marked by the three shallow platforms *b* and *c* with small enclosures attached to them, were set on top of this ridge and furrow, hence the short ridges just mentioned. But these little ridges continued to be ploughed, producing their own headland (southwest of *c*). Maybe the ridge and furrow of the rest of the furlong was

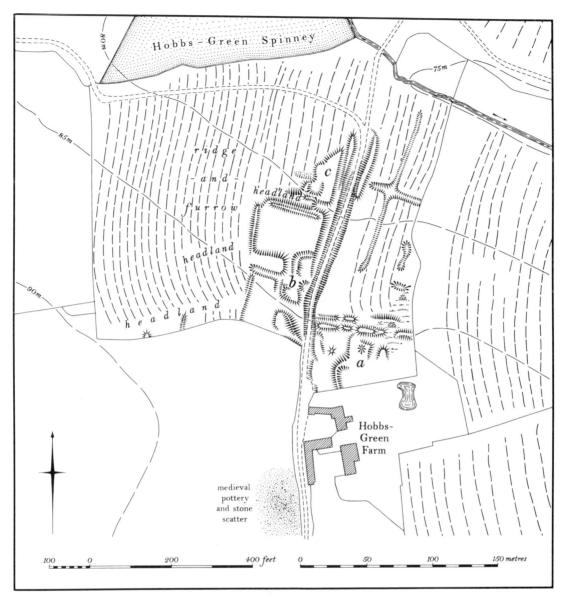

46   *Earthworks at Hobbs Green, Odell, Bedfordshire.*

relaid now to produce even widths and a graceful reversed S shape; the short, original ridges do not show these characteristics. But at a later date still the southeastern part of these new ridges ceased to be ploughed, the headland formed to the west of *b* resulting in the creation of a little area of pasture to the south of it.

In other instances it is the alignment of the series of earthworks which is significant. The way in which round barrows can be arranged in a row aligned upon a long barrow, as in the celebrated barrow cemetery at Winterbourne Stoke cross-roads in Wiltshire, and the manner in which part of the Dorset cursus has been laid out along the axis of a pre-existing long mound, are classic instances of the establishment of a sequence. Long barrows incorporated in the layout of certain Celtic fields in Wiltshire may have been the main determinant in the alignment of some of the large blocks of such fields (Bowen 1972, 48; 1975, 106). At Fen Ditton in Cambridgeshire the earthworks of a water garden are aligned upon the seventeenth-century south front of Fen Ditton Hall, which enables a date for them to be suggested (RCHME 1972, 56).

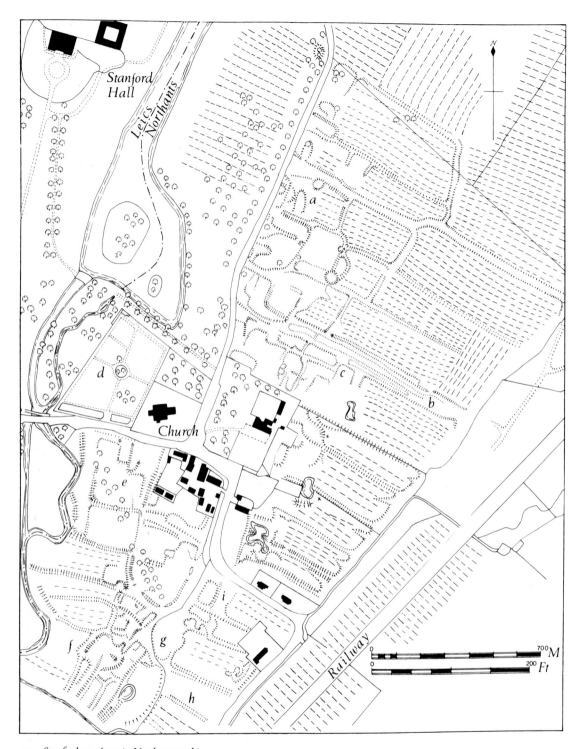

47   *Stanford-on-Avon in Northamptonshire.*

Differences in the overall plan of the remains from one part of a site to another may suggest differences in date. Fig. 47 shows the village of Stanford-on-Avon in Northamptonshire. There have probably been changes in the road system of this village. Now the village is entered from the south-east by a road which takes a complicated series of bends to cut through the medieval building plots at *i*; but the original line of the road probably came in at *h*; at *g* there was a junction with a north–south road which formed the original main street of the village; there were house plots on both sides of this. This was the core of the settlement. But north of this again, and on one side of a street only, is another series of building plots *a*, longer, and rather more regular in layout than the ones to the south. This and the fact that the plots sit on ridge and furrow suggest a later, planned extension. At Uphoe Manor Farm, Lavendon, Bucks. (Fig. 48), the general form of the earthworks of this moated site suggests two phases of development, starting with a relatively small sub-rectangular enclosure later considerably expanded.

In other places differences in the way banks or walls are constructed have been used to suggest a sequence. On the gritstone of Derbyshire, for example, Bronze Age field banks tend to be built of small stones; medieval ones had facings of substantial upright stones and where possible a ditch (Hart 1981, 63). On Dartmoor a typology has been tentatively established involving a sequence from prehistoric banks, which could be constructed in a variety of ways – piled stones, large boulders, large or small banks of earth; later, possibly Saxon or early medieval ones, consisting of block walls of large boulders and broad, linear piles of stone designated clearance walls; 'corn ditches' with a ditch on one side and a stone-revetted bank on the other, considered to be a response to the Forest Law of the eleventh century; ditched hedge banks of earth, mainly late medieval; massive wall banks of stone and earth with stone facings, late or post-medieval; and stone walls, eighteenth and nineteenth centuries (Fleming and Ralph 1982; Collis 1983).

Consider also Fig. 49. Here at Podington in Bedfordshire the bank *c* has been regarded as the edge of the bailey associated with the motte *a*. But this bank is relatively slight, particularly on the west, only 25 cm (10 in) high, with a very shallow outer ditch. A much better candidate for a bailey, more in keeping with the motte, is the scarp *b*, 2 m (6½ ft) high, which runs off the south-west corner of the motte; it has traces of an outer ditch. The bank *c* meets this at a curious angle, again suggesting that relatively speaking it is late; it also cuts through the easternmost ridge of a small block of ridge and furrow, and can perhaps be interpreted as part of a series of later manorial enclosures (including *d*) going with a manor house rather than a castle.

Differences in the state of preservation of earthworks can suggest differences in date. Obvious examples are the Iron Age hill forts at Scratchbury and Yarnbury (Wiltshire) and the Trundle (Sussex), which have denuded enclosures within them. That at the Trundle is Neolithic, but the other two are earlier in the Iron Age (Wilson 1982, 75). But this is not a universal rule, since the state of preservation of an earthwork will necessarily reflect its original size. There is a continuous run of bank and ditch along the north-eastern section of the parish of Fawsley in Northamptonshire. It can be broken down into three parts. The section along the north-west has a ditch on its southern side and a narrow bank

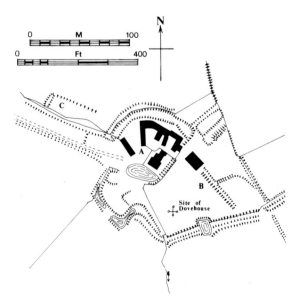

48   *Uphoe Manor, Lavendon, Buckinghamshire. A is probably the original enclosure, to which B could have been added. C is a fishpond.*

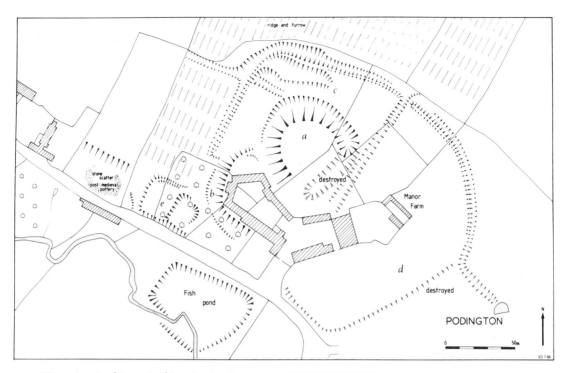

49   *The earthworks of the castle, fishpond and settlement at Podington, Bedfordshire.*

half a metre high with a sharp-pointed profile. The stretch along the north-east has a ditch on its northern side and a broad bank with a gently rounded profile 1·25 m (3½ ft) high. The stretch in the middle consists of a ditch only a few centimetres deep and a metre across. The north-western section belongs probably to the seventeenth century; the north-eastern was the dyke already mentioned (p.72) as old in an Anglo-Saxon charter of AD 944; the central section, the least well preserved, might belong to the late medieval deer park of Fawsley. In essence these earthworks perform much the same function as boundaries but are all of different dates, different styles and therefore different states of preservation; the oldest is not the least well preserved.

As a final example of acute observation in the establishment of landscape sequences, Fig. 50 shows in simplified yet pleasing form a set of earthworks planned by H. S. Toms, an associate of the great Lieutenant-General Pitt Rivers (Toms 1925). Barrows 2, 3, 4, 18 and 21 were in a perfect state of preservation when dug by the General; they had never been ploughed over. This means that lynchets 12 and 13, the formation of which

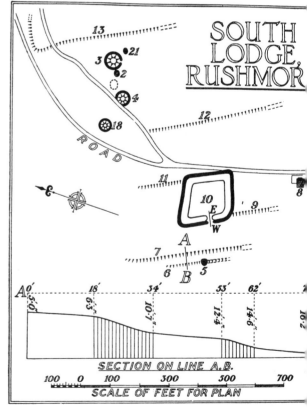

50   *South Lodge Camp, Dorset, as planned in the 1920s.*

required the movement of soil brought about by ploughing, must pre-date them; the barrows therefore sat on former arable. Similarly the squarish Bronze Age 'camp' 10 overlay lynchets 9 and 11 and its ditch cut through them. Its general form was determined by these earlier earthworks; like the barrows, it lay on land at one time under the plough.

This example serves to emphasize the importance of the kind of detail which favourable circumstances and good observation can provide. In many Midland village sites complete farm layouts can be made out, with rectangular depressions representing yards, access ways, house platforms and property boundaries still visible. At Thorpe in the Glebe, Nottinghamshire (Fig. 51), a site preserved in grassland, a series of such farm units lay along a main street. In enclosures 14, 15, 21 and 22, for example, a bank separates the farm from the street; behind the bank (i.e. to the north of the street) is a pair of raised platforms to

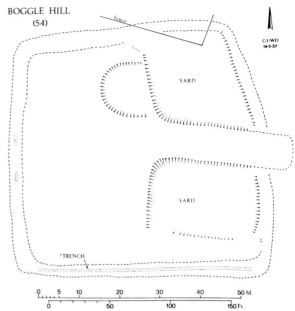

52   The earthwork at Boggle Hill, Thorneyburn, Northumberland.

51   The deserted village of Thorpe in the Glebe, Nottinghamshire.

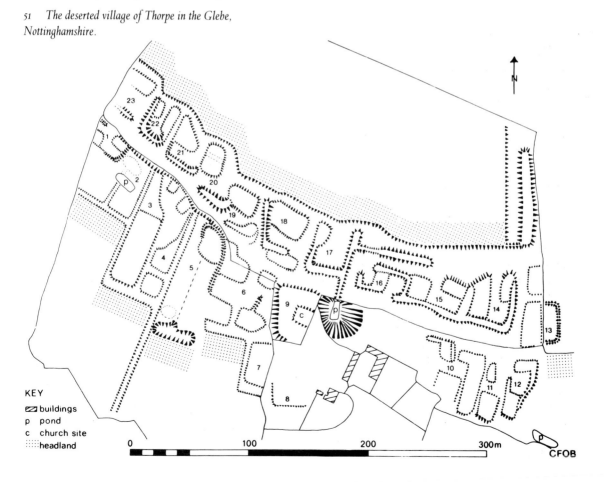

KEY
buildings
p   pond
c   church site
headland

accommodate buildings on either side of a depression representing the farmyard (Cameron and O'Brien 1981). At Kirby in Northamptonshire a clearance effected at a time − probably the seventeenth century − when domestic buildings were of stone, well-preserved earthworks show in remarkable detail the plan of a farmstead with the internal arrangement of the rooms clearly visible as well as the yard and outbuildings (RCHME 1975a, 33). Field survey can still sometimes retrieve significant detail from sites whose general state of preservation is mediocre. At Boggle Hill, Thorneyburn, Northumberland, a square enclosure contained a central causeway and two depressions which represented yards; behind one of these a small scarp probably marked the site of one of the round houses of this Romano-British farm (Fig. 52). Most significantly, slight grooves and differences in the colour of the grass probably indicated the line of a trench for an earlier timber palisade, probably prehistoric (Jobey 1984).

To appreciate how patchy the incidence of earthwork remains actually is and how their informativeness can vary necessitates an understanding of past land use. Parkland constitutes a particularly favourable location for the preservation of earthworks, and particular attention must be paid to it whenever possible. At Barnsley in Gloucestershire it was the park there which allowed the survival of 48 ha (120 acres) of Celtic fields associated with a Roman villa; they consisted in part of very low baulks up to 12 m (52 ft) across (RCHME 1976, 11). In the parish of Aldsworth in the same county, it was the existence of a racecourse at Bibury which permitted the preservation of parts of a remarkably regular Celtic field system with stony banks 0·3 m (1 ft) high (ibid. 2−3). Ancient woodland will quite frequently preserve earthworks in a very valuable way; at Micheldever in Hampshire a wood over 200 ha (500 acres) in area contained no less than

three Iron Age banjo enclosures, another small earthwork enclosure of Iron Age date, fields, tracks and linear earthworks of Iron Age and of Roman date as well as medieval wood banks; yet outside the wood, traces of such features existed only as soil and crop marks on aerial photographs and as flint and pottery scatters in ploughed fields (Fasham 1983). A survey of the site of Richmont Castle, East Harptree, Avon, in woodland, showed that a plan of the castle consisting of two baileys, with walls, towers and the (probable) site of the gatehouse could still be made out from the robbing trenches created when the place was demolished in the early sixteenth century to build a country house 2 km (1¼ miles) away; these trenches could be distinguished from later lead-mining trenches because of their shallowness and regularity (Iles 1984a). Old grassland is vital. The Port Meadow at Oxford, anciently common grazing, preserves the slight earthworks of prehistoric and Roman settlement sites (Miles 1980). In situations such as this even light ploughing will cause tremendous damage and make recording and interpretation difficult. At Porton Down a survey has shown that most of the area had in fact been ploughed at least for a time in the mid-nineteenth century; as a result the prehistoric boundary banks and ditches have been substantially reduced in emphasis, whereas the round barrows, larger features which could be avoided by the plough, survive (Bonney 1980, 47). A single ploughing will quickly remove all traces of such slight earthworks as those of the small isolated Roman settlements investigated by Professor Peter Fowler on Overton Down, Wiltshire (Bowen and Fowler 1966). All this serves to illustrate the very partial and biased nature of earthwork evidence in zones of continuous and intense human occupation, but also to emphasize its tremendous value and the urgency of recording it well.

5 Maps and the fieldworker

The Ordnance Survey has had a policy of marking antiquities in distinctive type on its maps since the early nineteenth century, and of course these indications are of prime importance in the preliminary identification of sites in a programme of field survey. Generally speaking the identifications will be accurate, and the fact that something is marked as an antiquity at all will serve usefully to draw attention to it. But the speed or otherwise of the revision process and the rapidity and completeness of modern destruction can easily mean that the available Ordnance map and the reality of the surviving ancient landscape can be severely out of phase. There can also be inconsistencies – the well-known hill fort at Sutton Walls, Hereford and Worcester, was marked in Gothic type as a 'camp' for years on one-inch maps until suddenly ceasing to be marked as an antiquity at all in 1947. There can also be errors in identification, as we have already seen. Sometimes errors in ascription to period occur; earthworks south of Brinsop church in the same county were marked in the script appropriate for a Roman site but must surely be those of a medieval settlement. On occasion there are near misses. On the eastern side of Spaunton Moor in Yorkshire are some small quarry-like excavations known locally as the 'glass holes' but marked on Ordnance maps as 'smelting works' or 'ancient smelting works', or more recently as 'iron workings'. In fact detailed excavation has shown them to have really been quarries designed to get at a sandy material suitable for making glass at a furnace at Rosedale probably in operation during the period 1580–1615 (Hayes and Hemingway 1984). The fact that the Survey has had a policy of indicating antiquities for so long is in itself a tremendous advantage, since sites which have since been forgotten or destroyed were marked on the basis on local knowledge in the nineteenth century. At Burton Lazars in Leicestershire a small spa was created in the eighteenth century, with a bathing room, a successor in a way to the medieval leper house. There are some generalized and repetitive references to its appearance and efficacy in the eighteenth-century literature, but nowhere is its location accurately stated. The only source for this is the nineteenth-century Ordnance Survey map.

There are also occasions when the Ordnance Survey can be misled in the location of antiquities. The site of the deserted village of Hardwick in the parish of Empingham, Leicestershire, has been taken to be represented by some irregular earthworks in a field close to Ermine Street, but these were probably old quarries, as their general form suggests; a fact supported by the field name, Pit Field. No pottery has been found there. The true site lay 600 m (half a mile) to the north-east, where the 1947 RAF vertical air photographs record earthworks, and where the field name Old Hardwick is suggestive.

Basic plans of earthwork field monuments can be obtained from the 25-inch plans. In terms of the actual location of scarps, banks and mounds, these surveys are of the high degree of accuracy one expects of the Ordnance Survey, but finer points of interpretation may be missed out, and low earthworks less than 0·5 m (1½ ft) certainly will be, because of Ordnance Survey policy in this regard. This means that an apparently straightforward site on the map can on inspection turn out to be vastly more complicated. Fig. 53 is a relatively simple example. Sometimes field inspection will enable an alternative explanation from the Ordnance Survey plan to be put forward. Fig. 54 shows the Ordnance Survey representation of Wood Walton castle in Cambridgeshire, an interpret-

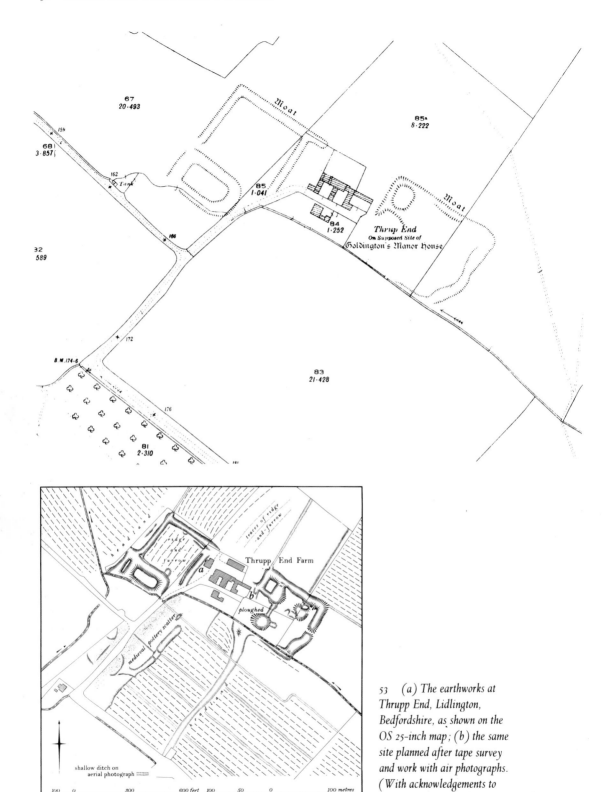

53   (a) The earthworks at Thrupp End, Lidlington, Bedfordshire, as shown on the OS 25-inch map; (b) the same site planned after tape survey and work with air photographs. (With acknowledgements to the Ordnance Survey)

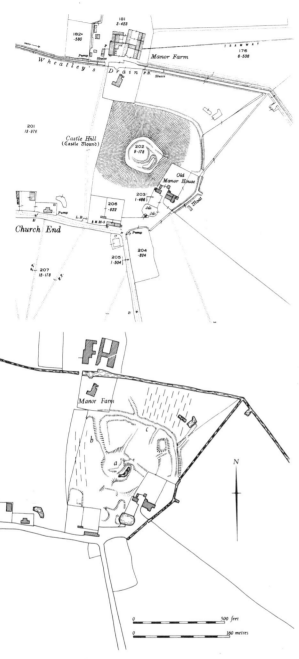

54   Wood Walton Castle, Cambridgeshire, (a) as shown on the OS 25-inch map and (b) as the result of fresh earthwork survey. (With acknowledgements to the Ordnance Survey)

ation followed subsequently by the Royal Commission on the Historical Monuments of England. Alongside it is a plan produced more recently by extra-mural students. The difference is due to the fact that the original surveyors regarded the low natural hillock on which the castle was placed as a motte, and drew it accordingly; but the motte has in fact been removed, and instead the more recent plan, because it shows the ramps leading down from the centre of the castle across the ditch, has been able to provide direct evidence for the way in which the actual process of removal took place.

Because the Ordnance Survey maps are so meticulous in their record of landscape detail, information will be given on them which will enable the reasonable suggestion to be made that an antiquity exists even if it has not been marked as such or even recognized when the map was made. Right-angled ponds can sometimes, but not always, turn out to be medieval moated sites. Narrow ponds strung out along the streams may be medieval fishponds; sometimes an isolated dam will turn out to be an indicator of a fishpond complex. These things may derive added significance from their juxtaposition to churches or manor farms. At Whissendine in Leicestershire the manor house marked as such on the Ordnance map has a broad earthwork bank marked northeast of it; a garden, probably of the seventeenth century, is indicated (Fig. 55). The narrow earthworks to the east must be a set of fishponds. Continuous hedge lines forming large enclosures containing inter alia areas of woodland and associated with appropriate place names – Park Farm, Park Wood, etc. – probably show the outlines of medieval deer parks (e.g. Fig. 57). On occasion earthworks which to judge from their plans are clearly ancient are beautifully drawn yet not marked as antiquities – the deserted village of Horn in Leicestershire is an example, where both the hollow way and moated site are shown (Fig. 55). In the same county the earthworks indicated at Leighfield Lodge are obviously those of a series of fishponds with associated embanked leats, linked with one of the administrative centres of the forest of Rutland. At Poston, Hereford and Worcester, an Iron Age promontory fort was recorded as a camp in Isaac Taylor's map of Herefordshire of 1754, and a substantial L-shaped earthwork bank in a small wood of the same shape has been marked clearly on the Ordnance maps for many years; but the site has only recently been labelled as an antiquity. On the other hand, not all earthworks so indicated will represent antiquities – quite a few will be quarries, stock ponds or other less significant disturbances. It is important

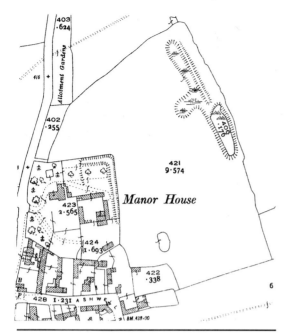

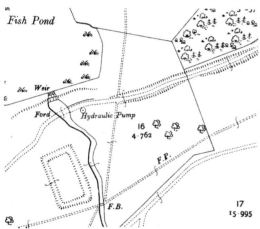

55   *25-inch Ordnance map extracts of (a) Whissendine and (b) the deserted village of Horn, in Empingham, Leicestershire. (With acknowledgements to the Ordnance Survey)*

to look at as many editions of the Ordnance maps as possible. Recent editions show how the south-eastern corner of Exton parish in Leicestershire projects in a very marked way into the parishes of Whitwell and Hambleton. The outline formed by the parish boundary is projected northwards by a continuous hedge line. The enclosure so formed contains a couple of woods, Barnsdale and Armley. This topographical evidence and documentary references make it certain that this was a

medieval deer park, known as Barnards Lilpark in the fifteenth century. But it is not until the Ordnance maps of the 1930s are consulted that an accurate plan is obtained of a feature not shown at all on the more recent maps and anyway since destroyed, a small moated site known as Robin Hood's Cave, probably a hunting lodge of the type well known from parks elsewhere. The first-edition one-inch maps are particularly important, since they will often be the earliest Ordnance maps of an area in existence, and structures marked on them as functioning entities may well be represented only by earthworks now. At Liddington in Leicestershire the first-edition one-inch map shows a windmill south-east of the village. Until recent destruction this was represented by a mound 18 m (59 ft) in diameter with a dished top, within which was a fragment of a millstone (Brown 1975, 17).

These are ways in which the Ordnance maps can help directly in the discovery and interpretation of sites. But these maps can help in more oblique ways. Isolated churches are a classic indicator of deserted village sites, although it cannot be assumed by any means that all solitary churches once had settlements close to them. The names of farms or of very small settlements printed in lettering too large for the size of the place can be another pointer; the general location of the lost village of Papley in Northamptonshire is thus indicated, supported by the way in which several tracks apparently converge on nothing, and by the presence of a moated site. After a while the field archaeologist develops a knack of picking out anomalies on Ordnance maps which on checking may well turn out to be indicative of something of archaeological interest. Fig. 56 shows a field outside the village of Thornby in North-amptonshire. The projection in the western corner looks odd, and on examination can be seen to run round the base of a windmill mound. Kinks and unexpected bends in streams can indicate mill sites or other early waterworks. At Yardley Hastings in the same county a massive dam is marked on no Ordnance map, yet a hint of it is given by the way in which the stream runs through three neat sharp right-angled bends to make its way through a breach (RCHME 1979a, 184). Similarly sharp differences in the shapes of the fields in different parts of the same parish can

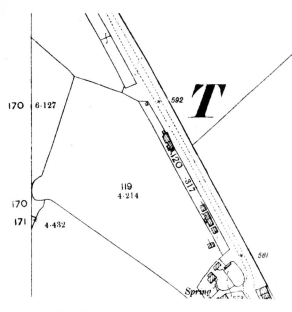

have great significance. At Liddington, Leicester-shire, the outline of the deer park belonging to the palace of the bishops of Lincoln is marked by continuous hedge lines, and the fields within it differ in character from the straight-sided ones to the north and east, the result of the Parliamentary enclosure of the open fields in 1799 (Fig. 57).

Very abrupt changes in the alignment of a road will normally require an explanation, as will anomalies in the plans of villages – streets unlined with houses, or lengths of road going nowhere, for example. Fig. 58 shows the 25-inch Ordnance Survey plan of the village of Hamerton in

56   Thornby in Northamptonshire. In this 25-inch Ordnance map extract, the odd projection in the western corner of the field indicates the site of a windmill. (With acknowledgements to the Ordnance Survey)

57   This six-inch map extract shows the area of the Bishop of Lincoln's deer park at Liddington, Leicestershire. An episcopal palace lay one km to the east in the village. Note the irregular fields within the area of the park, and the way in which they contrast with the much more geometrical fields along the northern side of the park, to the south of the parish boundary. (With acknowledgements to the Ordnance Survey)

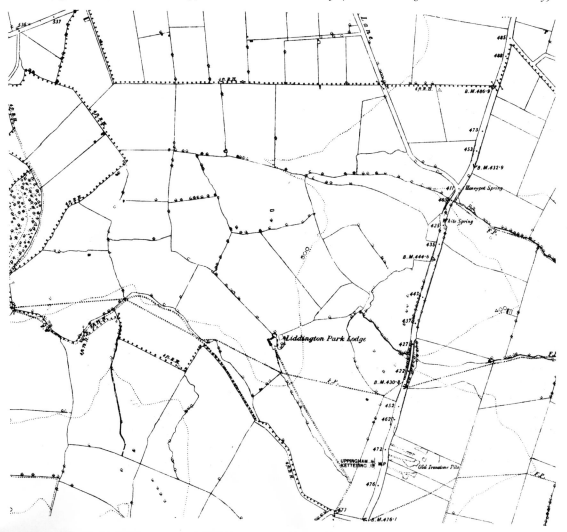

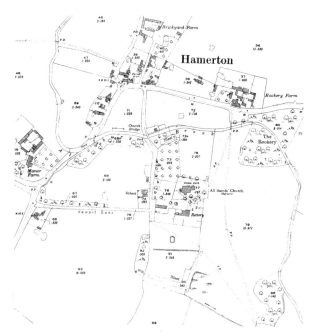

58   *Hamerton in Cambridgeshire, as on the 25-inch Ordnance map. (With acknowledgements to the Ordnance Survey)*

Cambridgeshire. The peculiar thing about this is the dispersed nature of the plan, curious for a village in this zone of tightly nucleated settlements. That this need not always have been the case is apparent from Fig. 59, produced as a result of a field survey. This indicates clearly that the village once had a different appearance. But one can go further and suggest that the plan of the place had undergone various changes consequent upon alterations in the pattern of communication – what traffic there is tends now to go east–west towards the A1, but the existence of a fine fourteenth-century bridge carrying the north–south road running past the church and now apparently leading nowhere suggests that this road must once have been an important axis of communication, connected perhaps with the development in the thirteenth century of Kimbolton eight miles away, as a market centre.

In towns and villages the shapes of building plots and the relationships between the blocks of land which go to form the plans of such places can be analysed in a rigorous manner to shed light upon the origins, development and function of these settlements. Little need be said here about this kind of analysis, since an excellent guide is

already available (Roberts 1982) and a worked example is given on p.124; but a couple of basic points can be made. First, although almost all the work which has so far been done in this country on village plan analysis has taken place on existing settlements, there is no reason why the earthworks of deserted or shrunken ones should not be similarly treated; and in some cases the existing plan of a village will be unintelligible without the addition of the earthworks anyway, as in the case of Hamerton. Secondly, the kinds of technique recommended above for the location and identification of archaeological features in the countryside using Ordnance maps can be used in a modified form for built-up areas. It is remarkable how in large towns the boundaries of ancient estates and their subdivisions can be traced even today on the large-scale Ordnance maps, with the aid of other maps and much documentary work. In Oxford the outlines of the very substantial block of land owned by the Grey Friars and in particular their orchard (known as Paradise) and their meadow (called Boleham) could still be made out on the late nineteenth-century 25-inch map in an area of very dense housing development. The street names Paradise Square and Friars

59   *The garden and village earthworks at Hamerton.*

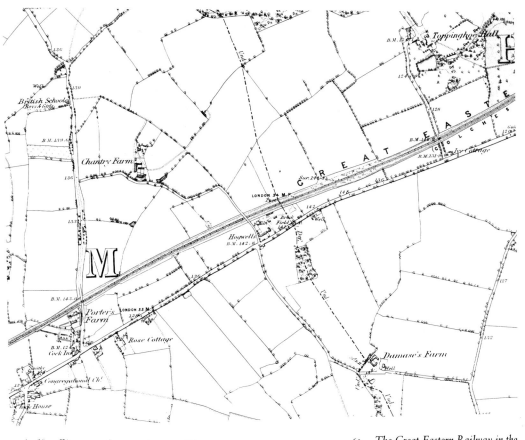

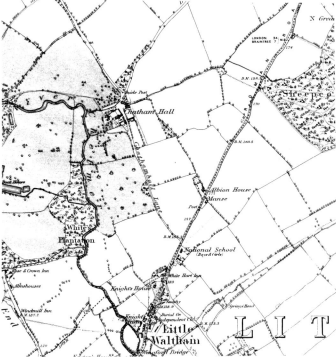

60 *The Great Eastern Railway in the parish of Boreham and the Roman road to Braintree near Little Waltham, Essex. (With acknowledgements to the Ordnance Survey)*

Street preserved a memory of the former owners of the land (Hassall *et al.* 1984, 269–75). This kind of observation can work at the level of the individual archaeological site. At Wollaston in Northamptonshire, for example, the curved building line of the houses to the north of a small ditched mound in the village could well represent the outline of the associated bailey (RCHME 1979a, 180); at Towcester (Fig. 32) the enclosed areas on either side of the motte known as Bury Mount might represent the same kind of feature.

Most important of all is the observation that, outside the zone which in the Middle Ages had highly developed open-field systems and tightly nucleated villages, in general terms stretching from Dorset *via* the Midlands to south and west Yorkshire, lie tracts of countryside with a different character embodying somewhat irregular hedged fields, winding lanes, many smallish woods and a dispersed settlement pattern of hamlets and farms. The landscape shown on the modern Ordnance map and still more so that of the nineteenth-century tithe maps, before the widespread recent destruction of hedgerows, represents the results of a slow process of change which in places must have started in prehistory. This is shown not just by fieldwalking (p.24), but by the map itself. Fig. 60 shows how the railway line from London to Colchester clearly cuts through the pattern of the fields; they obviously predate it. The same figure also indicates that the Roman road from Little Waltham in Essex to the Roman small town of Braintree can be regarded in exactly the same fashion as the nineteenth-century

railway; it cuts through the pattern of the field boundaries in a way which shows clearly that it is later. The general alignment of the underlying, presumably Iron Age, field system can be picked up by further map work, and the manner in which this behaves in relation to other roads to which it conforms enables the skeleton of this early landscape to be reconstructed (Drury 1978, 134–5).

The development of the Ordnance Survey in the nineteenth century eventually led to a decline in the production of county and other small-scale maps by private surveyors. It is sometimes said that these early privately produced maps are of little aid to the fieldworker, and it is easy to see why: often there is little topographical detail and overmuch picturesque decoration; they are sometimes inaccurate; they copy each other – Wistow and Newton Harcourt in Leicestershire were placed on the wrong side of the river Sence by Saxton in 1576 and the error was repeated in Morden's map of Leicestershire a century later (Fox 1982, 3). But such maps cannot really be ignored. Some early cartographers were interested in antiquities and went to some trouble to mark them. A possible hill fort at Icomb in Gloucestershire has now been almost entirely destroyed by ploughing; the only evidence for its probable original shape comes from Taylor's map of Gloucestershire of 1777 (RCHME 1976, 66). A number of county maps from Morden onwards marked the sites of depopulated villages, which had never in fact been forgotten. Fig. 61 shows a cartouche from Morden's map of Rutland where

61   *Explanatory cartouche from Morden's map of Rutland.*

the location of *loca devastata olim villae* is quite clearly given. Similarly deserted sites were indicated on the map drawn by Sir William Dugdale to accompany *The Antiquities of Warwickshire* in 1656. Many maps, such as Thomas Eyre's map of Northamptonshire published in 1791, were on a scale sufficiently large to enable thumbnail impressions of village plans to be given which are of great value in understanding subsequent changes. Sometimes these plans are useful in the interpretation of earthworks: compare Eyre's representation of the village of Hothorpe with the plan of the surviving traces, which can usefully be interpreted in the light of the eighteenth-century sketch (Fig. 35). Some of these maps show parks, important gardens, and the roads regarded as the most significant at the time, and industrial developments, as did Prior's map of Leicestershire of 1777, which included conventional symbols for coal mines and lime works. The non-appearance of early industrial features and their inclusion on early Ordnance maps can give a useful indication of the date for the inception of some of these early industrial remains (Palmer, M 1984).

The insets devoted to towns on these early

62   *The bowling green on Jeffery's map of Huntingdon, 1768.*

maps are of obvious importance in the study of urban topography and are valuable indicators of the state of growth at a particular period as well as such things as the lines of the defences, the locations of gates and now-demolished churches; and they can also explain quite small details of field archaeology. Fig. 62 is a detail from Thomas Jeffery's map of Huntingdon dated 1768. The feature, now destroyed, was being used as a bowling green at the time the map was made, but the corners show that in fact it had originally formed part of the Civil War defences of the town and could be described technically as a flanked redoubt.

So far we have discussed the usefulness of Ordnance Survey maps and earlier county maps. These will exist for just about everywhere. But there are other maps which can have tremendous value which are unfortunately not available for all parts of the country. Estate maps, produced in increasing numbers from the late sixteenth century, which can embrace whole parishes or just small parts of a parish or a township, vary very widely in their occurrence; generally speaking, except in the matter of field names, they cease to be really useful in the second half of the nineteenth century, when estate managers simply used Ordnance maps as a base and original surveys were no longer made. By no means all enclosure awards have maps going with them, and in any case the maps may only show those parts of the parish or township which were actually the subject of the enclosure award. Maps of this kind were made with specific purposes in mind, and information fieldworkers would consider of prime importance will frequently have been missed out. Fig. 63 shows part of the enclosure map of Daventry of 1804. Its purpose was to indicate the areas of land assigned to those in receipt of allotments under the terms of the enclosure award; no one looking at the map could possibly realize that at the time the map was made, within the part illustrated, lay a hill fort three times the size of Maiden Castle in Dorset, the site of a substantial Roman building still visible as earthworks, at least two prehistoric barrows and fourteen Roman ones, plus a variety of minor medieval earthworks of various kinds. The enclosure map of Bolnhurst in Bedfordshire, dated 1777, marks the building known as Manor

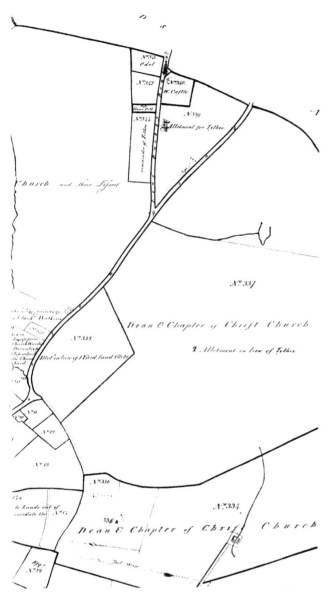

63   *An extract from the enclosure map of Daventry,*
Northamptonshire, 1804.

Farm which must occupy the site of the manor
house belonging to the abbey of Thorney, the
main landowner in the Middle Ages. The ditches
shown around it indicate that it had been moated,
but what the map does not show is the existence
of the large prehistoric earthwork already mentioned (Fig. 36), which lies in the field to the south
of the farm and out of which the moats had been
formed. Maps of this sort can be quite capricious
in their depiction of detail not central to their

purpose. Fig. 64 is an earthwork survey of the
remains of the small Augustinian house of
Stonely in Kimbolton parish, Cambridgeshire,
along with extracts from a pair of maps dated 1764
and 1769 showing the same piece of ground. The
earlier map is a careful representation, but even so
one of the lengths of ditch has been left out; the
later map makes no attempt to show anything in
this piece of ancient enclosed pasture – there was
simply no need to do so.

Maps and their makers in fact require very
careful critical appraisal before they can be used as
reliable guides to the contemporary appearance of
things. For example, three seventeenth-century
plans of the Civil War defences of Oxford, the
Royalist capital, are in existence in the Bodleian
Library. One of these is an obvious nonsense – half
of it is upside down. Another, actually printed in a
late seventeenth-century history of the University
of Oxford and accepted by some authorities as
accurate, can be seen on close inspection to be
extremely conventional, with a very regular
system of bastions set out mechanically around
the city, taking no regard of the possibilities of
local inundations available in the vicinity of this
low-lying town. Only a third plan, with careful
and accurate details and attributable to Sir Ber-
nard de Gomme, a professional military engineer
who probably helped to design their final form,
can be accepted as reliable (Lattey *et al.* 1936; Kemp
1977).

Tithe maps constitute an important mid-
nineteenth-century cartographic source, but
these generally finely drawn maps were only
made for places where tithes were still payable
after the passage of the Tithe Commutation Act
in 1836. It is quite common to encounter annoying
situations such as that exemplified by the neighbouring parishes of Foston and Kilby in Leicestershire. Kilby was enclosed in 1771 and the vicar
compensated with an allotment of land to make
up for the extinction of tithes. The enclosure
award gives an impression of the general disposition of the open fields, but the absence of
information about field names which would have
been provided by a tithe map means that the
location of the furlongs cannot be established
despite pre-enclosure documentation, which
gives their names. Foston on the other hand was
enclosed in the seventeenth century, but tithes

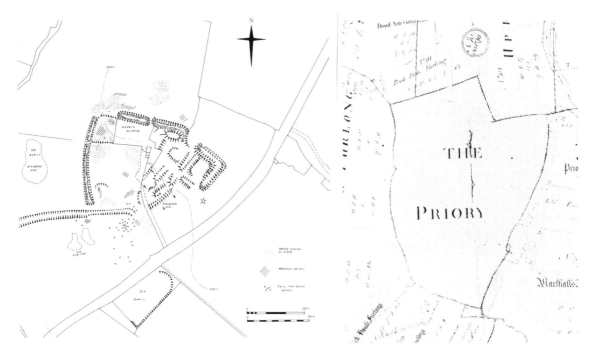

64   (a) An earthwork survey of Stonely Priory,
Cambridgeshire.
(b) The same area on a map of 1769; (c) the same area on a
map of 1764.

were not extinguished then. The tithe map produced in 1850 provides plenty of information about field names but, because there is no enclosure award, we can say very little about the broad outlines of the open field system. Sometimes the tithe map will cover only a part of a parish, and reasons must be sought for this. At Ridlington in Leicestershire an area shown as 'tithe-free' indicates the outline of the royal deer park known to have been there from medieval documents.

However, in places for which they exist, the information which can be derived from maps of these types can be of the highest value. The fine series of maps relating to the estates of the Coke family and preserved at Holkham Hall in Norfolk include examples which contain a great deal of material useful in the analysis of the development of the landscape. Fig. 65 is an instance where the moated site at Longham, surveyable now as an antiquity, is shown in a functioning state with the house, along with its porch and bridge, inside it (Wade Martins 1980). Mark Pierce's famous map of Laxton in Nottinghamshire, dated 1635, shows that a house, dovecote and barns, now gone, stood then in the outer bailey of the castle, and the motte had been turned into an ornamental garden feature. Old maps will sometimes show

65   *The manor house on a late sixteenth-century map of Longham, Norfolk.*

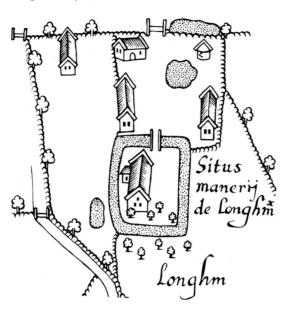

villages subsequently deserted or partially deserted still in position (e.g. Figs. 67 and 68); and can also explain why village earthworks take the form they have. At Brafield on the Green, Northamptonshire, a series of parallel-sided croft earthworks now in an out-of-the-way position south of the church can be seen to relate to a huge green which was not enclosed until 1827 and which gave the village its name (RCHME 1979a, 9). Early maps will also help to explain difficulties encountered in the interpretation of earthwork surveys. To the south of a moated site at Bushmead in Bedfordshire is a pair of wide but shallow ditches. These did not join the moat and it was hard to see what purpose they had, but an estate map of 1624 shows that at one time they were attached to the moat to form part of an elaborate drainage system. An earthwork on Hungry Hill near Aldershot was regarded as an Iron Age hill fort by Dr Williams Freeman, but a nineteenth-century military map proves that it was a redoubt put up for practice in the 1860s (Riall 1983).

A specialized variant of the estate map is the open-field strip map (Beresford and St Joseph 1979). These maps, which often provide representations of the associated settlements as well as details of mills, fishponds, gardens and so on, generally mark and name the furlongs of the open fields, the areas of pasture and meadow and enclosed land. The strips owned by the various farmers within the furlongs are also drawn, but not necessarily each plough ridge or land; sometimes a figure is inserted in each strip to show how many lands it contains, but not always — sometimes an area can be given or reference made to a field book which may or may not survive. Some tithe maps show fields still organized in this way in the 1840s in Leicestershire. Their value in reconstructing open-field systems is evident; and they are useful in the interpretation of specific problems — rectangular areas visible on top of certain plough ridges in the parish of Brixworth in Northamptonshire could be identified on a strip map of 1688 as rick places (RCHME 1981, 31). But some open-field maps listed in record office indexes can turn out to be a disappointment in that they only show the boundaries of the great fields, and not the furlongs they contain; and in any case such maps only show what the fields looked like at the time the map was made. A fine

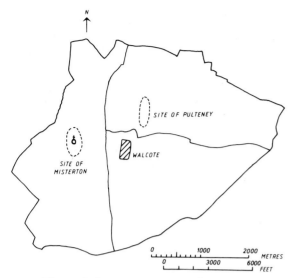

66   The parish of Misterton in Leicestershire.

strip map of Theddingworth, Leicestershire, dated 1696, for example, has an area of large hedged fields along the north-west edge of the parish, the result of early consolidation and enclosure; furlongs are not shown here, yet they certainly once existed.

Almost all the maps so far mentioned, including some of the later county maps, have the important merit of showing boundaries. Quite often we will be dealing with parish boundaries, but by no means always so. Fig. 66 shows the parish of Misterton in Leicestershire. In the south-eastern part of this there is a smallish hamlet known as Walcote. But not only was Walcote a separate settlement, it also had a tenurial history distinct from the other places in the parish, and its own entirely independent open-field system. The boundaries of this are clearly marked on the enclosure map of 1796. Misterton itself had its own field system, recoverable rather less certainly by means of field names listed in deeds (p.122); and we know from medieval sources that Pulteney had a field system of its own as well. These were economic units set within the ecclesiastical unit of the parish. Any attempt to reconstruct the medieval landscape of this area using field techniques must obviously take account of these boundaries. But the existence of these sub-units has implications for the field archaeology of settlement. The landscape of Pulteney today contains only a few scattered farms, but in this part of England the existence of a set of open fields

usually indicates the presence of a village; in fact a set of battered earthworks and a pottery scatter can be found. Not all parishes are subdivided in this way but many are; the subdivisions have a variety of names, hamlets, lordships, tithings and – particularly in the north of England where parishes can be very large – townships. Because of the possibility of subsequent changes boundaries derived from Ordnance maps should always be checked against older map sources to get back to the earliest form. Odd projections in parish boundaries are of interest in that they may indicate the territory of a deserted settlement; but other possible explanations for such things exist – deer parks sometimes jut out in this way, or the projection may be a relic of rights in a former area of moorland or of some trade-off in territory with a neighbouring settlement.

Such boundaries are also useful in indicating former territorial relationships. Misterton is an example of this, where, except for an odd unexplained projection on the north-west, the outer boundary forms a continuous perimeter and the internal ones indicate subdivisions. The ecclesiastical relationships of the three places concerned support this; Misterton as its name implies was the *minster-tun* where the head church of the area was; in the Middle Ages Pulteney and Walcote had chapels dependent upon it.

Maps and fieldwork combined can be used to reconstruct sequences of landscape development. At Overstone in Northamptonshire the modern Ordnance map depicts a large country house set within a park (now encroached upon by modern housing); the church stands within the park, but separated from the house by some half a kilometre (1,760 ft); the village is strung out along the road to Northampton, along the northern edge of the park. An explanation for this arrangement can be arrived at by looking at a sequence of maps for the parish, linked with an examination of the appropriate documentation. A late seventeenth-century map (Fig. 67) shows that the village of Overstone along with its church originally lay to the west of the manor house, the predecessor of the present great house; the houses were then somewhat dispersed, the effects possibly of shrinkage of population. The next available representation of Overstone, on the late eighteenth-century county map made by Thomas Eyre,

67   *Overstone in Northamptonshire, in the late seventeenth century.*

shows that a large park had been formed and the village moved to its present position outside it, but that the church remained still in its old location opposite the great house. Although the documents are silent on the point, the explanation can be offered that Henry Stratford, who is known to have bought Overstone in 1672 and who enclosed the parish in 1727, was responsible for moving the place; until recently the earthworks of the village, complete with hollow ways, house sites and property boundaries matching the features shown on the seventeenth-century map, survived. An estate map of 1832 shows further development in that the park has been enlarged still more, to take in part of the adjacent parish of Sywell as well as more of Overstone, and the church moved to its present position. These developments were the work of the late eighteenth- and early nineteenth-century owners of Overstone, particularly John Kipling; and the reasons for them are clear from the surviving

documentation; as a land valuer of 1791 said: 'There seems to be some material objection to Overstone House as a residence for a gentleman of large fortune ... a publick road immediately past the door and the church and some part of the glebe land directly in front of the house would be considered insurmountable bars to elbow room which the generality of people of fashion are accustomed to think a necessary article of ease, comfort and happiness' (Brown and Taylor 1975).

At Rockingham in the same county the development of the park can be largely reconstructed from a combination of cartographic evidence and fieldwork. A map of 1615 (Fig. 68) indicates a relatively small enclosure marked as Lime Kiln Quarter at the northern tip of the great park. The north-west side of this is the only portion of the circuit of any part of the park at Rockingham to have a classic medieval park pale earthwork, a bank 3 m (10 ft) wide, 2 m (6½ ft) high and an internal ditch. This enclosure was probably the original park going with the royal castle and mentioned in thirteenth-century documents. The park shown on the seventeenth-century map was the greatly enlarged one brought into being by Henry VIII in 1485; there was

68 Rockingham in Northamptonshire, in 1615. Compare with Fig. 40, and note in particular how the houses shown near the castle on this map have subsequently been removed and how changes have taken place in the road system of the village.

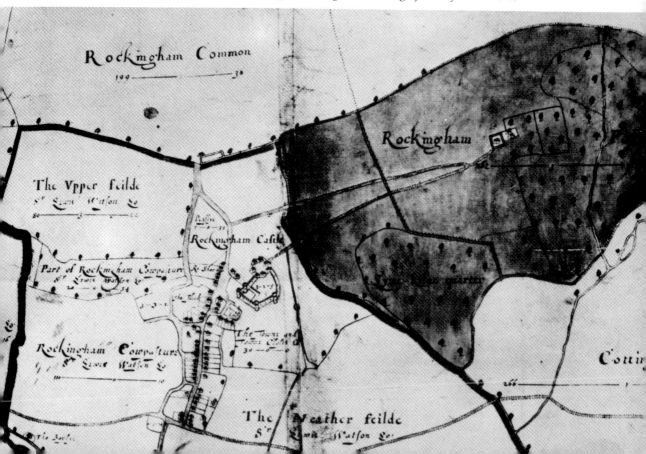

no substantial pale earthwork. But the boundary of this differs on the north-east from the park boundary shown on a series of nineteenth-century estate maps belonging to the Watson family, which finally obtained Rockingham Castle and park in the early seventeenth century. The explanation for this is that in 1638 Lewis Watson obtained a royal licence to enlarge the park; his new boundary can be traced as a ditch cutting through the ridge and furrow on that side ((a)–(k), Fig. 40). Finally, the first edition of the Ordnance Survey six-inch map shows further nineteenth-century additions along the northern side (Brown and Taylor 1974).

Maps are useful in the indications they give of past land use. This will have affected the survival of ancient monuments and any assessment of their significance must take the cartographic evidence into account. First-edition one-inch Ordnance maps are valuable in showing the areas under pasture in Dorset in the early nineteenth century. This explains the preservation of barrows in that area, which does not necessarily reflect their original distribution accurately. Tithe maps show land use at the time they were made, and have been used for example to show what land was under the plough in the Stonehenge area in the mid-nineteenth century. This and the consideration of medieval land use derived from enclosure awards as well as the accounts of such contemporary travellers as Daniel Defoe enabled the survival of certain barrows and Celtic field remains, and the loss of others, to be accounted for (RCHME 1979b).

A type of evidence conveniently considered here consists of old pictorial representations of the landscape (the sources are conveniently listed in Barley 1974). Some antiquarian drawings are of the highest value. William Stukeley's reputation for accurate observation is in general justified. He represented correctly the oval ditch that lies within the ramparts of the hill fort of Figsbury Rings, Wiltshire, and noted that it had no rampart – his idea that this had been removed to heighten (or make) the visible bank has been supported by recent work (Fig. 69; Guido and Smith 1982). The late seventeenth-century engravings of country houses and their formal gardens made by William Kip are essential in documenting a phase in the development of these places and in occasionally helping to understand earthwork remains. At Madingley in Cambridgeshire his drawing shows

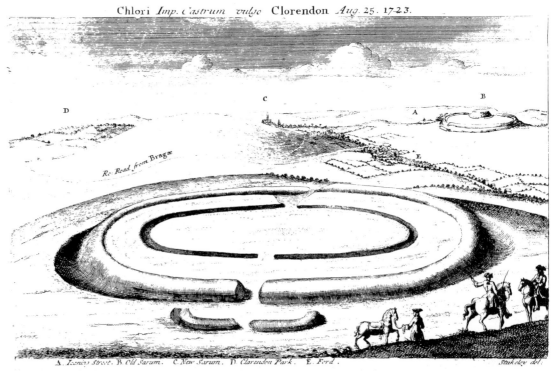

Chlori *Imp. Castrum vulgo* Clorendon *Aug. 25. 1723.*

A. *Icning Street.* B. *Old Sarum.* C. *New Sarum.* D. *Clarendon Park.* E. *Ford.*
Stukeley del.

69 *Stukeley's drawing of the Figsbury Rings hill fort in Wiltshire.*

the church, still in the position it occupies today, but with houses along a road running from it; these have gone and only a hollow way and some slight earthworks remain. At Dyrham Park, Gloucestershire, Kip's engraving shows a set of extremely elaborate gardens laid out c.1700 by William Blathwayt, Secretary of State to William III. These explain the few hillside terraces and ponds (actually remodelled medieval ones, as an estate map of 1688 indicates) which escaped a drastic alteration in the design of the park a century later (Iles 1984b and c). The productions of certain other antiquarian engravers, more concerned with architectural remains, can also be trusted. There is good evidence for the pains that Samuel and Nathaniel Buck, the well-known eighteenth-century artists, took over their work, using grids of squares for the accurate representation of quite fine detail; only the trees and vegetation and certain landscape details were worked up later to give effect (Wilks 1980). In the nineteenth century Thomas Bateman's views of Arbor Low, preserved in Sheffield Museum, are of value in the provision of information about the stones which once stood at the entrances of the monument. But the work of artists not primarily concerned with topographical matters and with other objectives can be trusted less. A barrow c. 2·4 m (8 ft) high near Stonehenge (Amesbury Barrow 39) recorded by Stukeley, which must at the time have been perfectly obvious, was in effect omitted from paintings of Stonehenge by Constable and Turner (Ashbee 1981). The artists were simply interested in the monument and its dramatic impact, not in the accurate representation of the surroundings. The same sort of point is made by a painting of Mousehold Heath in Norfolk by John Crome. This looks very much like an accurate representation of a piece of open countryside, yet cannot have been so since it was painted twenty years after the enclosure of the heath in the late eighteenth century (Fawcett 1982). David Austin has pointed out how Thomas Hearne's watercolour of Barnard Castle of c.1790 deliberately omits the chain factories, cloth mills and slum dwellings around the castle in order to present an attractive picture of a romantic ruin above a tree-covered hill overlooking a beautiful river (Austin 1984, 71–2). Paintings and drawings can be easily misinterpreted. Some small objects

drawn in outline on an early eighteenth-century representation of the Stonehenge area by J. Hassell were taken to indicate megalithic remains since removed, but must surely have been just bushes (Bonney 1981).

We must now briefly consider the usefulness of one of the commonest categories of information to be derived from the study of maps – place and field names. The value of Ordnance maps as a source for the former will be obvious; for the latter the schedules attached to tithe maps, estate maps, sale particulars relating to farms, some enclosure maps, and the field-name maps which have accumulated in record offices as a result of local effort by schoolchildren or the Women's Institute are the main cartographic sources.

As is well known, place and field names can indicate the existence of an archaeological site directly. The Old English words *beorg* and *hlaw*, meaning burial mound, which become 'barrow' and 'low' are obvious examples, although it is necessary to be aware of some possible difficulties. Names derived from *beorg* can be confused with those derived from *burh* (modern bury, borough), another significant name which implies a fortification, which could range in date and type from a prehistoric hill fort to a defended medieval manor house. Both *beorg* and *hlaw* may just mean hill, although the chances of their doing so are very much greater in the north of England (see Gelling 1978, 132–7 for details). Such names can refer to antiquities which are well known; in other instances the name may indicate a site largely destroyed, faint traces of which are recoverable as a result of detailed fieldwork. A Berkshire charter of AD 953 included a reference to 'the north gate of the raven's camp' (*hremnes byrig*). This particular place can be identified with Ram's Hill, where the ploughed-down rampart of an early enclosure was in fact identified by subsequent fieldwork (Bradley and Ellison 1975, 3). The earthen *burh* referred to in a charter of AD 995 relating to the parish of Ardley in Oxfordshire no longer exists as an earthwork, but a large rectangular enclosure intersecting a smaller banjo enclosure has been recognized on non-archaeological air photographs in the appropriate location (Bond 1984). The use of the Old English word *ceaster* (modern chester) to denote a Roman walled town is familiar, but there are several instances in which the term is found in connection with the sites of villas; for example, in Much Wenlock parish in Shropshire a villa lay in a field known as The Hairchester. Also note the village names Woodchester and Frocester in Gloucestershire, both of which have substantial villas. Many villa sites in the Cotswolds lay in fields known as the Chessells (from the Old English *ceastel*, a heap of stones); names with the element *stan* (stone) can have similar associations (RCHME 1976, lii–liii). The name street (from *straet*) usually signifies a paved road, quite possibly of Roman origin. There has always been a tendency to link ancient sites with the supernatural, from gods in the case of Wayland's Smithy chambered tomb in Wiltshire down to fairies – Margaret Faull has drawn attention to the place name Pugneys, near Wakefield (West Yorkshire) which includes the Old English element *puca* (fairy). This site produces quantities of Mesolithic flints, perhaps considered in the past to be the weapons of elves or goblins. Another example comes from the parish of Peterchurch, Hereford and Worcester, where a field next to Pucha Farm produces abundant Neolithic flintwork, including arrowheads, 'fairy bolts', from time to time (Faull 1978/9; Robinson 1934). Names referring to Grim's Dyke or Ditch in five townships east of Leeds led to the discovery that a denuded earthwork was not, as had been thought, a Roman road but a linear boundary, the course of which could be traced for seven miles (Faull 1978/9). Some place or field names commemorate trades or industries which may leave significant surface indications behind, such as pottery manufacture. Fields known as Potters Croft and Potters Hills at Great Munden, and the place names Potters Heath and Potters Crouch all belong to places which have produced evidence of medieval pottery manufacture in Hertfordshire (Renn 1964).

All this means that the evidence of field names must be taken into account in the matter of discovering sites. There will be many localities which contain a field known as Stone Fields, Blacklands or something similar, perhaps merely a descriptive name relating to the workability or colour of the soil, but quite possibly of archaeological significance – at Corby and Kings Sutton (Northamptonshire) large Roman sites occur in fields of the latter name (Brown 1970, 2–3; RCHME 1982, 93); near Woking (Surrey) a recently excavated Roman and later site lay in Black Close (Hawkins 1985); at Clipsham, Leicestershire, a Roman ironworking site lies in Black Piece. At Caldecott in the same county fields named as Windmill Close on a field-name map contain a mound which is all that is left of a windmill marked on the first-edition Ordnance Survey map (Brown 1975, 6). There is an important Iron Age and Roman site at Ash Furlong, Olney, Buckinghamshire. Records of old archaeological discoveries frequently refer to the names of the fields in which they were made, affording thereby a means of relocating them today. A furlong called the Shelven Stone on a map of Winterborne Monkton (Wiltshire), the location of which could be transferred to the modern Ordnance map, along with accurate topographical observations by Stukeley, enabled not only the location of the chambered tomb known as the Shelving Stone to be fixed but also the confusion between it and another known as Millbarrow to be finally sorted out (Barker 1983). At Market Overton, Leicestershire, a great quantity of Roman material, including a pottery kiln and two Anglo-Saxon cemeteries were discovered during ironstone digging in the early years of this century in Land Close. The local field-name map enabled the general area of these important finds to be located (Brown 1975, 18). At Podington (Bedfordshire) many Roman finds turned up in a field marked as Bellams on a map of c.1770. This must be the same as the field known as Bellum in which a Bronze Age figure of a helmeted soldier, possibly a Roman votive object, was ploughed up in the last century (Moore 1970, 12).

Field names are essential in the location of lost medieval settlements whose names are known from documents. In Leicestershire the location of the village of Sculthorp, which lay in the parish of North Luffenham, was indicated by a group of fields listed as Sculthorp Close, Scultrups and Bottom Scultrups on the tithe and field-name maps. In a similar way a series of fields known as Austrops and Top Austrips indicate the general location of the open fields belonging to the village of Alstoe in the parish of Burley (Brown 1975, 5, 20). The same technique can be used for locating lost settlements which were never much more than single farms. It is known from documentary sources that a place called Claverlay existed within the township of Upper Whitley in West Yorkshire. The tithe map marks a field named Clover Leys which gives its probable location (Faull 1978/9).

Field names can assist in the actual interpretation of the results of fieldwork. At Molesworth, Cambridgeshire, an extensive but confused series of earthworks incorporating what may once have been a substantial L-shaped bank and ditch lies in Hall Yard Close — possibly therefore a manor house site (Brown and Taylor 1981, 122–4). At Coppingford in the same county a small sub-rectangular moated site lies in a wood marked as Hermitage Wood on a map of 1716. Documentary sources confirm that the site was in fact a medieval hermitage given to Bushmead Priory in Bedfordshire in the early thirteenth century. Nearby lies the site of the deserted village of Coppingford, but between the hermitage and the village is a track running north-west/south-east, parallel with the main A1 road, marked on the Ordnance Survey six-inch map as the Bullock Road. The field survey of the village earthworks showed that the main street of the village was unusually wide. The road name helps to suggest an explanation; this track was used for the droving of cattle from the north of England in the post-medieval period. The map also shows that the track which lay along the main street of Coppingford village ran parallel with the Bullock Road. Both tracks eventually joined up to form a route still traceable on maps today by means of footpaths, tracks, minor roads and parish boundaries to a bridge over the river Nene at Wansford. The width of the village street at Coppingford is probably therefore to be ascribed to its use as a medieval and possibly later main road (Brown and Taylor 1978, 59–63). Field names can help sometimes to explain crop marks. At Stratford St Mary, Suffolk, a penannular ring discernible as a crop mark had for some years been regarded as a henge monument. Doubt began to be felt about this attribution because of the small size of the feature in relation to most known henges; also a cruciform feature was eventually noted from the air inside it. The identification of the site as a windmill was made certain by the field name, Mount Field, on the tithe map (Martin 1982).

Field and minor place names must be used with due care; the obvious interpretation is not always the right one. Not every Chapel Field will have contained a medieval stone ecclesiastical building; bones and stones of quite different origin may have turned up, not necessarily ancient. A group of three deer parks near Canterbury have been studied recently by Tim Tatton-Brown. Trenley Park is one of the oldest in England, being mentioned in Domesday Book. To the south-west is a small park which belonged to St Augustine's Abbey, Canterbury; it is labelled as the Old Park on a drawing of 1600. The third park dates only from c.1539 yet it is this one which today bears that quite misleading name (Tatton-Brown 1983). In Sharnbrook in Bedfordshire the name Moat House refers not to a medieval moated site but to some minor waterworks of the eighteenth century. Camp Farm in Aston Blank parish, Gloucestershire, takes its name from a series of quite natural ridges (RCHME 1976, 4). In the East Riding of Yorkshire the Howe Hills at Goodmanham contain the Old Norse element *haugr* (modern law) i.e. a burial mound. There are earthworks there, with suggestive local legends about the early propagation of Christianity in the region attached to them, but they are in fact the remains of medieval and post-medieval chalk pits (Faull 1978/9). The name Cold Harbour, often taken to denote a Roman site, is really a term applied in the seventeenth century in a derogatory way to a miserable house usually set at a distance from others (Coates 1984). In Norfolk a long southern projection of the parish of Sporle contains a farm called Petygards. Its situation on the map, along with the indication of an antiquity on the Ordnance map (the site of the Hall), led to the suggestion that there had once been a village of that name here. Detailed fieldwalking showed that a village had indeed existed in the Middle Ages, but the documentary evidence studied at the same time, particularly charters (p.120) showed that the name of the place had in reality been Cotes; Petygards had simply been one of the component farms (Davison 1982).

The ability to fix ancient field names on the map is very variable. An abundance of documentation with field-name information is almost useless to the fieldworker unless the maps exist which tell him just where the fields to which the names belong actually were; and as we have seen, not all places have tithe or estate maps. As will be explained later, an important function which field names fulfil is to assist in the reconstruction of pre-enclosure field systems, but the very fact of enclosure often had the effect of blotting out the open-field furlong names to a considerable degree. The hedged fields laid out after parliamentary enclosure on top of the old furlongs may or may not have been given the names of the furlongs they replaced and very often a series of uninteresting names such as Ten or Six Acre Field, Hut Close or Road Field is the result. In the case of early pre-parliamentary enclosure for sheep, the objective was to obtain a series of relatively large fields which would contain many of the pre-enclosure furlongs. Since each field had only one name, ancient furlong names came to be forgotten almost entirely; when the large hedged fields were subsequently subdivided, new names were found for the new fields then brought into being.

Moreover, not only were fields (and open-field furlongs) renamed from time to time, but the names themselves could undergo considerable change, attaining a final form which seems far removed from the original. The usual English word for an open-field plough ridge was a 'land'. In Shropshire we find field names containing such versions of this as lawn, lean, loan, loin, lunn and lunt. Similarly the word lynchet or lynch can appear as lunch or lancet; common dole makes an appearance as Commodores (Foxall 1980). It needs a certain degree of experience or, better still, expert help, to make a correct assessment of the significance of names which have travelled so far along the road of change as this.

A final point about place names. There has been a tendency for local historians to use them to give some chronological depth to the matter of dating the beginnings of settlements. Thus names in -ley or -hurst, which imply woodland, could be seen as the result of the foundation of new settlements at a time of clearance and intensive internal colonization in the early Middle Ages, for which there is abundant documentation. They were regarded as 'secondary' settlements in a temporal sense, i.e. they were founded *after* larger, parent settlements in more favourable locations somewhere else. But the drift of recent fieldwork has been to suggest that the place where these names occur were areas of ancient settlement, with the evidence pointing to Saxon, Roman or earlier occupation; the names are best seen as descriptive rather than as having any particular chronological implication. In a rather similar way names such as cotes or cotton (cottages) have been considered to indicate relatively late settlements. This need not *necessarily* be so; the names rather imply a position of dependence in a larger territorial unit; Walcote in Misterton parish would be an example of this. Names in -by and -thorpe do not automatically mean that the places that carry them were founded by Danish settlers in the ninth or tenth centuries, although the reality of Danish settlement and political and tenurial influence is not in question. An alternative explanation would be to see many of these names as the result of a change of name when a landowner with a Danish name replaced one with an English name, a process which could be linked with the break-up of larger estates. This kind of renaming was a long-drawn-out process. Some names in -by, especially in north-west England, contain the names of people known to have owned the villages in the eleventh and twelfth centuries; Gamblesby and Glassonby belonged to the Gamel and Glassam referred to in a writ of Henry I, and there are places in Yorkshire which contain the names of Normans, Selby and Barlby for example (Fellows Jensen 1984; Stafford 1985, 115–21). Fieldwork has its part to play in the resolution of these problems in that the fieldwalking of ploughed village sites and the watching of sites being levelled can sometimes result in the discovery of extensive pottery sequences starting before the Danish period. A Lincolnshire example would be Kingerby in Osgodby parish, where draining and levelling led to the recovery of pottery running right through from the Roman to the medieval periods without a break (MVRG 1980, 7).

6 Documents and the fieldworker

The aim of this chapter is to give some idea of the range of historical documents which is likely to be of particular interest to the fieldworker. Of course almost any document may prove to have a bearing on the archaeologist's concerns; every source which relates to a particular locality will help in filling out the picture. But in practice the fieldworker is going to find himself dealing with the development of individual structures – such things as castles, monasteries, or moated sites for example; settlements, their identification, history and the analysis of their form; and the physical evidence of man's use of the land, whether for agricultural or industrial purposes. So the documents considered here will represent a selection of those most likely to be useful in elucidating problems in the medieval and post-medieval periods connected with these topics. For other matters the reader is referred to the wide range of guides to historical sources now available (West 1962; Stephens 1973; Riden 1983).

At some stage the fieldworker will have to decide on the amount of time he is prepared to spend on documentary work. If done properly, as much if not more time will be spent in the local record office or in the library as in the field. The fieldworker will also have to make up his mind about the extent of his involvement with palaeography and with medieval Latin. Most post-medieval handwriting usually turns out not to be too much of a problem; many university extra-mural departments run evening courses on palaeography with the local historian very much in mind. Medieval hands and Latin present rather more of a difficulty but perhaps not an insuperable one; again, courses are held and it is easy to underestimate the willingness of local workers to come to grips with these unfamiliar matters.

The limitations of documentary evidence must be appreciated. There is a general tendency for medieval documents which relate *specifically* to topographical matters to be scarce; much of the surviving documentation about a locality will deal with tenurial matters which bear on the landscape in an oblique way and has to be subjected to a process of decoding before its significance can be understood by the fieldworker. It is always a disappointment and comes as a surprise to many to find that there is virtually no documentation at all about a magnificent castle site such as that shown in Fig. 70, which quite dominates its village. This was not a royal castle and so has no accounts relating to its repair and maintenance; it has no place in national history. The only historical reference to it occurs in an inquisition of 1361, which says that it was in ruins; even then it is not specifically described as a castle, simply as a manor. We know that it belonged to the Trailly family, which rose from modest beginnings in Domesday Book to head a small barony in the thirteenth century; presumably it was the administrative centre of their estates. This means that it is in fact the fieldworker who has the greatest contribution to make; he at least can produce a description of the site in archaeological terms. Similarly Deddington Castle in Oxfordshire, a structure with substantial earthworks and masonry remains and the head of a feudal honour, and which must on general grounds have been in existence by the late eleventh century, has hardly any secure documentation before 1204 (Ivens 1984). At Cranborne in Dorset a fine motte and bailey covering 1 ha ($2\frac{1}{2}$ acres) with the motte 55 m (180 ft) in diameter and 24 m (78 ft) high, has no history whatsoever (RCHME 1975b, 15). Some settlements remain anonymous. A series of moats discovered in Bottisham parish in Cambridgeshire clearly belong to a medieval

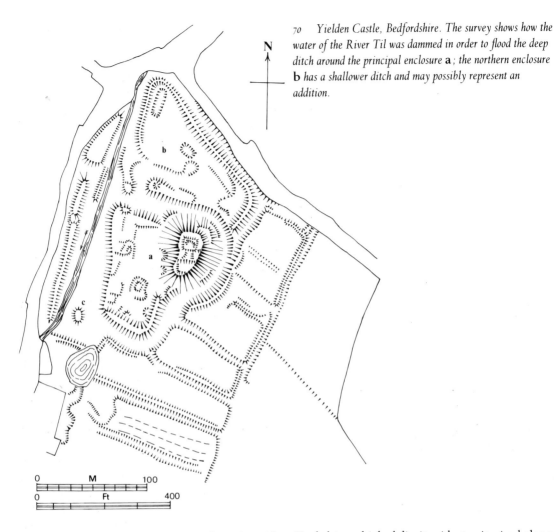

70   Yielden Castle, Bedfordshire. The survey shows how the water of the River Til was dammed in order to flood the deep ditch around the principal enclosure **a**; *the northern enclosure* **b** *has a shallower ditch and may possibly represent an addition.*

settlement; they are impressive earthworks with elaborate water channels, but the settlement has no certain name and so no record can be attributed to it (RCHME 1972, 15). In Dorset a hollow way, banks, scarps and twelfth- and thirteenth-century pottery indicated the remains of a settlement now in Charminster parish. The territory which belonged to the settlement can be defined – the tithe map of Frampton of 1839 shows that it was then a detached part of that parish, but the site, probably never much more than a single farm, has no name and no history (RCHME 1975b, 15).

Sometimes a great deal of work on documents will only serve to suggest the broad outlines of a solution to a problem without being able to provide an absolutely positive answer. As we have seen, there are several dyke systems in east

Yorkshire which delimit wide territories belonging to prehistoric people of the first millennium BC. Some of the systems are multiple, consisting of from four to six dykes, but one of these, the Cockmoor Dyke near Scamridge, is remarkable in that it consists of no less than twenty banks running parallel with each other from the limestone scarp down into a valley which eventually opens into the Vale of Pickering. This extraordinary concentration of earthworks requires explanation. Field survey showed how the Cockmoor Dykes could be divided into two types, six large and a variable number of smaller ones; how a known medieval road could be seen to cut through the large dykes, whereas the small ones stopped short on both sides of the road and respected it; and how the large dykes tended to follow sinuous courses whereas the small ones were straight – in one instance a straight length of small dyke had been built across the inside curve of a large one. So the small dykes were clearly later than the large ones. An indication of date was provided by a Duchy of Lancaster boundary perambulation of 1707, which referred to Snainton Six Dykes at this point, i.e. the large ones; there is no reference to the small ones until 1817, when they are mentioned in a book on the local history of Whitby. So these were constructed probably in the eighteenth century. Now it is known from books such as this local history that rabbit warrening was practised on a large scale in this part of Yorkshire in the early nineteenth century, although it went into decline soon after; as we have seen, the construction of special earthworks for rabbits was common practice for rabbit farming in medieval and subsequent periods, and the re-use of suitable existing earthworks such as castle mounds is well attested. So although no document can be shown to relate specifically to the Cockmoor Dykes as rabbit warrens, and there is no absolute proof, the evidence points very strongly in that direction (Spratt 1984).

Another example of the kind of long-drawn-out process sometimes involved in the application of documentary work to the results of fieldwork can be taken from the discovery of a large quantity of late post-medieval pottery at Hole Common, Lyme Regis, Dorset. This material suggested the existence of kilns, but the relevant tithe maps and other nineteenth-century estate maps did not show any, and there were no suggestive field names. Abundant eighteenth-century surveys and leases of the manor to which the area belonged were worked through, but said nothing about pottery manufacture. The explanation eventually arrived at was that the potters had been operating on the edge of common land which had been enclosed after the pottery had gone out of use; there were therefore no formal documents whatsoever about the site. What was found after diligent search were references to the potters themselves, indicated as such by their trades in local parish registers and wills (Draper 1982).

There is the obvious fact of differential survival – the relatively few good runs of medieval charters, court rolls and accounts in existence tend to have a bias towards places once the property of the Crown or of religious houses. In other instances the social structure of a locality will be a material factor. In the Middle Ages transactions involving free tenants tended to be conducted by means of charters, which may survive, loose or collected in ecclesiastical cartularies. But the transference of land by bond tenants might well have been registered in a different way, on manor court rolls. If one or other of these sources has not survived a distinct bias is introduced. At Daventry in Northamptonshire, for example, two cartularies survive, a fine example belonging to the priory there as well as a rather badly written lay one relating to the larger of the two medieval manors, but no court rolls. The two cartularies have much to say about the burgage tenements of the town, but the important villein holdings, around which the cultivation of the lords land revolved, go almost unrecorded. Similarly differences in land ownership within the same land unit can cause difficulties. At Knuston in the same county were two manors, one descended from the Domesday holding of Gunfrid de Cioches (the Chokes holding) and the other from that of William Peverel. The latter went on to become part of the Duchy of Lancaster estate administered from Higham Ferrers castle. Amongst the abundant documentation surviving from the Lancaster estates are documents which enable something to be said about the Lancaster manor in the Middle Ages, but there are hardly any records at all of the Chokes fee there (Brown and Taylor 1975). In West Yorkshire the township of Northowram is well covered by the court rolls of the huge manor of Wakefield except for part of it which was held by the Preceptory of Newland and administered from its centre at Batley. The reconstruction of the local medieval settlement pattern is made more difficult because of this (Moorhouse 1981, 603).

Even when documents survive, great care must be taken to give them their correct weight; their very existence is liable to create distortions in interpretation. Court rolls and accounts of the twelfth and thirteenth centuries have much to say about assarts, the clearance of fresh land for agricultural development at a time of rising population. The abundance of references to these has given rise to the impression that it was at this time that there was a major new phase of internal colonization with the creation of fresh settlements – the 'secondary settlements' of many history books – and the laying-out of new fields. Now the process of growth and assarting certainly took place at this time – both field archaeology and documents are clear about this, but this activity needs to be placed in the proper context made available by detailed fieldwork, particularly fieldwalking. As we have seen, this will indicate that these high medieval clearances came at the end of a long and complex process of expansion and reorganization, not uniform everywhere, but in places stretching far back into prehistory. It is situations like this that emphasize the need for documentary research and for fieldwork to go together.

How to start

A distinction can be drawn between sources in print and those which will have to be looked at in the original. An obvious point of departure will be the volumes of the *Victoria County History*. These will have valuable introductory chapters about the Domesday and related surveys, and on ecclesiastical history including lists of religious houses and chapters on agrarian and industrial history. The parish entries which follow this are arranged under hundreds and wapentakes, and except in the more recent volumes may not concern themselves in a direct way with the kinds of topographical questions with which the fieldworker is likely to be concerned. But there will be references to basic population statistics; surveys will be quoted; the fundamental facts about the enclosure history will be given. The footnotes are very useful indicators of primary and other sources which may be worthwhile following up. What the *VCH* will certainly attempt to do is to provide an account of the descent of the manor or manors in the locality. This is not a valueless feature, as will be explained later.

Eighteenth- or nineteenth-century county histories will in a way cover much the same ground, with a heavy emphasis on manorial and landowning matters, as one would expect, given the clientele for whom such weighty books were written. Some of this material will represent work of the highest quality; on occasion there is greater detail than the *VCH*, with extensive and valuable quotations from the medieval sources. An important point to remember is that these historians wrote when features we now regard as subjects of legitimate archaeological investigation were still a living reality (open field systems, for example); their books will often contain almost incidental references to assessments and the disposition of holdings which were still in force but of great antiquity. Descriptions of tithe collection arrangements, intercommoning, references to detached portions of lordships will quite often indicate traces of ancient estates. It is always worth trying to find out from the local record office what happened to the original papers from which these early accounts were written. These can contain much fuller information than was eventually printed, as for example do the Bridges papers for Northamptonshire in the Bodleian Library. Sometimes these monumental county works were conceived on too grand a scale and were never completed, yet the assembled raw materials survive. Bridges' successor, George Baker, produced only two volumes of a massive projected Northamptonshire county history, but the materials, well indexed by him, are still available in the Phillips Robinson collection in the Bodleian.

A number of lists emanating from the national archives at the Public Record Office will contain references to documents potentially of interest to the topographer; such lists include *Ministers' Accounts* (accounts relating to land for one reason or another in the hands of the Crown), *Records of the Duchy of Lancaster, Inquisitions ad quod damnum, Rentals and surveys, Lands of dissolved religious houses*; but these are lists only and simply indicate whether a document exists, giving its PRO class and reference number without details. To find out what the document actually says will entail a visit to the PRO itself (for information about the classes of document at the PRO see the *Guide to the Contents of the Public Record Office* (HMSO 1963–8)). For procedure there consult Riden (1983, 128–41). Certain PRO publications provide greater detail in the form of summaries of individual documents. These are the famous green-bound Calendars, runs of which are possessed by some county record offices. The ones likely to be of particular interest to the fieldworker are those recording grants made or licences given by the Crown (the *Patent, Charter* and *Close Rolls*), or dealing with the obtaining of information, usually for the purposes of maintaining royal financial rights, by means of an inquisition (*Inquisitions Post Mortem, Inquisitions Miscellaneous*). Other calendars relating to taxation matters and the holding of land are also useful (*The Book of Fees* [sometimes called the Testa De Nevill], *Feudal Aids* and *Ancient Deeds*). The *Letters and Papers of Henry VIII* are useful not just in determining the fate of property taken from dissolved religious houses but for affording references to contemporary descriptions of them, lists of fields and so on. However, these are calendars, not editions, and the kind of detailed descriptive information the fieldworker is likely to require is frequently omitted. If the word 'extent' appears in an entry, then the only way to get at this valuable information is to note the class number and to visit the PRO. A number of important texts were however completely transcribed in the first half of the nineteenth century by the Record Commissioners; notably the *Valor Ecclesiasticus*, the survey of church wealth made in 1535, and the *Hundred Rolls*, of which more will be said later; this edition must however be used with care, particularly in the matter of the correct division between the entries relating to individual manors.

Other valuable printed sources, or indexes to original sources, will include the early nineteenth-century edition of Dugdale's *Monasticon Anglicanum* (Dugdale 1817–30). This contains summary references to the surviving archives of the religious houses of England, useful footnotes and extracts from cartularies. To follow these up in the original it is necessary to consult G. R. C. Davis, *Medieval cartularies of Great Britain* (1958), which will indicate their locations. As a preliminary way of finding out about the very numerous charters available in the British Library other than cartularies, see the *Index to the charters and rolls in the British Museum*. The British Library manuscripts room has valuable handwritten calendars giving the substance of these documents, witness lists and some idea of their date, but not the actual detailed contents. A comparable list for the Bodleian Library is W. H. Turner and H. O. Cox, *Calendar of charters and rolls preserved in the Bodleian Library* (1878). Further historical sources are conveniently discussed in C. Platt, *Medieval archaeology in England, a guide to the historical sources* (Isle of Wight, 1969); this has a useful list of early county

histories. At the local level there are the runs of edited documents published by such bodies as the Bedfordshire Historical Record Society, the Northamptonshire Record Society, the Lincoln Record Society, the Record Society of Lancashire and Cheshire and so on – cartularies, fines, bishops' registers, *inquisitions post mortem*, feodaries, estate papers. These societies are listed in E. L. C. Mullins, *Texts and calendars, an analytical guide to serial publications*, London, 1958. In cases where a body such as this does not exist, then the *Transactions* of the local historical and archaeological society may contain useful material.

Finally, the local record office and original documents. Most of these house parish or township indexes which in theory list the holdings relating to any particular locality, with their reference numbers. Some of these items (school records, WI scrapbooks and the like) will be of little obvious use to the fieldworker. But, depending on the nature of the project, the others will have to be followed up. Sometimes a calendar, in varying degrees of detail, will be available for the collections to which individual items belong. Very often this will contain enough detail in itself and there will be no need to order up the document; if open-field terriers are being sought, the list ought to say whether a schedule has been appended or not to a deed, thus enabling only those documents of real value to be asked for. If the index is very general, or the documents are un-indexed, they will have to be looked at, but again a fairly quick inspection will detect those with the kind of information the fieldworker is likely to want (field names, for example). Record offices also have separate indexes for maps and for material on enclosures and sometimes indexes of material kept in record offices elsewhere but which relate to their own locality. For advice on record office procedure, photocopying and notetaking, the reader is again referred to Riden (1983, 40–8).

How documents can help the fieldworker: surveys

This term covers a wide range of documents. Some are straightforward descriptions of properties and it is a fortunate fieldworker whose site has one of these. As an example we may instance a survey made in 1526 of the priory of Bradwell in Buckinghamshire by William Brabazon on the occasion of its dissolution; the document was reproduced in both Lipscomb's *County History* and Dugdale's *Monasticon* (Mynard 1974). The survey describes, frequently with dimensions, the gateway to and houses and barns around the outer court; the gate to the inner court, the houses, kitchens, hall and various rooms associated with it; the cloisters, chapter house and church along with a 'little chapell withowte the Church'. It then goes on to list the various closes around the priory with their names and condition; the dovehouse, the wood, and several fishponds. Many of the buildings were derelict. There are recommendations for the demolition of some and the repair of others. Taking all this into account, and making allowance for the 'beautification' of what was left of the priory buildings in the eighteenth century, it is possible to offer a reasonably accurate reconstruction of what the priory and its surroundings looked like at the end of its days. This is so because one of the medieval buildings survives − the chapel; others can be recognized as forming the core of what later became the farmhouse, and their measurements agree with those of the survey; certain points − the site of the church, for example − have been checked by excavation. The fishpond is still visible as an earthwork; the site of the dovehouse was marked by a stony mound in Dovehouse Close. Some of the buildings in the outer court could be matched up with earthworks of the right dimensions in the correct relationship to each other, given that the survey seems to have proceeded in a systematic way; the medieval road which ran across the north of the site was still there as a hollow way and helped to fix the site of the gatehouse to the outer court, where the survey began.

This survey was a complete one. Others simply consist of a list of defects and afford only a partial view. A survey of Rockingham Castle taken in 1250 is of this type, although the amount of repair work to the keep, hall, bailey walls and chapel means that the description is a fairly full one. There is a prominent ledge around the bailey of this hilltop castle, hardly helpful to the defensive capabilities of the place; this is explained by the survey, which states that the ditch around the outside of the castle was nearly levelled (Brown

and Taylor 1974). Surveys are useful in describing features which have been totally removed or substantially altered by later activity. A Parliamentary survey of the palace of the Bishop of Lincoln at Buckden in Cambridgeshire shows that the inner court, many of the buildings of which still stand, had formerly been moated; it describes a little park with three fishponds encircled by a raised path. This private enclosure with its path is still there, but the fishponds have been converted into a small ornamental lake and the moat filled in (*VCH* 1932, 261).

These surveys are relatively straightforward examples of the genre. Others, whether medieval or their post-medieval successors, which set out to describe the resources of whole *manors*, are more complex. Now in the same way as the surveys just mentioned, these documents can contain detailed descriptions of fishponds, mills, parks, woods and other manorial appurtenances which are of direct relevance to the fieldworker. For example, the actual site of the manor house belonging to the Cromwell manor of Lambley in Nottinghamshire was uncertain until a detailed manorial rental of 1459 was examined. This contained a description of the manor house giving information not only of its internal arrangements but of its method of construction; it stood on a mound (*mota*) which was surrounded by a moat (*fossa aquatica*), over which a wooden bridge led to a courtyard with outbuildings, the functions of which were specified. Some of these were said to be near the churchyard. This enabled the site of the manor to be recognized as the moated site lying south of the church (Weir 1981).

But in other matters manorial surveys have to be handled with care, particularly with respect to the areas of the agricultural holdings and plots of land listed in them. This is because they are not always surveys in the modern sense, involving observation and measurement; they are statements about obligations and rents, and where measurements are given they may well be customary ones, not necessarily actual statements of surface area. The surveyors were not engaged in the measurement of land; the surveys were compiled from the statements made by jurors − the whole process of compilation resembled a legal proceeding rather than a survey in the modern sense. These documents are of fundamental importance in the reconstruction of medieval field systems (p.117) but can also sometimes contain information about the houses and associated closes of the manorial tenants. Only in some cases will the survey list these in the order in which they lay; sometimes they will be listed according to the type of tenure, or by the manor if more than one is being surveyed; then considerable effort will have to be made to put the tenements in the right sequence by tracing their ownership forwards in time, using deeds and any other topographical hints that come to hand. An attempt must then be made to match what the survey says with large-scale Ordnance Survey maps, using whatever topographical pointers can be derived from the survey itself, deeds, earlier maps and general probability. Consider the following example, which is taken from a survey of Daventry; although dated 1571 it is basically medieval in concept.

The north side of the high street

Knightley	1 tenement			
	1 backyerde	1 close	1 garden	2 acres
Christchurch	1 cottage	1 close	1 garden	1½ roods
Christchurch	1 cottage	1 close		1½ roods
Knightley	1 cottage			
	1 parcell of grounde			1 rood
Christchurch	1 cottage			
	1 backside			1 rood
John Smalebone	1 cottage			
	1 backside called the Swanne			1 rood

It would be natural to assume that the measurements given in this survey, which is complete and in sequence, were accurate surface areas, but an attempt to reconstruct Daventry as it was in 1571 by a process of dead reckoning soon ran into serious difficulties. The explanation came from a list of burgage tenants and fractions of them given in the (lay) cartulary of the principal manor, and some early charters in the cartulary of the Cluniac priory there, which refer to grants of properties described as 'acres' in burgage. A close study of the first-edition 25-inch Ordnance Survey map reveals that the boundaries between many of the Daventry properties are 60 ft (18 m) apart; they are sometimes curved in the same way as medieval plough ridges; they are frequently long and narrow. The medieval documents can be interpreted as meaning that each of the parallel-sided plots 60 feet apart was regarded as an 'acre' (or if short, as half an acre), even though its true surface area might be considerably more or less than that. As time went on the original acre or half-acre properties became split up, or amalgamated, but the surface areas tended still to be thought of as fractions or otherwise of the original nominal acreages. These are the measurements still current as late as 1571; this explains why a block of land really occupying 4 acres was in fact said to contain $5\frac{1}{2}$ – there were eleven half-acre burgage properties, each 60 feet across, there (these are the Newland burgages, Fig. 73).

The *inquisition post mortem* is another type of document which is sometimes useful in providing a brief contemporary description of an estate. These documents were produced whenever someone holding land directly of the king died, and were intended to ensure that the king's rights by way of relief and wardship were maintained. The fact that a series of inquisitions relating to the same manor can sometimes be found is of great value in detecting significant changes. For example, there are three inquisitions of the manor of Waterhall which lay in the vill of Abingdon, in Cold Brayfield parish, Buckinghamshire, dated 1308, 1324 and 1370. Whereas in general terms the size of the demesne remained constant in these documents, its value dropped sharply between 1308 and 1324, from sixpence to twopence an acre. In 1308 and 1324 the actual manor house was said to be worth two shillings, but nothing in 1370. Now it is known from other sources that in 1280 Waterhall Manor was sold to Reginald de Gray, who had already inherited a neighbouring manor at Snelston. An extent of Snelston dated 1323 gave a valuation of the manor house there, together with the fruit of the garden at Le Waterhalle. Taken together with the inquisitions, the implication is that the manor house at Abingdon had been abandoned and the estate run from Snelston; and in the hard economic conditions of the early fourteenth century the demesne arable produced so little that it was hardly worth ploughing. It is not surprising therefore to find that Abingdon in due course became a deserted village (Britnell 1980).

Settlements and population

Information about the bare existence and relative sizes and prosperity of settlements can quite often be obtained from the records of lay taxation. In 1290 an impost called a subsidy was instituted which involved an assessment of the value of a person's moveable property, and the levy of a tax rated as a fraction of this — usually one-tenth in the case of towns and royal demesne, one-fifteenth in rural places. Except in 1301 there were exemptions, and a minimum value below which the tax was not levied was always set. The records of these lay subsidies can be found at the PRO, either as county lists with the totals of tax paid given against each vill, or better still, lists of individual taxpayers, with their assessment set alongside them. Quite a few of these useful documents have been printed by local record societies. But they ceased to be produced after 1334 when the sums of money from each vill became fixed; the assessments for this year, vill by vill, have been published for the whole country by R. Glasscock (*The Lay Subsidy of 1334*, London, 1975). The lay subsidy documents will not provide information about population levels as such, but about the relative distribution of wealth between one place and another; they will show which places were richer or poorer than their neighbours.

In 1377 the poll tax, levied at the rate of fourpence per head, was introduced. The receipts relating to this tax and its successors at the PRO will give some impression of minimum population levels, but the degree of evasion was high, and the survival rate of the documentation very variable. (Local record offices usually have microfilm copies of these documents for their localities. For a useful discussion of medieval lay taxation records see Beresford 1963.)

Apart from their inherent limitations all these medieval documents suffer from the fact that they were put together on the basis of vills — i.e. the basic local administrative unit, which could consist of one *or more* of the economic units described on p.101 — and not on the basis of individual settlements. Thus the entry for Polebrook in Northamptonshire in 1334 for example includes (without mentioning them) the sums raised from the villages of Kingsthorpe and Armston, and there is no way of telling how the sum of money is to be apportioned between the three places. Even in areas of highly nucleated settlements such as Oxfordshire, Northamptonshire and Leicestershire, a very high proportion of the entries in medieval taxation records was of this type; very often it is impossible to determine the relative standing or population of the site whose earthworks are under investigation.

For the end of the Middle Ages, the returns of the Enclosure Commission of 1517, which are in print (Leadam 1897), will provide specific evidence for actual depopulation, usually on a small scale. Later, there are the early sixteenth-century lay subsidies, the various censuses taken in connection with the concern of the government with the numbers of communicants, sometimes on the basis of families as in 1563 or of actual communicants, as in 1603 and 1676 (Canterbury archdiocese only). The hearth taxes of the late seventeenth century are also valuable (for all these sources see Thirsk 1965). We have moved now into the age of emparkment and country house building, and there is a natural tendency to link the desertion of a village entirely with the creation of the park in which its earthworks are to be found. Certainly depopulation for sheep did occur; for example the enclosure commissioners recorded that in 1499 the occupants of fifteen houses at Wormleighton in Warwickshire had been forced by the Spencers to leave and 240 acres of arable were enclosed. Similarly, examples of depopulation for emparkment can be found: at Normanton in Leicestershire the village was finally cleared away around 1764 by Sir Gilbert Heathcote and the remaining inhabitants housed at Empingham; at Hothorpe in Northamptonshire the remaining people were moved about 1830 and housed at Theddingworth in Leicestershire. But it is usually the case with enclosure both for sheep and for emparkment that the final act of depopulation involved the last relatively small number of inhabitants of a place which had been in decline for other reasons for very many years; enclosure and emparkment came at the end of a long-drawn-out process and was not necessarily the main cause of the desertion. In the late fifteenth century John Rous regarded the desertion of the village of Fulbrook in Warwickshire as the result of the creation of a park by the Duke of Bedford in 1421, but other documents show that half the tenants' arable had already been abandoned some years before (Dyer 1982).

One further point can be made about the use of population figures in attempting to explain the existence of village earthworks. It is possible to get a situation in which such figures can remain relatively stable for a parish or township, yet village desertion can occur; the bare population figures can conceal profound changes. At East Matfen in Northumberland, for example, the village was gradually depopulated during the late seventeenth century as a new proprietor, John Douglas, bought up the houses in the village; there were about a dozen of them. But new farms were established in regularly laid-out enclosed fields throughout the township's territory; by 1760 there were nine, not very many fewer than the village had contained before Douglas bought the place. Here it is the survival of estate management papers and deeds in the county record office which enabled the change in the way the land was managed to be understood (Wrathmell 1980). Similarly, changes in the plan of a village brought about by alterations in the local pattern of communications, or by replanning by the manorial lord, may involve no major change in the level of population, but could produce extensive spreads of earthworks. Conversely, some large earthwork sites may only represent single farms or small hamlets, the bulk of the earthworks consisting of paddocks and close boundaries, not house sites; here the documents affording information about the size of the place, if available, are of real value as an indication of the true nature of the site.

The lists of taxpayers which survive for some of the earlier fourteenth-century subsidies are a source of the greatest value in dealing with areas of dispersed settlement. This is because many of the surnames of the people listed will be the names of the places where they lived. These places may be farms or small settlements still in existence today, with names clearly derived from medieval ones, visible on the tithe or Ordnance maps. Or they may be deserted sites, in many cases still detectable as earthworks, whose names have vanished from the Ordnance map but are preserved as field names on tithe or estate maps. In west Somerset detailed work on the subsidy returns of 1327, which have been in print since 1889, and on

tithe maps of 1836–44 has shown that out of 137 deserted farm sites no less than 46 can be matched up with surnames on the medieval list. Many more are still in existence as working farms. In the parish of Brompton Regis, for example, Richard Bitelescombe clearly came from a place known still as Bittescombe; Walter de Hicumbe from Hiccombe; Hugh de Luteleghe from Lotley; John de Smalemor from Smarmoor (now a deserted site). In this way a picture can be built up of the pattern of settlement in the early fourteenth century (Aston 1983). The difficulties of using this method can be illustrated by the parish of Thurleigh in Bedfordshire. Here there is a village, with its church, but also a number of other settlements of varying types, some deserted and represented by earthworks, some not. The subsidy list of 1309 gives the names of 47 people. Setting aside the moated and fortified manorial sites, only one of the names can be matched up with a farm marked on any of the fairly numerous estate and other maps which exist for this parish. The tax list includes William Aspey; a sixteenth-century lease enables this name to be equated with a farm known as Aspie's End. Yet by the time of the earliest relevant maps the name of this farm had changed to Coplar Farm (Fig. 75); only the names of the immediately surrounding fields and their sizes enabled it to be identified with the Aspie's End of the earlier deed.

The agrarian landscape

The purely archaeological techniques for the reconstruction of pre-enclosure open-field systems have already been described (p.62). But the full value of this kind of fieldwork cannot be realized until the documents pertaining to the system in question have been studied and some attempt made to produce a reconstruction of the way in which the furlongs, represented by the blocks of ridge and furrow, were organized as a field system.

Open-field maps have already been discussed. But an enormous amount can be achieved in the absence of these if a field (or drag) book is available for the system under study. These documents consist of a detailed description of every furlong, listing in order the number of lands (plough ridges) held by each owner and sometimes giving their sizes; generally these will be in acres and roods (i.e. quarter-acres) – purely conventional terms; if the areas are expressed in acres, roods and perches the measurements will be the result of (hopefully accurate) superficial computation and generally speaking less useful, since they will not relate to the medieval system of land tenure (p.121). The orientation of the furlongs should be provided. The descriptions of the furlongs usually follow on from each other; the furlongs are grouped into their respective great fields; the meadow is similarly described and the sizes of the various portions given. Information will now have to be collected about the post-enclosure field names of the area under study, using the kind of map sources already cited. A certain proportion of these names will probably match up with the furlong names of the field book. This fact, taken together with topographical pointers contained within the document itself, such as references to roads, the orientation of the furlongs and the number of lands they contain in relation to the number still to be counted on the ground or visible on air photographs, will enable a reconstruction of the field system to be made. Fig. 71 is such a reconstruction, based on the survey of Daventry made by the Duchy of Lancaster in 1571; it shows a parish with two settlements, Daventry and Drayton, each with its own three-field system.

If no field book or map is available – and this will generally be the case – the work of reconstruction becomes much less certain and a great deal more difficult. If a Parliamentary enclosure award exists, a useful start can be made by transcribing the bare details of the allotments made therein – the names of the people involved, the area allotted to each and their abuttals, and in particular the information contained in the award about the open-field system and the relationship of the newly set-out blocks of enclosed land to it. The award will often give the name of the former open field in which any particular allotment lies, while the description of the roads and paths set out by the award will sometimes provide the names of the furlongs over which they pass. The next step will be to copy on to a 1:10,000 Ordnance Survey map the acreages of the fields, taken from the earliest available edition of the 25-inch map. On the assumption that at least a proportion of the hedges on the 25-inch map represent the boundaries of blocks of land set out at the time of enclosure, it should be possible to reconstruct the award using the topographical indicators contained in it about such matters as the relationship between the allotments and the village, the roads and boundaries of neighbouring places, and about the relationship between the allotments themselves, as well as their sizes. Since the award may give the names of the open fields in which the various allotments lie, the general arrangement of the field system will have been achieved. The precise boundaries between the fields can be much more of a problem; clearly they will usually run along the junction of the furlongs drawn on the ridge-and-furrow map, and they tend to follow roads or obvious natural features such as streams, but in the case of a large or (from our point of view) awkwardly placed allotment lying in two or more of the former open fields, the award offers little beyond general help.

This problem may be overcome, and the reconstruction advanced further, by attempting to name the individual furlongs on the open-field map. As before, information about field names has to be sought from cartographic sources; but a search has also to be made in record offices for terriers relating to this particular field system. Very often glebe terriers will exist, describing the property of the church; and deeds will have to be worked through in search of those which have terriers annexed to them or which contain detailed descriptions of open-field holdings within the body of the document itself. These terriers differ from field books in that they relate to one holding only, and do not describe the whole system. They will set out the furlongs in which the lands lie, give their names and the names of the great fields to which they belong; the number of lands each tenurial strip contains will be given and quite often their abuttals and their conventional (open-field) areas; the direction of the furlongs is also sometimes stated or can be worked out. This information now has to be matched up with the ridge-and-furrow map, the information about the great fields and furlongs derived from the enclosure award, and the assembled field names. If the field-name and other information is adequate, a reconstruction of what the field system looked like before the enclosure can be produced with some confidence. But not all

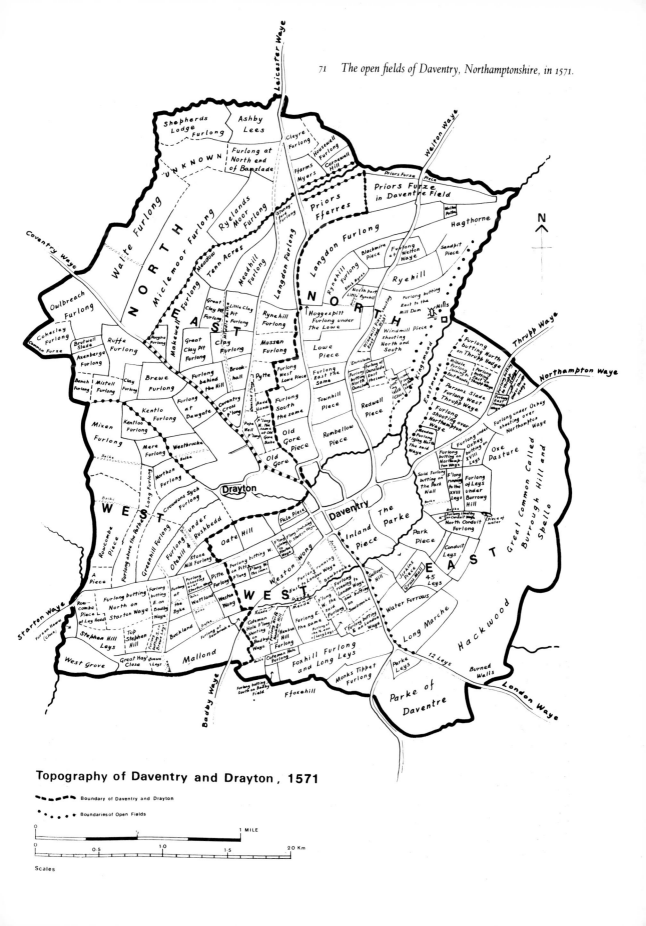

Topography of Daventry and Drayton, 1571

■ ■ ■ ■ ■ Boundary of Daventry and Drayton

• • • • • Boundaries of Open Fields

0   1 MILE

0   0.5   1.0   1.5   2.0 Km

Scales

enclosure awards say much about the earlier field system, particularly the pre-Parliamentary ones; as we have seen, not all places have good field-name information, and one's reconstructions will operate on a descending scale of confidence until places are reached for which ridge-and-furrow maps can be produced on the evidence of fieldwork, but very little can be said about the actual organization of the field system it represents.

Ideally the production of maps of this kind should be seen as the start of a process of analysis. Given the survival of the right kind of document-ation it is sometimes possible to work back towards an understanding of earlier phases. Quite significant changes may well have been made during the post-medieval period − field bound-aries may have been rearranged, some land laid down to grass, consolidation of holdings and partial enclosure effected. But it will be necessary to proceed beyond these to analyse the medieval documentation, if it exists, notably terriers but particularly − because they are more commonly found − the deeds known as charters. An import-ant point to be made is that although these documents are being described here in the con-text of the reconstruction of field systems, they can provide useful information about almost everything in the medieval landscape: tenements in villages and towns, with sometimes their sizes and abuttals, agreements about mills, fishponds, woods and parks; the way in which features are described will help to fix the lines of roads and tracks; the witness lists will provide surnames indicative of farms and settlements which may no longer exist or have subsequently changed their names. At the most basic level they will help to indicate whether a place had its own open-field system or not. Not all charters will be helpful − some will be bereft of topographical detail but some can be remarkably informative about the location of the land they specify in terms of fields and furlong names, orientation, the names of the neighbouring owners, and sizes. Dating is obvi-ously crucial and may present some problems. Later documents can be dated in terms of saints' days and years, either regnal or calendar; recourse will have to be had to the handbooks which deal with these matters (Powicke and Fryde 1961; Cheyney 1970). But earlier ones will have to be

dated by means of the known dates of the people mentioned in them, whether the principals or witnesses; aids such as the lists of abbots given in Dugdale, manorial descents in the *VCH* or other sources will be useful for this.

It is not always easy to understand the correct significance of the field and furlong names given in these charters. Sometimes they will give the impression of a field system of enormous com-plexity, with several great fields. Now in some instances this picture will be the correct one. But there will be times when the documents mislead. Consider the following examples from Daventry. At Daventry a document of 1277 records an agreement mentioning land which is described as lying in four fields − north, south, east and west. But what seems to be a clear indication of a four-field system can be placed in perspective by looking at two more charters; in one, of 1346, Robert Symons is granted rent from land includ-ing 'one acre in the south field over Daventry Maweland; half an acre over the Loch; one rood beneath the Lyde' and another, of 1349, which describes *inter alia* 'half an acre in the southern field above the Lok ... half an acre in the western under the Lyche'. In the first document the Lyche or Lyde is placed in the south field; in the second in the west.

Now it is reasonable to conclude from other charters, early post-medieval terriers and manorial accounts that it is extremely unlikely that the number of fields in the Daventry system ever exceeded three. The charters are misleading because they are simply setting out to describe as accurately as they can the precise location of the land they are concerned with; the fields they describe are nothing to do with the way in which the field system was organized, but simply the zones into which it was divided by the road system. So to say that a piece of land lay in the West Field meant that it was to be found in a certain furlong which lay between the roads to Badby and Staverton. The lesson here is that the whole range of documentation has to be taken into account and the fieldworker must be fully aware of the limitations of the evidence available.

Fig. 71 is useful to illustrate the way in which charters and other documentation can illuminate changes in a reconstructed open-field system. The drawing shows how a substantial area in the

North Field of Drayton was said not to have any known owners at the time the survey was made (marked as 'unknown'). What this means is that this block of land had been put down to grass and was being used as common pasture. Yet the fieldwork shows that it had been covered with ridge and furrow; and some of the charters in the cartulary of Daventry priory strongly suggest that these furlongs had once formed part of the normal open-field system. Similarly the area known as Hackwood in the south-eastern corner of the Daventry field system, pasture in 1571, had once been arable, as the ridge-and-furrow survey showed; the way in which some farmers claimed to hold grassed-down plough ridges there at the time of the enclosure in 1804 suggests that this too had once formed part of the arable system. So fieldwork and documents both indicate a degree of contraction in the area under the plough. What is more, there have obviously been changes in the way the great fields have been arranged. The North Field of Drayton has a very odd L-shaped outline; and the boundary between the North and West Fields of Drayton cuts through the furlong called Kentloo and a northern portion of Mixen Furlong. Now thirteenth-century charters make it clear that there were only two fields in Drayton at that time, not three; and that Owlebreach furlong, in 1571 in the North Field of Drayton, lay then in South Field. It looks very much as if the boundary between the original two great fields once ran along the Coventry road. No documents exist to say when the rearrangement into three took place beyond the fact that it had happened before 1571. Daventry had undergone a similar transmutation but there the division between the two original great fields is harder to work out because it so happens that charters with the right information do not exist.

It is worth trying to take the business of reconstruction further by attempting to match up the tenurial structure of the field system with the reconstruction produced by fieldwork and documentary evidence. Medieval common-field systems were organized tenurially on the basis of a unit known as a *virgate* (the corresponding English word is the *yardland*), or in the north of England around similar units called *bovates* (in English, *oxgangs*). Land could be held as complete virgates or bovates or as fractions of them; they would carry with them a proportionate allotment of meadow land and rights in the common pasture. The sizes of these units were not uniform and they varied from field system to field system; a virgate was generally in the region of thirty customary open-field (not statute) acres, and a bovate half this. This land would be held in lands (plough ridges) generally a quarter (i.e. a rood) or half an acre in area (customary measurement) scattered around the furlongs of the open fields as described in terriers. Information about the size of the virgate or bovate in any particular field system has to be sought, not always with success, in charters and deeds which not only give the acreage of the land concerned but also specify that it is a virgate or bovate or fraction thereof; in surveys and court rolls; in *inquisitions post mortem* and estate papers – odd statements about such essential matters are liable to turn up almost anywhere. The size of the virgate did not always stay the same – in Drayton, for example, it went up from 30 or 31 acres to 33 or thereabouts (p.129). Also as time went on some virgate holdings lost acres, some gained, and a terrier of a particular example may or may not reflect reasonably well what its original size had been. Rather similar problems will arise in trying to find out how many virgates any particular field system was said to contain. County histories, enclosure acts and awards sometimes provide this information, or it may be obtained from the kinds of medieval documents already mentioned, although many surveys have a tendency not to specify the number of virgates freeholders have, just their rents. A valuable source which exists for certain parts of the country is the Hundred Rolls (p.113). Edward I's great survey enquired into many things, but the returns which are of particular interest in this context are those which specify in great detail the demesne and tenant holdings of the vills surveyed. In cases where holdings are small and described in acres and roods it will be necessary to convert the totals thus expressed into virgates, using the size of the virgate appropriate to that particular field system.

These calculations are important because, as will be discussed later on (p.129), they can have a bearing upon the interpretation of the development of medieval field systems recovered by fieldwork; and also upon the interpretation of settlement plans, whether a place is still in existence or represented by earthworks. At present it will be sufficient to point out that a close examination of field books will frequently reveal a repetitious pattern in the way in which the names of the various owners seem to occur; charters which specify land regularly abutted by the same people suggest the same kind of regular ordering. When the cycle has been worked out, it will often be found to correspond to the number of virgates the system is said to contain. In the case of Daventry and Drayton, for example, information derived from documents produced in connection with Parliamentary enclosure enables one to say that each system had 44 virgates; this explains why the names Goodman and Hitchcock occur regularly at intervals of 22 lands in the field book and why the boundary between the two systems is so indented – it is a by-product of the re-allocation of the lands carried out when the two systems were expanded from 40 virgates to 44 in the late twelfth century, when they were counted out in batches of 22 or 11 and the original boundary between the two systems, which had corresponded earlier to a north–south trackway following the line of the valley between the two places, was finally obliterated.

Another aspect of this marriage between field and documentary work on open-field systems is the ability it provides to identify specific features relating to cultivation practice and to recover the meaning of the now-forgotten language of the open-field system. For example, terriers frequently mention the existence of 'hades' as things sometimes belonging to lands; these turn out to be parts of the plough ridges deliberately left unploughed at the end, a way of obtaining a little extra grazing.

Finally, post-medieval non-open-field deeds. There are plenty of guides available to explain the various types – lease and release, bargain and sale, final concord (Dibben 1971). Just like medieval charters, these can contain useful descriptions of archaeological sites. For example, at a humble level, a bargain and sale of 1589 locates a windmill in the parish of Clipston in Northamptonshire in the following terms: a 'wyndemill with all manner of implements, furniture and appurtenances ... sett lying and being upon a furlonge called Middecrofte in the ffields of Newbolde

within the p[ar]ishe of Clipstone and also one half half roode of grounde by marke, boundes and stones as ys alredye sett out and appoynted'. But a series of deeds can also be used to unravel the development of a landscape. The parish of Haselbech in Northamptonshire was enclosed in 1599. A long series of deeds taken in conjunction with maps showing field names goes some way towards a reconstruction of the process whereby the large fields of the sixteenth century gave way to the much smaller ones of the nineteenth century (Fig. 72). In the same county similar documentary work enables the earthworks of the deserted village of Knuston to be explained. An early eighteenth-century deed shows that Benjamin Kidney bought the manor. In 1769 he effected the enclosure of the open fields; a map made about this time shows that the hamlet was still there, but that efforts had been made to turn the old manor house into a respectable country seat with a park around it. But Knuston changed hands several times during the course of the eighteenth century. Each time this happened an abstract of title was drawn up which described the estate in full, field by field and house by house. Since these documents repeat each other and at the same time provide a contemporary picture of the estate it is possible to trace the development of the landscape from that shown on Kidney's map to the one shown on the Ordnance Survey 25-inch map. The documents show how one by one the farms of the village were bought up by the successive owners of Knuston; the names of their successive tenants are listed but eventually give way to blanks; some houses and cottages are turned to other uses; various small closes in the area of the hamlet are thrown together and ultimately cast into the park around the country house. Three new farms were set up in the enclosed fields. This process has been completed by 1791 (Brown and Taylor 1975).

Manors and manorial descents

As has been said (p.112), the earlier literature about the history of a locality will almost certainly contain a great deal of information about the manorial structure and much energy will have been spent in the compilation of manorial descents, often set out in rather abstruse and obscure terms. A glance at the footnotes of the average

72   *The fields of Haselbech, Northamptonshire, from the seventeenth to the nineteenth century.*

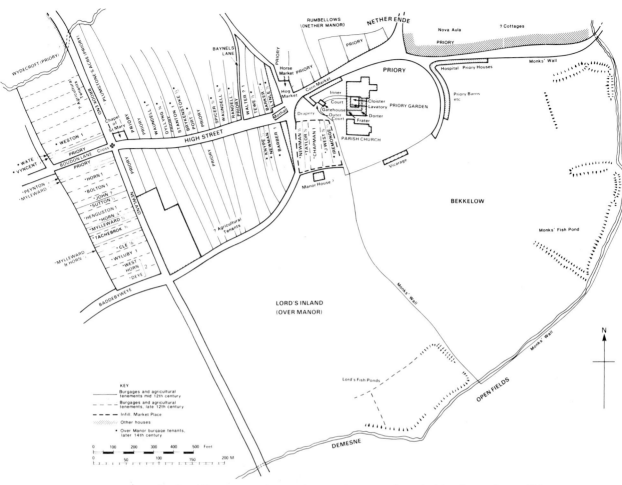

73   *A reconstruction of medieval Daventry, Northamptonshire.*

VCH volume will quickly show the range of documents used in producing these accounts. Now few beyond a handful of devoted local historians will have the time and knowledge to match the detail of this work, but it is essential for the fieldworker to be able to pick his way through these accounts and appreciate their significance for topographical studies. He must also know enough about the basic sources (p.113) to be able to check such things from time to time, since the *VCH* accounts are not always accurate.

In the first place the existence of more than one manor can have a profound effect upon the form of a settlement. Consider Fig. 73, Daventry again. This plan is the result of three phases of development. The first, undocumented, phase probably involved settlement in the general area of the church; these houses were removed when the

priory was founded in the early twelfth century. When this was done, charters in the priory cartulary and later manorial surveys suggest that a complete reorganization took place, involving the setting out of free and bond tenements on earlier ploughed land along both sides of the High Street (p.128); with the exception of a few, given to the priory, these belonged to the lord of the principal (or Over) manor. But the cartulary tells us that a sub-manor (the Nether manor) was set up at much the same time, with land mainly taken out of the demesne of the main manor; its properties were laid out on a piece of land north of the church; again the curved boundaries show that the operation involved earlier ploughed land. So we end up with a very neat, quartered plan; along the High Street free burgage tenants along the north, mainly agricultural bond tenants along the south; to the north-east of the High Street the tenants of the sub-manor; opposite, the

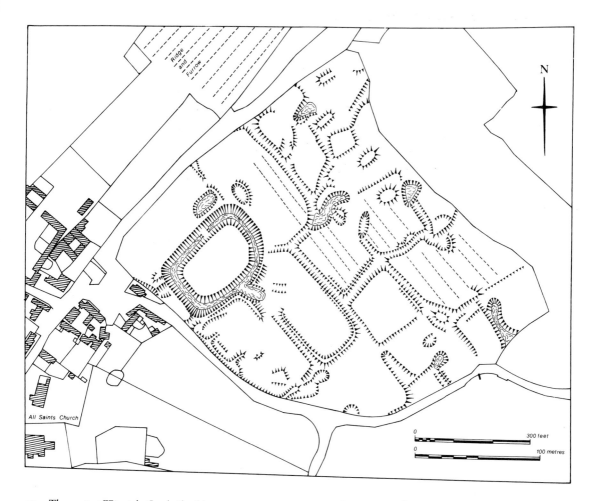

Ridge and Furrow

N

All Saints Church

0   300 feet

0   100 metres

74   *The moat at Winwick, Cambridgeshire.*

church and priory, in effect an ecclesiastical quarter.

This is an example involving an entire settlement, but sometimes quite small changes in a village layout can be attributed to manorial developments. Fig. 74 represents a moated site and associated enclosures at Winwick in Cambridgeshire. Because of their relationship with ridge and furrow the enclosures quite clearly sit on earlier ploughed land. But who owned the place? The matter is not absolutely certain, but a reasonable possibility would be to link it with the Caxton family, which held a substantial estate in Winwick which had been detached from one of the principal manors some time in the late twelfth century; on occasion they called themselves by the name de Winwick, implying that they actually lived there; their capital messuage is referred to from time to time in medieval deeds.

These examples relate to nucleated settle-

ments. In an area of more dispersed settlement, an understanding of the manorial structure of a parish or township will help to explain the moated sites which occur so frequently in this kind of landscape. In the parish of Bolnhurst in Bedfordshire are four moated sites. One encloses the rectory and lay outside the manorial system. But the others can be identified with the three medieval manors of the parish. The monastery of Thorney owned land in Bolnhurst from before the Norman conquest; the cartulary, the Red Book of Thorney, clearly shows that their Bolnhurst houses lay around the present Manor Farm; this lies within the moated site carved out of a prehistoric earthwork already mentioned (Fig. 36). A second manor known as Mavorns or Glentells in post-medieval documents, and descended from the land formerly held by Canons Ashby Priory in Northamptonshire, can be linked with the moated site in the south-western corner of the parish still known as Mavourns and occupied by a descendant of the Franklin family, former tenants of the priory. A third moat, Greensbury, represents the site of the manor of Grymsbury, known from the Grym family which acquired it in the late thirteenth century. In other places it is the social structure of the local manors which assists in the interpretation of the fieldwork. Fig. 75, the parish of Thurleigh in Bedfordshire, includes five moated sites and a castle mound. A feature of the social structure of this and neighbouring parishes, as evidenced in the detailed lists of the Hundred Rolls, is the existence of large numbers of freemen. The castle is the centre belonging to the largest manor in the parish, which in the thirteenth century belonged to the Grey family. Because of its name, the moat known as Blackburn Hall can be identified with the manor known as Blackborne, held by John Fitz Geoffrey in 1536; its descent enables it to be traced back to one of the small Domesday holdings here. But two of the others, College Farm near Backnoe End and Whitwick represent estates which did not figure as manors at all in earlier medieval records such as the Hundred Rolls; they represent the holdings of successful free tenants belonging to manors already in existence who rose through royal service, acquired arms and were able to convert their estates into manors in their own right in the fourteenth century.

In other instances the details of manorial history enable such matters as village desertion to be understood. As an example we may take Thorpe in the Glebe in Nottinghamshire. By 1310 this village for the first time had a single landowner and a single manor, having previously been divided between two owners. This situation did not last long, and after the death of John de Darley, the lord, between 1348 and 1352, possibly as a result of the Black Death, the manor was divided up again. Half went to his daughter Margaret, who married into the Armstrong family, and who did not live there; the other half went to Nicholas Darley, who was resident. There is evidence in the form of leases to suggest that in the mid-fifteenth century the Armstrong estate had been turned over to grass; the Enclosure Commission of 1517 records the final enclosure of the remaining 90 acres. There were probably several factors contributing to the final depopulation of Thorpe, but one reason for the ultimate desertion of the village must have been the fragmentation in land

ownership which took place at a time of economic difficulty when, if the village was to survive, decisive action by a single lord would have been needed (Cameron and O'Brien 1981).

This discussion of the need to appreciate the manorial structure of a locality leads inexorably to the question of the relationship of Domesday Book and fieldwork. It is usual to enumerate the difficulties of relating this source to features actually to be found in the landscape and there is perhaps a tendency to leave matters at that; but these are counsels of despair. No one doubts that the problems are formidable. Domesday Book concerns itself with the taxation rating and value, past and present, of estates listed under their holders, along with some kind of statement about the resources of these units of land. Within certain limits the entries were intended to be standardized and so cover every possible variation in the layout of the landscape. For example, as Professor Hoskins showed in a famous article, the entries for many Devon estates, which look much the same as any other Domesday entries, can be shown to relate to a landscape of dispersed settlement; the demesne and villein farms enumerated in Domesday can with the aid of nineteenth-century maps be identified with working farms still in existence (Hoskins 1965). Yet a broadly similar entry for places in the open-field region of the Midlands may well relate to a totally different settlement pattern involving nucleated villages. But because Domesday is concerned with manors the arguments set out above for the importance of an understanding of manorial structure in relation to landscape development continue to carry weight.

At Raunds in Northamptonshire the Domesday entry records two landowners. But this may be a reflection of much earlier arrangements, since excavation and topographical studies have located two distinct settlement foci at the core of the present large village, in position in the seventh century, long before Domesday Book was drawn up (Cadman and Foard 1984). Christopher Taylor has drawn attention to several other examples in widely dispersed parts of the country of villages with separate foci embedded within their present plan or existing as earthworks, each of which can be equated with separate Domesday holdings (Taylor 1977). This raises the hope that Domesday

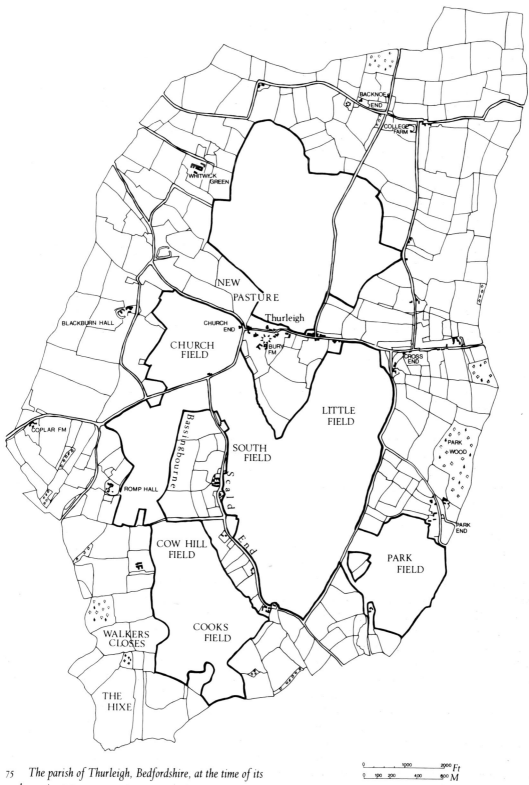

BACKNOE
END

COLLEGE
FARM

WHITWICK
GREEN

NEW
PASTURE

Thurleigh

BLACKBURN HALL

CHURCH
END

CHURCH
FIELD

BURY
FM

CROSS
END

LITTLE
FIELD

COPLAR FM

Bassingbourne

SOUTH
FIELD

PARK
WOOD

ROMP HALL

Scald End

PARK
END

COW HILL
FIELD

PARK
FIELD

WALKERS
CLOSES

COOKS
FIELD

THE
HIXE

75 *The parish of Thurleigh, Bedfordshire, at the time of its*
enclosure in 1808.

entries in regions of nucleated settlement may have something to contribute in the study of settlement plans. Yet a settlement which is a nucleated village now may not necessarily have been one at the time of Domesday Book, and caution is always going to be required in asserting that a particular component in a village plan was in place in 1086. At Wawne in Yorkshire there are strong grounds for believing that the now destroyed village earthworks there fell into two distinct zones; early medieval documents including Domesday Book indicate two estates. Yet the collection of pottery during the bulldozing of the earthworks in 1961 produced no material earlier than the late twelfth century (Hayfield 1984); just what the Domesday entry actually meant in terms of the settlement pattern is quite unknown. Similarly the *manors* now represented in Bolnhurst by the moated sites can all be traced back to estates listed in Domesday Book, but we have really no idea where the halls of these manors, if they existed, actually were or where the tenants of these estates lived at that time. Fieldwalking rather than earthwork survey provides a better chance of solving this kind of problem.

Domesday will provide information about the tax assessment of each estate, expressed in hides or carucates, about the number of ploughs at work on the demesne and belonging to the tenants, and about the possible taxable capacity of the land in terms of the number of ploughs it could carry. Whole books have been devoted to the meaning of these terms and there can be no question of entering into a detailed discussion of these things here. But the point can be made that it is always worth comparing the tenurial structure of an open-field system recovered by the methods already described with the Domesday entry, bearing in mind the late Saxon taxation system — four fiscal virgates to the hide, eight oxgangs/bovates to the carucate. The exercise may not always yield profitable results, but can on occasion be suggestive. For example, at Butterwick on the Yorkshire Wolds, Domesday records twelve carucates ie 96 bovates; the open fields contained 98 oxgangs in 1563. At Fangfoss in the Vale of York Domesday has eight carucates, 64 bovates; there were 64 oxgangs in the sixteenth century (Harvey 1984). This means that the *possibility* exists (not the proof) that the open fields were in existence at these places in 1086, and did not expand very much after that.

At Lidlington in Bedfordshire, a single-manor vill owned by Barking Abbey, Domesday records the existence of land for two demesne ploughs and eight villein and bordar ploughs, i.e. eight and 32 virgates respectively. Manorial surveys of the early seventeenth century set out the tenurial structure of the parish in detail and show that the open fields still contained almost exactly the same number of demesne and copyhold virgates as Domesday stated. Yet the seventeenth-century virgate total had gone up to 55, an increase of 15 over Domesday Book, all to be accounted for by the free tenants conspicuous in the post-medieval documentation. So it may be that in this case the open fields did expand; but the argument can be taken further, for the open fields of Lidlington contain a number of discrete but regularly laid-out blocks of settlement earthworks, clearly shown by ground survey and air photography to be set on top of earlier ridge and furrow (e.g. Fig. 53(b)); fieldwalking has shown that the house sites produce twelfth-century and later pottery. So perhaps there is evidence not just for an expansion of the open fields and for the tenurial basis of this but for a parallel development of planned settlement sites.

Daventry affords another example of the way in which Domesday, later documents and the physical evidence relating to both fields and settlements together can enable an interpretation of the development of the landscape to be put forward. Here the implication of the Domesday entry is that there was land for ten ploughs — 40 virgates. It so happens that the charters in the priory cartulary, taken with post-medieval manorial surveys, enable the ownership of the virgates contained in the early medieval open fields to be determined with some certainty. Twelve originally belonged to the lord as his demesne; twelve formed the basic endowment of the priory, to which another, isolated virgate was subsequently added by charter; three tenant virgates went to establish the Nether manor; twelve virgates remained as villein holdings belonging to the main, Over manor (i.e. the twelve 60 ft (18 m) wide properties along the south of the High Street not regarded as burgages in the lay cartulary, Fig. 73); 40 all together, exactly as

Domesday says. Yet as we have seen, there were 44 virgates at the time of enclosure. What happened was that in the late twelfth century the fields expanded to take in the Hackwood area (a significant name, Fig. 71) adding 120 acres to the open-field system, four more virgates; and when new burgages were added along the main Coventry road in Newland (another significant name, Fig. 73), four 60 ft (18 m) wide agricultural tenements were laid out as well to the north of them. Exactly the same procedure took place in Drayton. Here the original 40 virgates were increased to 44 (probably by taking in an area of rough pasture in the north-west of the parish; note the furlong names there, Miclemoor – the great moor, and Walte Furlong – derived from the Old English word 'holt' or wood). But because the area thus added to the Drayton field system was larger than the corresponding area added to the Daventry system at the same time, the size of the Drayton virgate was increased from 30 to 33 acres or thereabouts; there seems to have been a strong desire to limit the expansion of the Drayton field to 4 virgates to match the Daventry figure, perhaps because of concern with the added pressure to be placed on the now-depleted commons that the creation of fresh farms would entail. As for the location of the new farms in Drayton, field survey has revealed a regularly laid-out zone of settlement earthworks on earlier ridge and furrow in the southern part of the hamlet on land said in the 1571 survey to contain exactly eight acres. Documentary proof is lacking, but maybe here we have the farms set out now to go with the expansion of the open fields, at the rate of an acre to the half-virgate.

The fact that a place does not appear in Domesday does not mean that it was not in existence in 1086; the entries of some places silently include material relating to others. There are no less than eleven entries in Domesday Book for Sharnbrook in Bedfordshire yet two of them do not belong to the present village of Sharnbrook at all. By working back through the manorial descents of all these holdings it can be shown that one relates to Colmworth, a hamlet of Sharnbrook to the west, and another to Souldrop, a small parish to the north of it. The significance of this is that not only were these places there in some form, but also that Domesday preserves an indication that once all three formed one large unit called Sharnbrook; the place names containing the elements -worth and -thorp indicate a subordinate position within it.

Finally, Domesday Book and population. Many accounts of deserted villages take the Domesday population figures, with a suitable multiplier (say $3\frac{1}{2}$ or 5), as a reasonable index of their population. As an indication of relative population these figures are useful; for example, places with low Domesday Book population figures tend to be the ones with low lay subsidy figures and ultimate desertion. But Domesday presents a very minimal view, and there is reason to believe that quite substantial segments of the population could be left out altogether – rent-paying freemen, for example. In the case of the estates of Burton Abbey early twelfth-century surveys record large numbers of *censarii*, rent-payers who constituted some 35 to 43 per cent of the total population of the places concerned. Such people must have existed at the time of Domesday, not long before, but are nowhere directly mentioned (Walmsley 1968). At Daventry it is certain that half the population of the parish, presumably in the Drayton half, has been left out altogether, only the villeins and the bordars and slaves necessary to the cultivation of the demesne being mentioned.

Documents relating to boundaries

Boundary perambulations using fixed points can be found in a variety of documents. Anglo-Saxon land books recording grants will sometimes contain a clause in Old English describing the bounds of the estate (Reed 1984); forest eyres will describe the boundaries of the royal forests at various dates; monastic cartularies will record agreements about tracts of land of all kinds which may incorporate boundary descriptions; some surveys such as those compiled for the Duchy of Lancaster will set out parish or township boundaries; enclosure awards will contain boundary descriptions in cases in which it was felt necessary to produce clarification.

Such boundaries have an intrinsic value as part of the history of the landscape; some of them are of great antiquity (Bonney 1972). Fieldwork can add a dimension to the reconstruction of old boundaries. Consider the case of certain Anglo-Saxon land books relating to Badby, Northamptonshire (Brown *et al.* 1977). Here earlier work by the editors of the county volume of the English Place-Name Society had shown that this land grant followed the boundaries of the present parishes of Badby, Newnham, Dodford and Everdon. But a fresh look at the long boundary clause in relation to the landscape itself was able to show that really quite large boundary banks still existed in places where the documents said they should; several of the tracks mentioned could still be traced as hollow ways, and their recoverable destinations indicated changes in the relative importance of different elements in the local settlement pattern; a gate mentioned in the rampart of a hillfort could be equated with a causeway still extant across the fort ditch. In all these instances the fieldwork added something new to the work, and on occasion was the decisive factor enabling the bounds to be determined. As so often in fieldwork, the possibility of matching up field names taken from a variety of sources with boundary points is essential in making sure that the interpretation being offered is the right one. In Somerset, for example, an investigator has been able to show that the *Wydencumb* of a charter of AD 936 relating to Marksbury was preserved as a tithe map field name Widecombe; *Kalwendowne* and *Colwedonne* were now Callydown; the *Maere Maede* of a charter of AD 941 relating to Corston in the same county were the Mare Meads of the tithe map (Costen 1983). But in many cases a diligent search of the field-name sources may well yield nothing. Many of the boundary points will describe topographical features — rivers, streams, areas of meadow and moorland, woods, natural ridges, valleys, hills (often with useful qualifying adjectives, bold, cloven, earthen, black). Now indoor work with maps may go a long way in solving this kind of boundary problem on general topographical grounds, but there will usually come a time when only exploration in the field will confirm or otherwise the physical reality of a purely theoretical interpretation. Such an approach is evident in the solution recently proposed for a charter of AD 956 granting an estate at Panborough in Somerset to Glastonbury Abbey, which has only six boundary points in it, none of which really survived as field or place names; yet the sort of features they referred to — a fish weir (implying a river), a piece of meadow land, a

clearing in woodland, an enclosure (for pasture) and a (peat) moor enabled a general outline of the estate to be established which could be refined by documentary work and the general drift of the local place names, as well as field checking (Hudson and Neale 1983). Note, however, that the solution arrived at indicated that most of the boundary of this estate still survived as later estate and parish boundaries. The boundaries of parishes or other land units always form a useful starting point for the solution of charter perambulations; if the ancient boundary is truly lost and there are no place- or field-name checks the chances of its recovery are slight.

A prime requirement for the study of these ancient documents is a good text, from which an accurate translation will have to be made by someone knowledgeable about Old English and aware of the specialized meanings many of the words used are now considered to have had (Hooke 1981; Gelling 1984); the well-known editions of Birch (1885–99) and Kemble (1839–48) ought if possible to be checked in the original. Many bounds in fact exist only in later medieval copies, and serious copying mistakes can produce errors, alterations and additions, some of which may be relatively easy to spot. At Marksbury, for example, the charter of AD 936 has a rabbit warren as one of the boundary points (*conigravi*); yet rabbits were not introduced into England until the twelfth century. But some copying errors can attain grotesque proportions. In the *History of Essex* published in 1768 by Philip Morant is a translation of a charter of 1046 in which Edward the Confessor gave land at Mersea to the monastery of St Ouen at Rouen. But the translator misunderstood such a basic matter as the script in which the document was written and rendered the Old English letter for 'th' (a barred 'd', ð) as 'der'. So 'dam' in the original (i.e. the) became 'deram'; to this a 'y' and a capital letter were added to produce Deramy, a totally imaginary personal name. So all the boundary points in the charter, which had the definite article in front of them in the original document, were rendered instead as Deramy's diche (instead of simply 'the ditch'), Deramy's strete, Deramy's stone and so on. Not surprisingly, this has led to certain mistaken local identifications (Crummy 1982). One should also be prepared for the unexpected — most charter boundaries proceed clockwise, but the occasional anti-clockwise set, as at Panborough or Blockley in Gloucestershire is encountered (Finberg 1957, 7); and very rarely freaks are met with in which there can be a systematic error of ninety degrees in the orientation of the directions given.

Medieval accounts and court rolls

Unless printed versions exist, these sources can take up an enormous amount of time and require a good knowledge of medieval writing and Latin, with the possibility always of unusual and difficult words and phrases; also much of the routine business listed by them will be of marginal interest to the fieldworker. But court rolls will record such matters as surnames which may be the same as those belonging to scattered settlements, as well as fines for assarts, and for offences involving such things as parks, woods and rabbit warrens. Manorial accounts may well refer to repairs to fishponds, watermills and windmills, sometimes in great detail, as well as manor houses, granges and other manorial appurtenances, and may mention industries such as lime-burning, for example. Both types of document can sometimes help in sorting out details of the tenurial basis of common field agriculture in a lordship. But at a more general level, if good runs of these documents are available, they, more than any other source, can provide a contemporary version of economic and social change which will enable the fortunes of individual settlements to be followed. A series of account rolls for the Warwickshire manor of Hatton for the period 1371–93 illustrate this. In the 1370s and 1380s they indicate crop failures and drought; the failure to harvest demesne crops in 1375; the growth in sheep rearing; the late fourteenth-century letting of land to tenants in the neighbouring village of Hampton; towards the end of the fourteenth century a declining number of virgates still tenanted; until in the middle of the fifteenth century no tenant was left and the whole manor was turned over to pasture (Dyer 1967–8). At Brookend, a manor in Oxfordshire in which Oseney Abbey had substantial interests, late fourteenth-century accounts show an uncultivated demesne, a decline in tithe and an increase in sheep farming; at the same time the court rolls indicate depopulation – tenants running away, or

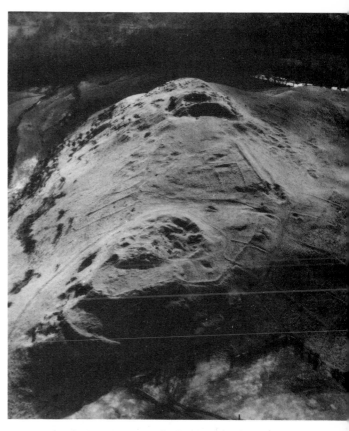

76 The hill fort and castles at Cefnllys, Powys. The later castle is the square one at the top of the photograph, nearest the river. Note also the rectangular enclosures set around the hill nearer to the camera; these may be connected with the borough which we know to have existed here in the fourteenth century. (Cambridge University collection: copyright reserved)

legally leaving the manor by paying a fine, becoming priests, or marrying outside the lordship. As a result rents were gradually reduced and tenants induced to enlarge their holdings and take on more land. This policy had no success, houses became ruinous; four farms and earthworks now remain (Lloyd 1964–5).

Narrative sources

Very occasionally the interpretation of sites represented now by earthworks will be aided by their appearance in a narrative historical source, readily available in print (e.g. those available in the famous Rolls Series published during the last century). There are occasions when such historical documents can provide the complete answer to a field problem. Fig. 76 shows a complicated set of earthworks on top of a hill at Cefnllys within a bend of the river Ieithon, near Llandrindod Wells in Powys. Field survey shows a hill fort, with the remains of two castles, the easternmost a motte with two baileys, the motte making use of a natural crag and one of the baileys part of the hill fort defences; the westernmost a square affair, cut off from the interior of the hill fort by a deep rock-cut ditch. But which castle is the earlier? Medieval chronicles record that during the wars of the mid-thirteenth century some Welshmen were able to kill the porters of this Mortimer castle and seize the constable. The Mortimers got the castle back by a treaty of 1267, but it was the understanding of the Welsh prince Llewellyn that Roger Mortimer was allowed only to repair it under the terms of the agreement. But in 1273 or 1274 we find Llewellyn writing to Henry III to complain that Roger had built a new work with a wide and deep ditch, having brought in stone and timber. The sequence and the reason for it are now clear. The square castle, with its ditch, was the new one, placed in the best position far inside the loop of the river; the motte and bailey the earlier, its site dictated by the presence of a natural outcrop of rock which in fact did not sufficiently command the ground around it, a piece of bad judgement by the Marchers that allowed the Welsh to surprise it with ease in 1260 (Brown 1972b).

7 *Envoi*

It goes without saying that fieldwork, as excavation, is useless unless published (for the practicalities of the publication process see Grinsell, Rahtz and Price Williams 1974; Barker 1977, chapter 13; Riden 1983, chapter 7). New and cheaper printing processes mean that there are now more outlets for archaeological and local historical publications than ever before, from traditional county journals and the magazines of smaller societies to the humbler bulletins of *ad hoc* research groups. The important point to make about publications of the latter type is that it is always possible for their existence to pass almost unnoticed in the ever-increasing tide of archaeological and historical literature. It is therefore vital that information about them and their contents should find its way into the bibliographical services operated by the Council for British Archaeology (p.147) so that a permanent and widely accessible reference will always be available; copies should always be sent to the national copyright agencies, such as the British Library, as well as to local libraries and record offices.

Finally, it is essential to think about the wider significance of one's fieldwork. This book has concentrated on practical matters, how to walk fields, survey earthworks, the kinds of historical documents likely to be of most immediate use to the fieldworker. It is easy to become engrossed in the details of discovery and site interpretation and to forget that the real subjects of study are not so much potsherds and field monuments as the people who were originally responsible for them; and that field survey is only one aspect of the wider study of the past and must be combined with everything else, the results of excavation and environmental studies, anthropological work and general historical studies, to have its fullest effect. So it is worth while from time to time to take a detached look at the objectives and results of field studies, not so much to put them into some sort of context but rather to provide a synthesis of all the evidence, which will offer a picture of society in the past and a reasoned account of the changes which took place within it. The work of Andrew Fleming and his colleagues on the stone boundaries on Dartmoor known as reaves has been mentioned more than once. Because the work has been pursued for some time and because the moorland terrain means that the evidence is rather more complete than in lowland situations for example, it has been possible for Fleming to make suggestions about their significance in social terms (Fleming 1984). Carbon-14 dates derived from excavation show that they were built around 1600–1200 BC, on land which was generally free of peat and on which cereals could be grown. They can be divided into three classes – groups of parallel reaves running at right angles to the contours covering large areas and ending on the upward, moorland, side on terminal reaves; single radial reaves which run beyond the parallel systems on to the moorland, marking out areas of unenclosed pasture belonging to the people who occupied the parallel systems; and contour reaves which, separated from the blocks of parallel reaves, follow the line of the higher ground. Within the parallel-reave systems are huts and enclosures of various types, sometimes single or in pairs or sometimes in larger groups, representing archaeologically the people responsible for the actual farming of the parallel systems. But the scale and regularity of the parallel systems suggests for each of the groups a high degree of planning by an overall authority; the existence of common pasture delineated by the radial reaves again implies for its successful management some kind of general oversight. But the contour reaves may indicate a level of authority operating at a wider level still, at what can be described as a regional level. These reaves behave in a way which suggests that they were later than the radial ones; in some cases they truncate the original zones of grazing delimited by them. The contour reaves can be interpreted as the imposition of a physical boundary to mark off (and on occasion to reduce in area) the grazing land belonging to the communities operating the parallel-reave systems, from the wider area beyond, subject still to intercommoning. The fact that the contour-reave system is incomplete might be taken as an indication of the collapse of the wider authority, or of its relative ineffectiveness. But the fieldwork is a key element in the line of argument which enables the existence of this authority and of the hierarchical system below it to be suggested, just as the way in which barrows, henges and other monuments cluster in certain areas in southern England has been taken to indicate the presence of powerful regional authorities there in the late Neolithic and early Bronze Age.

A rather different picture has been produced by Don Spratt's work of synthesis in north-eastern Yorkshire (Spratt 1892(b)). The collation of the observations of earlier workers and of information derived from mainly nineteenth-century barrow excavations, along with original field survey, has shown how land was utilized in the early Bronze Age and indicated something of the society that exploited it. Here blocks of land delineated by natural topographical features, streams and watersheds, can be seen to contain valley occupation sites, in places still recoverable as earthworks, as well as indicated more generally by loose finds. Each block contains a group of small cairns, some of them very numerous and running into hundreds, linked to the valleys by hollow ways. These cairnfields do not contain hut sites and can be regarded as areas used during the summer months for both arable and pasture. Higher up, the watersheds were marked by round barrows containing cremation burials in collared urns. So a scheme of land management involving permanent valley settlements and upland grazing within well-defined units of land can be put forward. But the proposed Bronze Age territories, which incidentally often have the same boundaries as the medieval townships, look very much

the same in composition and area; the barrow burials look like those of important local figures of the same rank. There is no evidence such as has been forthcoming on Dartmoor to indicate any wider overall authority.

For historic periods, enough has been said already about the way in which field surveys can act as a corrective to the bias inherent in the documentary evidence (p.111). Here the moated manorial site will be taken to illustrate the manner in which both the field and the historical sources, tending in the same direction, can be used to produce a more rounded picture of contemporary life. Much has been written about the rise of the knightly and gentry classes in the England of the thirteenth and fourteenth centuries, their ambitions and their wish to emphasize their standing by copying the manners and life style of their noble overlords. The construction of moated sites can reasonably be seen as part of this trend, as visible evidence of status and wealth in a society much given to display; but the wider political and social history of the time shows that there was a more serious purpose. Both narrative and judicial sources indicate the common use of violence and a contempt for the law widespread in all social classes, from the political factions of the nobility which could produce civil wars like the Wars of the Roses to the long-standing criminal activities of groups of robbers and murderers led by representatives of the gentry class, of which the Folvilles of Ashby Folville, who terrorized Leicestershire for sixteen years in the early fourteenth century, are the best known. Ostentatious building projects might generate a rivalry which could easily turn into violence; at Whitwick in the same county the crenellated manor of Henry de Beaumont was attacked, entered and the owners and their livestock driven away in 1331 by their local rival Sir John Talbot (Williams 1974/5). At a much lower level in the social scale the records of local judicial administration contain quite horrifying accounts of forcible entries and robberies with violence by gangs of common thieves. The Coroners' Rolls for Bedfordshire for example describe a raid in November 1269 when thieves broke down a wall of a house in Roxton and robbed it of its contents; did the same to the next house, killing the two occupants with axes; proceeded to another house, broke the door and windows and dragged the owner into the street and killed him, also severely wounding his wife, daughter and servants (Hunnisett 1961, 12). Such entries are not uncommon, and indicate that even the modest protection afforded by a rela- tively narrow moat was not something to be lightly ignored. Moats can quite rightly be seen as the markers of an aspiring social class, but also as an index of the fragility of public order; two aspects, not unconnected, of the same society.

Abbreviations

Aerial Archaeol .... Aerial Archaeology
Amateur Hist .... Amateur Historian
Antiq J .... Antiquaries Journal
Archaeol Aeliana .... Archaeologia Aeliana
Archaeol Cambrensis .... Archaeologia Cambrensis
Archaeol Cantiana .... Archaeologia Cantiana
Archaeol J .... Archaeological Journal
Bedfordshire Archaeol J .... Bedfordshire Archaeological Journal
Berkshire Archaeol J .... Berkshire Archaeological Journal
Brecon Beacons Nat Park Newslett .... Brecon Beacons National Park Newsletter
Bristol Avon Archaeol .... Bristol and Avon Archaeology
Brit Archaeol Rep (Brit Ser) .... British Archaeological Reports (British Series)
Bull Board Celtic Stud .... Bulletin of the Board of Celtic Studies
Bull Northamptonshire Fed Archaeol Socs .... Bulletin of the Northamptonshire
Federation of Archaeological Societies
CBA .... Council for British Archaeology
Cornish Archaeol .... Cornish Archaeology
Curr Archaeol .... Current Archaeology
Derbyshire Archaeol J .... Derbyshire Archaeological Journal
Durham Archaeol J .... Durham Archaeological Journal
E Anglian Archaeol .... East Anglian Archaeology
E Riding Archaeol .... East Riding Archaeologist
Econ Hist Rev .... Economic History Review
Essex Archaeol Hist .... Essex Archaeology and History
Ind Arch .... Industrial Archaeology
Ind Archaeol Rev .... Industrial Archaeology Review
J Brit Archaeol Ass .... Journal of the British Archaeological Association
J Engl Place Name Soc .... Journal of the English Place Name Society
J Field Archaeol .... Journal of Field Archaeology
Landscape Hist .... Landscape History
Lincolnshire Hist Archaeol .... Lincolnshire History and Archaeology
London Archaeol .... London Archaeologist
Medieval Archaeol .... Medieval Archaeology
Milton Keynes J Archaeol Hist .... Milton Keynes Journal of Archaeology and History
MVRG .... Medieval Village Research Group
Norfolk Archaeol .... Norfolk Archaeology
Northamptonshire Archaeol .... Northamptonshire Archaeology
Northamptonshire Past Present .... Northamptonshire Past and Present
Northern Archaeol .... Northern Archaeology

N Staffordshire J Fld Stud ....*North Staffordshire Journal of Field Studies*

Post Medieval Archaeol ....*Post Medieval Archaeology*

Proc Cambridge Antiq Soc..................*Proceedings of the Cambridge Antiquarian Society*

Proc Devon Archaeol Soc ....*Proceedings of the Devonshire Archaeological Society*

Proc Dorset Natur Hist Archaeol Soc........................*Proceedings of the Dorset Natural History and Archaeological Society*

Proc Hampshire Fld Club Archaeol Soc....................*Proceedings of the Hampshire Field Club and Archaeological Society*

Proc Prehist Soc ....*Proceedings of the Prehistoric Society*

Proc Suffolk Inst Archaeol Hist ....*Proceedings of the Suffolk Institute of Archaeology and History*

Proc Univ Bristol Spelaeol Soc ... *Proceedings of the University of Bristol Spelaeological Society*

RCAHMW .... Royal Commission on Ancient and Historical Monuments in Wales

RCHME .... Royal Commission on the Historical Monuments of England

Rec Buckinghamshire ....*Records of Buckinghamshire*

Rep Pap Lincolnshire Architect Archaeol Soc ....*Reports and Papers of the Lincolnshire Architectural and Archaeological Society*

Rep Pap Northamptonshire Antiq Soc............................... *Reports and Papers of the Northamptonshire Antiquarian Society*

Rep Trans Devonshire Ass............. *Reports and Transactions of the Devonshire Association*

Ryedale Hist .... *Ryedale Historian*

Scot Archaeol Forum.. *Scottish Archaeological Forum*

Scot Archaeol Rev... *Scottish Archaeological Review*

Somerset Archaeol Natur Hist .... *Somerset Archaeology and Natural History*

Surrey Archaeol Collect ....*Surrey Archaeological Collections*

Sussex Archaeol Collect ....*Sussex Archaeological Collections*

Trans Birmingham Warwickshire Archaeol Soc ....*Transactions of the Birmingham and Warwickshire Archaeological Society*

Trans Bristol Gloucestershire Archaeol Soc...................... *Transactions of the Bristol and Gloucestershire Archaeological Society*

Trans Caernarvonshire Hist Soc........ *Transactions of the Caernarvonshire Historical Society*

Trans Cumberland Westmorland Antiq Archaeol Soc ......*Transactions of the Cumberland and Westmorland Antiquarian and Archaeological Society*

Trans Lancashire Cheshire Antiq Soc .... *Transactions of the Lancashire and Cheshire Antiquarian Society*

Trans Leicestershire Archaeol Hist Soc ....*Transactions of the Leicestershire Archaeological and Historical Society*

Trans Radnorshire Soc............................. *Transactions of the Radnorshire Society*

Trans Thoroton Soc Nottinghamshire ...*Transactions of the Thoroton Society of Nottinghamshire*

Trans Woolhope Natur Fld Club......... *Transactions of the Woolhope Naturalists' Field Club*

Vale of Evesham Hist Soc Res Pap .... *Vale of Evesham Historical Society Research Papers*

VCH ....*The Victoria History of the Counties of England*

Wiltshire Archaeol Natur Hist Mag .... *Wiltshire Archaeological and Natural History Magazine*

World Archaeol .... *World Archaeology*

Yorkshire Archaeol J .... *Yorkshire Archaeological Journal*

Bibliography and references

Aberg, F A (ed), 1978 *Medieval moated sites*, CBA Research Report 17, London

Addyman, P V, 1964 A dark-age settlement at Maxey, Northants, *Medieval Archaeol*, 8, 20–73

Allen, M, 1984 Plumpton Roman villa, a cursory note, *Sussex Archaeol Collect*, 122, 219–20

Ashbee, P, 1981 Amesbury barrow 39: excavations 1960, *Wiltshire Archaeol Natur Hist Mag*, 74/75, 3–34

Aston, M, 1983 Deserted farmsteads on Exmoor and the lay subsidy of 1327 in West Somerset, *Somerset Archaeol Natur Hist*, 127, 71–103

Aston, M, 1985 *Interpreting the landscape. Landscape archaeology in local studies*, London

Austin, D, 1984 The castle and the landscape, *Landscape Hist*, 6, 69–81

Austin, D, and Burnham, B C, 1984 A new milling and processing complex at Dolaucothi: some recent fieldwork results, *Bull Board Celtic Stud*, 31, 304–313

Barfield, L, and Hodder, M, 1981 Birmingham's Bronze Age, *Curr Archaeol*, 78, 198–200

Barford, P M, 1984 Some possible quern quarries in the Bristol area – a preliminary survey, *Bristol Avon Archaeol*, 3, 13–17

Barker, C T, 1983 Millbarrow and Shelving Stone – finally at rest?, *Wiltshire Archaeol Natur Hist Mag*, 78, 115–17

Barker, P, 1977 *Techniques of archaeological excavation*, London

Barley, M W, 1974 *A guide to British topographical collections*, CBA, London

Barrett, J, Bradley, R, Green, M, and Lewis, B, 1981 The earlier prehistoric settlement of Cranborne Chase – the first results of current fieldwork, *Antiq J*, 61, 203–37

Bedwin, O, and Orton, C, 1984 The excavation of the eastern terminal of the Devil's Ditch (Chichester Dykes), Boxgrove, West Sussex, 1982, *Sussex Archaeol Collect*, 122, 63–74

Bell, M, 1983 Valley sediments as evidence of prehistoric land use on the South Downs, *Proc Prehist Soc*, 49, 119–50

Beresford, M W, 1963 *Lay subsidies and poll taxes*, Canterbury

Beresford, M W, and St. Joseph, J K, 1979 *Medieval England, an aerial survey*, Cambridge

Birch, W de G, 1885–1899 *Cartularium Saxonicum*, 3 vols, London

Bond, C J, 1973 The estates of Evesham Abbey: a preliminary survey of their medieval topography, *Vale Evesham Hist Soc Res Pap*, 4, 1–61

Bond, C J, 1978 The recording and survey of moats, in *Medieval moated sites* (ed F A Aberg), CBA Research Report 17, London, 14–20

Bond, C J, 1984 The Ardley charter, in Rahtz, S, and Rowley, T, *Middleton Stoney; excavation and survey in a north Oxfordshire parish*, University of Oxford Department for External Studies, 5–7

Bond D, 1982 An examination of a scheduled area and fields at Black Hill, Cerne Abbas, Dorset, *Proc Dorset Natur Hist Archaeol Soc*, 104, 67–70

Bonney, D J, 1972 Early boundaries in Wessex, in *Archaeology and the landscape* (ed P J Fowler), London, 168–86

Bonney, D J, 1980 Damage by medieval and later cultivation in Wessex, in *The past under the plough* (eds J Hinchliffe and R T Schadla-Hall), Directorate of Ancient Monuments and Historic Buildings, Department of the Environment, Occasional Paper No 3, 41–7

Bonney, D J, 1981 Megaliths near Stonehenge, *Wiltshire Archaeol Natur Hist Mag*, 76, 166–7

Borthwick, A, and Hartgroves, S, 1982 A wrongly identified barrow on Clapperton Down, Tilshead, *Wiltshire Archaeol Natur Hist Mag*, 77, 139–142

Bowen, H C, 1972 Air photography: some implications

in the south of England, in *Field survey in British archaeology* (ed E Fowler), CBA, London, 38–49

Bowen, H C, 1975 Air photography and the development of the landscape in central parts of southern England, in *Aerial reconnaissance for archaeology* (ed D R Wilson), CBA Research Report 12, London, 103–118

Bowen, H C, and Fowler, P J, 1966 Romano-British rural settlements in Dorset and Wiltshire, in *Rural settlement in Roman Britain* (ed C Thomas), CBA Research Report 7, London, 43–67

Bradley, R, 1978 *The prehistoric settlement of Britain*, London

Bradley, R, and Ellison, A, 1975 Rams Hill, *Brit Archaeol Rep (Brit Ser)*, 19

Bradley, R, Cleal, R, Gardiner, J, and Green, M, 1984 The Neolithic sequence in Cranborne Chase, in *Neolithic studies. A review of some current research* (ed R Bradley and J Gardiner), *Brit Archaeol Rep (Brit Ser)*, 133, 87–105

Bradley, R, and Holgate, R, 1984 The Neolithic sequence in the Upper Thames valley, ibid., 107–34

Briggs, S, 1984 An eroding asset – archaeology on the Beacons, *Brecon Beacons Nat Park Newslett*, 35

Britnell, R H, 1980 Abingdon: a lost Buckinghamshire hamlet, *Rec Buckinghamshire*, 22, 48–51

British Museum, 1968 *Flint implements*, London

Brown, A E (ed), 1970 Archaeology in Northamptonshire, 1969, *Bull Northamptonshire Fed Archaeol Socs*, 4, 2–48

Brown, A E, 1972a Round barrows in Herefordshire, *Trans Woolhope Natur Fld Club*, 40, 315–16

Brown, A E, 1972b The castle, borough and park of Cefnllys, *Trans Radnorshire Soc*, 42, 11–22

Brown, A E, 1975 *Archaeological sites and finds in Rutland: a preliminary list*, University of Leicester, Department of Adult Education

Brown, A E, 1978 Chester on the Water, a deserted medieval hamlet, *Northamptonshire Past Present*, 6 (1), 15–19

Brown, A E, and Sheldon, H L, 1969 Early Roman pottery factory in N London, *London Archaeol*, 3, 38–44

Brown, A E, and Taylor, C C, 1972 The gardens at Lyveden, Northamptonshire, *Archaeol J*, 129, 154–60

Brown, A E, and Taylor, C C, 1974 The earthworks of Rockingham and its neighbourhood, *Northamptonshire Archaeol*, 9, 68–79

Brown, A E, and Taylor, C C, 1975 Four deserted settlements in Northamptonshire, *Northamptonshire Past Present*, 5 (3), 178–195

Brown, A E, and Taylor, C C, 1978 Cambridgeshire earthwork surveys III, *Proc Cambridge Antiq Soc*, 69, 59–75

Brown, A E, Key, T R, and Orr, C, 1977 Some Anglo-Saxon estates and their boundaries in South West Northamptonshire, *Northamptonshire Archaeol*, 12, 155–76

Brown, A E, and Taylor, C C, 1981 Cambridgeshire earthwork surveys IV, *Proc Cambridge Antiq Soc*, 70, 113–125

Brown, A E, Key, T R, Orr, C, and Woodfield, C T P, 1981 The Stowe charter – a revision and some implications, *Northamptonshire Archaeol*, 16, 136–47

Brown, A E, and Woodfield, C, 1983 Excavations at Towcester, Northamptonshire, the Alchester road suburb, *Northamptonshire Archaeol*, 18, 43–140

Cadman, G, and Foard, G, 1984 Raunds; manorial and village origins, in *Studies in late Anglo-Saxon settlement* (ed M L Faull), Oxford, 81–100

Cameron, A, and O'Brien, C, 1981 The deserted medieval village of Thorpe in the Glebe, Nottinghamshire, *Trans Thoroton Soc Nottinghamshire*, 85, 56–67

Cantor, L, 1983 *The medieval parks of England, a gazetteer*, Department of Education, Loughborough University of Technology

Challands, A, 1982 Thoughts on the survival of pre-Iron Age landscapes in the East Midlands, *Landscape Hist*, 4, 5–9

Charge, B, 1985 Archaeology in Haverhill, *Curr Archaeol*, 98, 78–80

Cheney, R (ed), 1970 *Handbook of dates for students of English history*, Royal Historical Society

Coates, R, 1984 Coldharbour – for the last time? *Nomina*, 8, 73–8

Coles, J, 1972 *Field archaeology in Britain*, London

Collis, J, 1983 Field systems and boundaries on Shaugh Moor and at Wotter, Dartmoor, *Proc Devon Archaeol Soc*, 41, 47–61

Corney, M, 1984 Field survey of the extra-mural region, in M Fulford, *Silchester defences 1974–1980*, Britannia monograph series, 5, London

Costen, M, 1983 Stantonbury and district in the 10th century, *Bristol Avon Archaeol*, 2, 25–34

Crawford, O G S, 1960 *Archaeology in the field*, London

Crew, P, 1983 Antiquarian references to burial cairns and long cists around Snowdon, *Trans Caernarvonshire Hist Soc*, 44, 155–62

Crowther, D, 1983 Old land surfaces and modern ploughsoil: implications of recent work at Maxey, Cambs, *Scot Archaeol Rev*, 2 (1), 31–44

Crummy, N, 1982 Mersea island: the 11th-century boundaries, *Essex Archaeol Hist*, 14, 87–93

Cunliffe, B, 1973 Chalton, Hants: the evolution of a landscape, *Antiq J*, 53, 173–90

Curnow, P E, and Thompson, M W, 1969 Excavations at Richards Castle, Herefordshire, 1962–64, *J Brit Archaeol Ass*, 32, 102–27

Darvill, T, and Timby, J, 1984 Excavations at the Buckles, Frocester, 1983: first interim report, *Glevensis*, 18, 19–24

Davison, A, 1982 Petygards and the medieval hamlet of Cotes, *E Anglian Archaeol*, 14, 102–7

Davison, B K, 1972 The burghal hidage fort of *Eorpeburnan*: a suggested identification, *Medieval Archaeol*, 16, 123–27

Dibben, A A, 1971 *Title deeds*, The Historical Association

Dickinson, G C, 1969 *Maps and air photographs*, London

Dix, B, 1983 An excavation at Sharpenhoe Clappers, Streetley, Bedfordshire, *Bedfordshire Archaeol J*, 16, 65–73

Draper, J, 1982 An eighteenth-century kiln at Hole Common, Lyme Regis, Dorset, *Proc Dorset Natur Hist Archaeol Soc*, 104, 137–42

Drewett, P L, 1980 The Sussex plough damage survey, in *The past under the plough* (eds J Hinchliffe and R T Schadla-Hall), Directorate of Ancient Monuments and Historic Buildings, Department of the Environment, Occasional Paper No 3, 69–73

Drewett, P L, 1982 *The archaeology of Bullock Down, Eastbourne, East Sussex: the development of a landscape*, Sussex Archaeological Society Monograph 1

Drury, P J, 1978 *Excavations at Little Waltham 1970–71*, CBA Research Report 26, London

Dugdale, Sir W, 1817–30 *Monasticon Anglicanum* (eds J Caley, H Ellis, B Bandinel), 6 vols, London

Dyer, C, 1967–8 Population and agriculture on a Warwickshire manor in the late Middle Ages, *University of Birmingham Historical Journal*, 11, 113–27.

Dyer, C, 1982 Deserted medieval villages in the West Midlands, *Econ Hist Rev*, 35, 19–34

Eddy, M R, 1983 A Roman settlement and early medieval motte at Moot Hill, Great Driffield, North Humberside, *E Riding Archaeol*, 7, 40–51

Evans, J, and Richards, C, 1984 Ad Axium – fact or fantasy? *Bristol Avon Archaeol*, 3, 2–7

Everson, P, 1983 Aerial photography and fieldwork in north Lincolnshire, in *The impact of aerial reconnaissance on archaeology* (ed G S Maxwell), CBA Research Report 49, London, 14–26

Farrar, R, 1980 *Survey by prismatic compass*, CBA, London

Fasham, P J, 1983 Fieldwork in and around Micheldever Wood, Hampshire, 1973–80, *Proc Hampshire Fld Club Archaeol Soc*, 39, 5–45

Fasham, P J, Schadla-Hall, R T, Shennan, S J, and Bates P J, 1980 *Fieldwalking for archaeologists*, Hampshire Field Club and Archaeological Society

Faull, M L, 1978/9 Place names and past landscapes, *J Engl Place Name Soc*, 11, 24–46

Fawcett, T, 1982 John Crome and the idea of Mousehold, *Norfolk Archaeol*, 38 (2), 168–81

Fellows-Jensen, G, 1984 Place names and settlements: some problems of dating as exemplified by place names in *by*, *Nomina*, 8, 29–39

Finberg, H P R (ed), 1957, *Gloucestershire studies*, Leicester

Fleming, A, 1978 Dartmoor reaves: a nineteenth-century fiasco, *Antiquity*, 52, 16–20

Fleming, A, 1984 The prehistoric landscape of Dartmoor: wider implications, *Landscape Hist*, 6, 5–19

Fleming, A, and Ralph, N, 1982 Medieval settlement and land use on Holne Moor, Dartmoor; the landscape evidence, *Medieval Archaeol*, 26, 101–37

Foard, G, 1978 Systematic fieldwalking and the investigation of Saxon settlement in Northamptonshire, *World Archaeol*, 9 (3), 357–74

Foley, R, 1981 A model of regional archaeological structure, *Proc Prehist Soc*, 47, 1–17

Fowler, P J, 1964 Cross ridge dykes on the Ebble-Nadder ridge, *Wiltshire Archaeol Natur Hist Mag*, 59, 46–57

Fowler, P J, 1983 *The farming of prehistoric Britain*, Cambridge

Fox, Sir C, 1955 *Offa's Dyke*, Oxford

Fox, H S A, 1982 *Local history through maps*, exhibition catalogue, Department of English Local History, University of Leicester

Foxall, H D G, 1980 *Shropshire field names*, Shropshire Archaeological Society

Fryer, D H, 1961 *Surveying for archaeologists*, University of Durham

Fulford, M, 1984 *Silchester defences 1974–80*, Britannia monograph series, 5, London

Garton, D, and Beswick, P, 1983 The survey and excavation of a Neolithic settlement area at Mount Pleasant, Kenslow, 1980–83, *Derbyshire Archaeol J*, 103, 7–39

Gaffney, C, Gaffney, V, and Tingle, M, 1985 Settlement, economy or behaviour? Micro-regional land-use models and the interpretation of surface artefact patterns, in *Archaeology from the ploughsoil* (eds C Haselgrove, M Millett and I Smith), Sheffield, 95–107

Gelling, M, 1978 *Signposts to the past : place names and the history of England*, London

Gelling, M, 1984 *Place names in the landscape*, London

Gerrish, E J S, 1982 Fieldwalking in the White Peak : recent results, *Derbyshire Archaeol J*, 102, 45–48

Green, H J M, 1973 Roman Godmanchester III. Emmanuel Knoll, *Proc Cambridge Antiq Soc*, 64, 51–23

Greene, K, 1978 Apperley Dene 'Roman fortlet': a re-examination, *Archaeol Aeliana*, 5th ser, 6, 29–59

Grinsell, L; Rahtz, P, and Price Williams, D, 1974 *The preparation of archaeological reports*, London

Guido, M, and Smith, I F, 1982 Figsbury Rings: a consideration of the inner enclosure, *Wiltshire Archaeol Natur Hist Mag*, 76, 21–5

Hart, C R, 1981 *The north Derbyshire archaeological survey to AD 1500*, Chesterfield

Harvey, M, 1984 Open field structure and landholding arrangements in Eastern Yorkshire, *Transactions of the Insitute of British Geographers*, 9, 60–74

Hassall, T G; Halpin, C E, and Mellor, M, 1984 Excavations in St Ebbe's, *Oxoniensia*, 49, 153–275

Hawkins, N, 1985 Excavation of a Romano-British and later site at Black Close, Mayford, Woking, *Surrey Archaeol Collect*, 76, 69–76

Hayes, R H, and Hemingway, J E, 1984 The glass holes of Spaunton Moor, *Ryedale Hist*, 12, 5–11

Hayfield, C (ed), 1980 *Fieldwalking as a method of archaeological research*, Directorate of Ancient Monuments and Historic Buildings, Department of the Environment, Occasional Paper No 2

Hayfield, C, 1984 Wawne, East Riding of Yorkshire, a case study in settlement morphology, *Landscape Hist*, 6, 41–67

Healy, F, 1983 Are first impressions only topsoil deep? The evidence from Tattershall Thorpe, Lincolnshire, *Lithics*, 4, 28–33

Hills, M, and Liddon, A, 1981 The Vale of Belvoir survey, *Trans Thoroton Soc Nottinghamshire*, 85, 13–25

Hinchliffe, J, 1980 Effects of ploughing on archaeological sites: assessment of the problem and some suggested approaches, in *The Past under the plough* (eds J Hinchliffe and R T Schadla-Hall), Directorate of Ancient Monuments and Historic Buildings, Department of the Environment, Occasional Paper No 3, 11–17

Hingley, R, 1982 Recent discoveries of the Roman period at the Noah's Ark Inn, Frilford, South Oxfordshire, *Britannia*, 13, 305–9

Hinton, D, 1981 Hampshire's Anglo-Saxon origins, in *The archaeology of Hampshire* (eds S J Shennan and R T Schadla-Hall), Hampshire Field Club and Archaeological Society Monograph No 1, 56–65

Hollowell, R, 1971 Aerial photography and fieldwork in the Upper Nene valley, (ed A E Brown), *Bull Northamptonshire Fed Archaeol Socs*, 6

Hooke, D, 1981 *Anglo-Saxon landscapes in the West Midlands : the charter evidence*, Brit Archaeol Rep (Brit Ser), 95

Hoskins, W G, 1965 The Highland Zone in Domesday Book, in *Provincial England*, London, 15–52

Howell, C, 1983 *Land, family and inheritance in transition. Kibworth Harcourt 1280–1700*, Cambridge

Hudson, H, and Neale, F, 1983 The Panborough Saxon charter, AD 956, *Somerset Archaeol Natur Hist*, 127, 55–67

Hunn, J 1980 The earthworks of Prae Wood; an interim account, *Britannia*, 11, 21–30

Hunnisett, R F, 1961 *Bedfordshire coroners' rolls*, Bedfordshire Historical Record Society, vol 41

Hurst, H, 1977 The prehistoric occupation on Churchdown Hill, *Trans Bristol Gloucestershire Archaeol Soc*, 95, 5–10

Hurst, J G, 1984 The Wharram research project: results to 1983, *Medieval Archaeol*, 28, 77–111

Iles, R, 1984a Avon archaeology 1983, *Bristol Avon Archaeol*, 3, 54–65

Iles, R, 1984b The medieval landscape of the southern Cotswolds, *Bristol Avon Archaeol*, 3, 39–46

Iles, R, 1984c Lost paradise found, *Avon Conservation News*, 19, 3–5

Ivens, R J, 1984 Deddington castle and Odo of Bayeux, *Oxoniensia*, 49, 101–10

Jackson, D A, 1976 The excavation of Neolithic and Bronze Age sites at Aldwincle, Northants, 1967–71, *Northamptonshire Archaeol*, 11, 12–70

Jackson, D A, 1984 The excavation of a Bronze Age barrow at Earls Barton, Northants, *Northamptonshire Archaeol*, 19, 3–30

Jacobi, R M, 1981 The last hunters in Hampshire, in *The archaeology of Hampshire*, (eds S J Shennan and R T Schadla-Hall), Hampshire Field Club and Archaeological Society Monograph No 1, 10–25

Jobey, G, 1965 Stott's House 'Tumulus' and the Military Way, Walker, *Archaeol Aeliana*, 4th ser, 43, 77–85

Jobey, G, 1981 Groups of small cairns and the excavation of a cairnfield on Millstone Hill, Northumberland, *Archaeol Aeliana*, 5th ser, 9, 23–43

Jobey, G, 1984 A settlement on Boggle Hill, Thorneyburn, *Archaeol Aeliana*, 5th ser, 12, 241–2

Johnson, N, 1980 The Bolster Bank, St Agnes – a survey, *Cornish Archaeol*, 19, 77–88

Jones, M, and Dimblebey, G (eds), 1981 *The environment of man: the Iron Age to the Anglo-Saxon period*, Brit Archaeol Rep (Brit Ser), 87

Keen, L, 1983 Bindon Abbey, *Archaeol J*, 140, 58–60

Keighley, J J, 1981 The Iron Age, in *West Yorkshire, an archaeological survey to AD 1500*, vol 1 (eds M L Faull and S A Moorhouse), Wakefield, 115–135

Kelly, D B, 1971 Quarry Wood camp, Loose, a Belgic oppidum, *Archaeol Cantiana*, 86, 55–84

Kelly, R S, 1974 The probable sites of some disappeared chambered tombs in Caernarvonshire in the light of antiquarian references, *Archaeol Cambrensis*, 123, 175–79

Kemble, J M, 1839–1848 *Codex diplomaticus Aevi Saxonici*, 6 vols, London

Kemp, A, 1977 The fortification of Oxford during the Civil War, *Oxoniensia*, 42, 237–46

Kitchen, F, 1984 The *Burghal Hidage*: towards the identification of *Eorpeburnan*, *Medieval Archaeol*, 28, 175–78

Lattey, R T; Parsons, E T S, and Philip, I G, 1936 A contemporary map of the defences of Oxford in 1644, *Oxoniensia*, 1, 161–72

Leadam, I S, 1897 *The Domesday of enclosures*, Royal Historical Society

Liddle, P, 1985 *Community archaeology: a fieldworker's handbook of organization and techniques*, Leicestershire Museums, Art Galleries and Records Service

Lloyd, T H, 1964–5 Some sidelights on the deserted Oxfordshire village of Brookend, *Oxoniensia*, 29/30, 29–30

Manley, J, 1984 The late Saxon settlement of Cledemutha (Rhuddlan), Clwyd, in *Studies in late Anglo-Saxon settlement* (ed M Faull), Oxford University Department for External Studies, 55–64

Margary, I D, 1948 *Roman ways in the Weald*, London

Martin, E A, 1975 The excavation of two tumuli on Waterhall Farm, Chippenham, Cambridgeshire, 1973, *Proc Cambridgeshire Antiq Soc*, 66, 1–13

Martin, E A, 1982 When is a henge not a henge?, *Proc Suffolk Inst Archaeol Hist*, 35 (2), 141–3

Mercer, R J, 1980 The evaluation of modern ploughing threats to prehistoric sites, in *The past under the plough*, (eds J Hinchliffe and R T Schadla-Hall), Directorate of Ancient Monuments and Historic Buildings, Department of the Environment, Occasional Paper No 3, 105–8

Miles, D, 1980 Some comments on the effect of agriculture in the Upper Thames valley, *ibid*, 78–81

Miles, H, 1977 The A38 roadworks 1970–3, *Proc Devon Archaeol Soc*, 35, 43–51

Millett, M, and James, S, 1983 Excavations at Cowdery's Down, Basingstoke, Hampshire, 1978–81, *Archaeol J*, 140, 151–279

Moore, W R G, 1970 Note in Archaeology in Northamptonshire 1969 (ed A E Brown), *Bull Northamptonshire Fed Archaeol Socs*, 4, 12

Moorhouse, S A, 1981 The rural medieval landscape, in *West Yorkshire, an archaeological survey to AD 1500*, vol 3, (eds M L Faull and S A Moorhouse), Wakefield

MVRG, 1980 Research in 1980, *Medieval Village Research Group, 28th Annual Report*

Mynard, D C, 1974 Excavations at Bradwell Priory, *Milton Keynes J Archaeol Hist*, 3, 31–66

Nichols, J, 1798 *The history and antiquities of the county of Leicester. Vol 2 (2), Gartre Hundred*, London

Norman, C, 1982 Mesolithic hunter-gatherers 9000–4000 BC, in *The archaeology of Somerset* (eds M Aston and I Burrow), Somerset County Council, 15–21

O'Connell, M, and Poulton, R, 1983 An excavation at Castle Hill, Godstone, *Surrey Archaeol Collect*, 74, 213–15

Palmer, M, 1984 Industrial landscapes, in *Discovering past landscapes* (ed M Reed), London, 83–131

Palmer, R, 1983 Analysis of settlement features in the landscape of prehistoric Wessex, in *The impact of aerial reconnaissance on archaeology* (ed G S Maxwell), CBA Research Report 49, London

Palmer, R, 1984 *Danebury – an Iron Age hillfort in Hampshire: an aerial photographic interpretation of its environs*, RCHME Supplementary series, 6, London

Parker Pearson, M, 1981 A Neolithic and Bronze Age site at Churston, South Devon, *Proc Devon Archaeol Soc*, 39, 17–22

Philp, B, 1973 *Excavations in West Kent 1960–1970*, Dover

Pierpoint, S, 1981 *Prehistoric flintwork in Britain*, Highworth

Pitts, M W, 1980 *Later stone implements*, Shire Archaeology, Princes Risborough

Postles, D, 1979 Grain issues from some properties of Oseney Abbey 1274–1348, *Oxoniensia*, 44, 30–37

Powicke, F M, and Fryde, E B, 1961 *Handbook of British chronology*, Royal Historical Society

Pryor, F M M, 1983a Down the drain, *Curr Archaeol*, 87, 102–6

Pryor, F M M, 1983b South-west fen edge survey, *Northamptonshire Archaeol*, 18, 165–9

Pryor, F M M, and French, C A I, 1985 Archaeology and environment in the Lower Welland valley, vol 1, *E Anglian Archaeol*, 27

Pryor, F M M, and Palmer, R, 1980 Aerial photography and rescue archaeology – a case study, *Aerial Archaeol*, 6, 5–8

Putnam, W, 1982 Eggardon, *Proc Dorset Natur Hist Archaeol Soc*, 104, 181

Rackham, O, 1976 *Trees and woodland in the British landscape*, London

Rackham, O, 1986 *The history of the countryside*, London

Radley, J, 1968 The origin of Arbor Low henge monument, *Derbyshire Archaeol J*, 88, 100–3

Rahtz, P, 1962 Excavations at Shearplace Hill, Sydling St. Nicholas, Dorset, *Proc Prehist Soc*, 28, 289–328

Rahtz, S, and Rowley, T, 1984 *Middleton Stoney. Excavation and survey in a north Oxfordshire parish 1970–1982*, University of Oxford Department for External Studies

RCAHMW, 1976 *An inventory of the ancient monuments of Glamorgan. Vol 1, Pre-Norman. Part 2, the Iron Age and Roman occupation*, Cardiff

RCHME, 1932 *An inventory of the historical monuments in Herefordshire. Vol 2. East*, London

RCHME, 1970a *An inventory of the historical monuments in the county of Dorset. Vol 2. South-east (part 3)*, London

RCHME, 1970b *An inventory of historical monuments in the county of Dorset. Vol 3 (part 1). Central Dorset*, London

RCHME, 1972 *An inventory of historical monuments in the county of Cambridge. Vol 2. North-east Cambridgeshire*, London

RCHME, 1975a *An inventory of the historical monuments in the county of Northampton. Vol 1. Archaeological sites in north-east Northamptonshire*, London

RCHME, 1975b *An inventory of the historical monuments in the county of Dorset. Vol 5. East Dorset*, London

RCHME, 1976 *Ancient and historical monuments in the county of Gloucester. Vol 1. Iron Age and Romano-British monuments in the Gloucestershire Cotswolds*, London

RCHME, 1979a *An inventory of the historical monuments in the county of Northampton. Vol 2. Archaeological sites in central Northamptonshire*, London

RCHME, 1979b *Stonehenge and its environs: monuments and land use*, Edinburgh

RCHME, 1982 *An inventory of the historical monuments in the county of Northampton. Vol 4. Archaeological sites in south-west Northamptonshire*, London

Reed, M, 1984 Anglo-Saxon charter boundaries, in *Discovering past landscapes*, (ed M Reed), London, 261–306

Renn, D, 1964 *Potters and kilns in medieval Hertfordshire*, Hertfordshire Local History Council

Riall, N, 1983 Hungry Hill, Aldershot, a note, *Proc Hampshire Fld Club Archaeol Soc*, 39, 53–5

Richards, J C, 1978 *The archaeology of the Berkshire Downs: an introductory survey*, Berkshire Archaeological Committee, publication no 3, Reading

Riden, R, 1983 *Local history, a handbook for beginners*, London

Roberts, B K, 1982 *Village plans*, Shire Archaeology, Princes Risborough

Robinson, R S G, 1934 Flint workers and flint users in the Golden Valley, *Trans Woolhope Natur Fld Club*, 28, 54–63

Rose, E, 1982 A linear earthwork at Horning, *E Anglian Archaeol*, 14, 35–9

Scollar, I, 1975 Transformation of extreme oblique aerial photographs to maps or plans by conventional means or by computer, in *Aerial reconnaissance for archaeology* (ed D R Wilson), CBA Research Report 12, London, 52–8

Searight, S, 1984 The Mesolithic on Jura, *Curr Archaeol*, 90, 209–14

Selkirk, A, 1978 Hampstead Heath, a Mesolithic site in Greater London, *Curr Archaeol*, 60, 24–6

Shennan, S J, 1981 Settlement history in east Hampshire, in *The archaeology of Hampshire* (eds S J Shennan and R T Schadla-Hall), Hampshire Field Club and Archaeological Society Monograph No 1, 106–21

Shennan, S J, 1985 *Experiments in the collection and analysis of archaeological survey data: the East Hampshire survey*, Sheffield

Simco, A, 1984 *The Roman period*, Survey of Bedfordshire, Royal Commission on the Historical Monuments of England and Bedfordshire County Council

Simmons, B B, 1975 *The Lincolnshire Car Dyke*, Car Dyke Research Group, Publication No 1, Boston (Lincs)

Simmons, I, and Tooley, M, (eds) 1981 *The environment in British prehistory*, London

Spratt, D A, 1982a The Cleave Dyke system, *Yorkshire Archaeol J*, 54, 33–52

Spratt, D A, (ed) 1982b *Prehistoric and Roman archaeology of north-east Yorkshire*, Brit Archaeol Rep (Brit Ser), 104

Spratt, D A, 1984 Cockmoor Dykes and rabbit warrening, *Ryedale Hist*, 12, 21–30

Stafford, P, 1985 *The East Midlands in the early Middle Ages*, Leicester

Stamper, P A, 1984 Excavations on a mid-twelfth-century siege castle at Bentley, Hampshire, *Proc Hampshire Fld Club Archaeol Soc*, 40, 81–8

Steane, J M, and Dix, B, 1978 *Peopling past landscapes*, CBA, London

Stephens, W B, 1973 *Sources for English local history*, Manchester

Strong, R, 1979 *The Renaissance garden in England*, London

Tatton-Brown, T, 1983 Recent fieldwork around Canterbury, *Archaeol Cantiana*, 99, 115–32

Taylor, C C, 1975 Roman settlement in the Nene valley: the impact of recent archaeology, in *Recent work in rural archaeology* (ed P J Fowler), Bradford on Avon, 107–120

Taylor, C C, 1977 Polyfocal settlement and the English village, *Medieval Archaeol*, 21, 189–93

Taylor, C C, 1983a *Village and farmstead*, London

Taylor, C C, 1983b *The archaeology of gardens*, Shire Archaeology, Princes Risborough

Taylor, J, and Smart, R, 1983 An investigation of surface concentrations: Priddy 1977, *Bristol Avon Archaeol*, 2, 2–11

Thirsk, J, 1965 *Sources of information on population 1500–1760*, Canterbury

Thomas, A C, 1964 The henge at Castilly, Lanivet, *Cornish Archaeol*, 3, 3–12

Thomas, R, 1984 Bronze Age metalwork from the Thames at Wallingford, *Oxoniensia*, 49, 9–18

Thompson, F H (ed) 1980 *Archaeology and coastal change*, London

Thompson, M W, 1955 The excavation of two moated sites at Cherry Holt near Grantham and at Epperstone near Nottingham, *Rep Pap Lincolnshire Architect Archaeol Soc*, 6 (1), 72–82

Toms, H S, 1925 Bronze Age, or earlier, lynchets, *Proc Dorset Natur Hist Archaeol Soc*, 46, 89–100

Topping, P, 1983 Observations on the stratigraphy of early agricultural remains in the Kirknewton area of the Northumberland Cheviots, *Northern Archaeol*, 4 (1), 21–31

VCH, 1908 *The Victoria history of the county of Hereford. Vol 1*

VCH, 1932 *The Victoria history of the county of Huntingdon. Vol 2*

Wade Martins, P, 1980 Fieldwork and excavation on village sites in Launditch Hundred, Norfolk, *E Anglian Archaeol*, 10

Wadmore, B, 1920 *Earthworks of Bedfordshire*, Bedford

Walmsley, J F R, 1968 The *censarii* of Burton Abbey and the Domesday population, *N Staffordshire J Fld Stud*, 8

Weir, C, 1981 The site of the Cromwells' medieval manor house at Lambley, Nottinghamshire, *Trans Thoroton Soc Nottinghamshire*, 74, 75–7

West, J, 1962 *Village records*, London

Wheeler, R E M, 1954 *The Stanwick fortifications*, Reports of the Research Committee of the Society of Antiquaries of London, 17

Wheeler, R E M, 1956 *Archaeology from the earth*, Pelican Books, London

White, A J, 1984 Medieval fisheries in the Witham and its tributaries, *Lincolnshire Hist Archaeol*, 19, 29–35

Wilks, A, 1980 Pioneers of topographic printmaking: some comparisons, *Landscape Hist*, 2, 59–69

Williams, D, 1974–5 Fortified manor houses, *Trans Leicestershire Archaeol Hist Soc*, 50, 1–16

Williams, J, 1905 *General history of the County of Radnor*, Brecknock

Williams, J H; Shaw, M, and Denham, V, 1985 *Middle Saxon palaces at Northampton*, Northampton Development Corporation Archaeological Monograph 4

Williams Freeman, J P, 1915 *Field archaeology as illustrated by Hampshire*, London

Williamson, T M, 1984 The Roman countryside: settlement and agriculture in NW Essex, *Britannia*, 15, 225–30

Wilson, D R (ed) 1975 *Aerial reconnaissance for archaeology*, CBA Research Report 12

Wilson, D R, 1977 A first-century fort near Gosbecks, Essex, *Britannia*, 8, 185–7

Wilson, D R, 1982 *Air photo interpretation for archaeologists*, London

Wise, C, 1899 *The compotus of the manor of Kettering AD 1292*, Kettering

Woodward, P J, 1978 Flint distribution, ring ditches and Bronze Age settlement patterns in the Great Ouse Valley: the problem, a field survey technique and some preliminary results, *Archaeol J*, 135, 32–56

Wrathmell, S, 1980 Village depopulation in the 17th and 18th centuries: examples from Northumberland, *Post-medieval Archaeol*, 14, 113–26

Wymer, J, 1985 Bawsey, *Curr Archaeol*, 97, 42–5

Yarwood, R E, 1981 The natural environment, in *West Yorkshire: an archaeological survey to AD 1500* vol 1, (eds M L Faull and S A Moorhouse), Wakefield, 33–72

Appendix 1
Useful Addresses

Royal Commission on the Historical Monuments of England
(including National Monuments Record)
Fortress House
23 Savile Row
London WIX IAB

Tel: (01) 734–6010

Council for British Archaeology
112 Kennington Road
London SE11 6RE

Tel: (01) 582–0494

University of Cambridge Committee for Aerial Photography
Mond Building
Free School Lane
Cambridge CB2 3RF

Tel: (0223) 334575

Ordnance Survey
Romsey Road
Maybush
Southampton SO9 4DH

Tel: (0703) 792687

British Geological Survey
The Library
British Geological Survey
Keyworth
Nottingham NG12 5GG

Tel: (06077) 6111

Appendix 2
Field monuments in England and Wales

The aim of this section is to provide a basic check list of archaeological field monuments, with references to sources which will supply illustrations and descriptions as an aid to recognition.

Note that books and articles mentioned already in the main text are not given full bibliographical descriptions again, but simply Harvard-style references to the main bibliography on pp 139–46.

GENERAL
Reference must be made to the *Inventories* published during the last twenty years or so by the RCHME and RCAHMW, which contain a wide variety of plans of sites of all kinds as well as valuable introductory prefaces which sometimes have sections which concentrate on particular field problems; the preface to the *Inventory of historical monuments in the County of Cambridge: Vol. 1, West* (1968) for example has a section on moated sites; the volumes on *Archaeological sites in north west Northamptonshire* (1981) and *South west Northamptonshire* (1982) have sections on village earthworks and plans. Hart 1981 is a general introduction to the field archaeology of northern Derbyshire and contains plans of sites of all periods. For more specifically medieval earthworks, see the two earthwork survey volumes recently published by the Leicestershire Museums, Art Galleries and Records Service; Hartley, R F, 1983 *The medieval earthworks of Rutland* (Archaeological Report 7); idem, 1984 *The medieval earthworks of north west Leicestershire* (Archaeological Report 9).

As examples of comprehensive multi-period surveys involving not just traditional field survey but also excavation and environmental studies the reader can consult Drewett 1982 (Bullock Down, East Sussex); the field surveys cover a wide variety of sites including trackways, lynchets, marling pits, medieval farmsteads and post-medieval buildings and pits; Fasham 1983 (Micheldever Wood, Hampshire; barrows, Iron Age banjo enclosures, hollow ways, Romano-British fields, medieval wood banks); also Balaam, N D, Smith K, Wainwright, G J, 1982 The Shaugh Moor project,

Dartmoor; fourth report – environment, contexts and conclusion, *Proc Prehist Soc*, 48, 203–78.

MOUNDS

Long

Long barrows
Ashbee, P, 1970 *The earthen long barrow in Britain*, London.
RCHME, 1979 *Long barrows in Hampshire and the Isle of Wight*, London.
Bradley, R, 1983 The bank barrows and related monuments of Dorset in the light of recent fieldwork, *Proc Dorset Natur Hist Archaeol Soc*, 105, 15–20.

Long cairns
Masters, L, 1984 The Neolithic long cairns of Cumbria and Northumberland, in *Between and beyond the walls. Essays in the prehistory and history of North Britain in honour of George Jobey* (eds R Miket and C Burgess), Edinburgh, 52–73.
Herring, P, 1983 A long cairn on Catshole Tor, Altarnum, *Cornish Archaeol*, 22, 81–3.

Pillow mounds
In addition to references in the text (p 68), see RCHME, 1970 *Inventory of historical monuments in the county of Dorset. Vol 2. South east, Part 1*, 48 (Ridgway Hill, Church Knowle); Iles, R, 1983 Avon archaeology 1982, *Bristol Avon Archaeol*, 2, 53 (Dyrham Park); RCHME 1975a, 47, 92 (Fotheringhay and Stoke Doyle, Northamptonshire).

Peat stools
RCAHMW, 1956 *An inventory of the ancient monuments in Caernarvonshire. Vol 1. East*, lxxviii.

Oval

Oval barrows
Drewett, P, 1974 The excavation of an oval burial mound of the 3rd millennium at Alfriston, East Sussex, *Proc Prehist Soc*, 41, 119–52.
Berridge, G, 1983 An oval barrow (?) at Triffle, St. Germans, *Cornish Archaeol*, 22, 85–91.

Round

Round barrows
Ashbee, P, 1960 *The Bronze Age round barrow in Britain*, London.
Grinsell, L V, 1953 *Ancient burial mounds of England*, London (all periods).
Grinsell, L V, 1979 *Barrows in England and Wales*, Shire Archaeology, Princes Risborough.
Lawson, A, Martin, E A, Priddy, D, 1981 The barrows of East Anglia, *E Anglian Archaeol*, 12.

Roman barrows
Jessup, R F, 1959 Barrows and walled cemeteries in Roman Britain, *J Brit Archaeol Ass*, 22, 1–32; for a Roman barrow cemetery, Charlton, B and Mitcheson, M, 1984 The Roman cemetery at Petty Knowes, Rochester, Northumberland, *Archaeol Aeliana*, 5th ser 12, 1–31.

Cairns
RCAHMW, 1976 *An inventory of the ancient monuments in Glamorgan. Vol 1. Pre-Norman. Part I, the Stone and Bronze Ages*, 43–105.
Trahair, J E R, 1978 A survey of cairns on Bodmin Moor, *Cornish Archaeol*, 17, 3–24.

Small (clearance) cairns
Jobey, G, 1981 (Northumberland); Leech, R H, 1983 Settlements and groups of small cairns on Birkby and Birker Fells, Cumbria, *Trans Cumberland Westmorland Antiq Archaeol Soc*, 83, 15–23; Spratt 1982b, 145–56 (Yorkshire); RCAHMW, 1976 *Glamorgan. Vol 1. Part 1*, 105–20.

Mottes (see also Castles)
King, D J C, and Spurgeon, C J, 1965 The mottes in the vale of Montgomery, *Archaeol Cambrensis*, 114, 69–86.
Renn, D F, 1959 Mottes, a classification, *Antiquity*, 33, 106–12.

Windmill mounds
Posnansky, M, 1956 The Lamport post mill, *Rep Pap Northamptonshire Antiq Soc*, 33, 66–79.
Rahtz, P A, 1958 A barrow and windmill at Butcombe, North Somerset, *Proc Univ Bristol Spelaeol Soc*, 8, 89–96.
Zeepvat, R J, 1980 Post mills and archaeology, *Curr Archaeol*, 71, 375–7 (Great Linford, Buckinghamshire).

Beacons
Russell, P, 1955 Fire beacons in Devon, *Rep Trans Devonshire Ass*, 87, 250–302 (no illustrations, but descriptive list with grid references).

Tree mounds
Brown and Taylor, 1974 (Rockingham, Northamptonshire); RCHME 1970a, 481–2 (East Holme, Dorset); RCHME, 1972 *An inventory of historical monuments in the county of Dorset. Vol 4, North*, 93 (Tarrant Gunville).

Meeting place mounds
Adkins, R A, and Petchey, M R, 1984 Secklow hundred mound and other meeting place mounds in England, *Archaeol J*, 141, 243–51.

Less regular mounds and other circular features

Cooking mounds
Passmore, A H, and Pallister, J, 1967 Boiling mounds in the New Forest, *Proc Hampshire Fld Club Archaeol Soc*, 24, 14–9.
RCAHMW, 1976 *Glamorgan. Vol 1, Part 1*, 125–7.

Shell middens
Smith, P D E, Allan, J P, Hamlin, A, Orme, B, Wootton, R, 1983 The investigation of a medieval shell midden in Braunton Burrows, *Proc Devon Archaeol Soc*, 41, 75–80.

Stack stands
Ramm, H G and McDowall, R W, 1970 *Shielings and bastles*, RCHME, 56 (Cumbria and Northumberland).

Sheep shelters and sow kilns (for lime production)
Jobey, G, 1968 Excavation of cairns at Chatton, Sandyford, Northumberland, *Archaeol Aeliana*, 4th ser, 46, 44–6.

ENCLOSURES

Neolithic causewayed camps
Mercer, R, 1980 *Hambledon Hill, a Neolithic landscape*, Edinburgh.
Smith, I F, 1971 Causewayed enclosures, in *Economy and settlement in Neolithic and Early Bronze Age Britain and Europe* (ed D D A Simpson), Leicester, 89–112.

Neolithic/Bronze Age henge monuments
Atkinson, R J C, 1951 The henge monuments of Great Britain, in R J C Atkinson, C M Piggott, and N K Sandars, *Excavations at Dorchester, Oxon*, Ashmolean Museum, Oxford, 81–107, has definitions and basic descriptive list.
For plans of particular monuments, RCHME, 1975b, 113–15 (Knowlton, Dorset); RCHME 1979b, 8–18 (Stonehenge, Coneybury, Durrington Walls, Woodhenge, Wiltshire).

Neolithic cursus monuments
RCHME 1979b, 13–15 (Stonehenge cursus); RCHME 1975b, 24–5 (Dorset cursus).

Ring banks/cairns (enclosed cremation cemeteries)
RCAHMW, 1976 *Glamorgan. Vol 1, Part 1*, 43–105.

Hill forts
Hogg, A H A, 1975 *Hill forts of Britain*, London.
Forde-Johnston, J, 1976 *Hill forts of the Iron Age in England and Wales*, Liverpool.

Dyer, J, 1981 *Hill forts of England and Wales*, Shire Archaeology, Princes Risborough.
Conventionally regarded as late Bronze or Iron Age: but see Bedwin, O, 1984 The excavation of a small hill top enclosure on Court Hill, Singleton, West Sussex, 1982, *Sussex Archaeol Collect*, 122, 13–22 (early Neolithic); and Burrow, I, 1981 Hill forts after the Iron Age: the relevance of surface fieldwork, in *Hill fort studies* (ed G Guilbert), Leicester, 122–49. Dark Age forts in Wales: RCAHMW, 1964, *An inventory of ancient monuments in Caernarvonshire. Vol 3. West*, cxv-cxviii.

Roman military sites
Nash Williams, V E, 1969 *The Roman frontier in Wales* (ed M G Jarrett), Cardiff.
Collingwood, R G, and Richmond, I, 1969 *The archaeology of Roman Britain*, London, 8–94.
Frere, S S, and St. Joseph, J K, 1983 *Roman Britain from the air*, Cambridge, 19–144.
Wilson, R, 1980 *Roman forts. An illustrated introduction to the garrison posts of Roman Britain*, London.
Daniels, C M, (ed) 1978 *Handbook to the Roman Wall*, Newcastle upon Tyne.

Anglo Saxon burhs
Biddle, M, 1981 Towns, in *The archaeology of Saxon England* (ed D M Wilson), Cambridge, 99–150.
Haslam, J, 1985 *Early medieval towns in Britain*, Shire Archaeology, Princes Risborough.
Haslam, J, (ed) 1984 *Anglo Saxon towns in southern England*, Chichester.

Medieval ringworks
King, D J C, and Alcock, L, 1969 Ringworks of England and Wales, In *Chateau Gaillard. European castle studies III: conference at Battle, Sussex, September, 1966* (ed A. J. Taylor), 90–127.

Medieval moated sites
Aberg, F A, (ed), 1978; also Wilson, D, 1985 *Moated sites*, Shire Archaeology, Princes Risborough.
Spurgeon, C J, 1981 Moated sites in Wales, in *Medieval moated sites in north-west Europe* (eds F A Aberg and A E Brown), Brit Archaeol Rep (Int Ser), 121, 19–70.

Early Christian cemeteries
Thomas, A C, 1967 *Christian antiquities of Camborne*, St. Austell.

Enclosed rabbit warrens (see also pillow mounds, medieval hamlets and farms).
Tebbutt, C F, 1968 Rabbit warrens in Ashdown Forest, *Sussex Notes and Queries*, 17, 52–7.
RCHME, 1972 12 and 113 (warren for hares, Swaffham Bulbeck).

Sheepfolds
RCAHMW, 1956 *Caernarvonshire. Vol 1. East*, lxxvii.

Ramm, H, 1957 Survey of an earthwork at Kingsterndale, *Derbyshire Archaeol J*, 78, 53.

FIELDS AND SETTLEMENTS
For fields generally, Bowen, H C, 1961, *Ancient fields*, 1970, Wakefield, and Taylor, C C, 1975, *Fields in the English Landscape*, London.

PREHISTORIC AND ROMAN SETTLEMENTS AND FIELDS
Useful recent general accounts with numerous maps and plans are:
Bowen, H C, and Fowler, P J, 1978 *Early land allotment in the British Isles. A survey of recent work*, Brit Archaeol Rep (Brit Ser), 48.
Spratt, D, and Burgess, C (eds) 1985 *Upland settlement in Britain*, Brit Archaeol Rep (Brit Ser), 143.
Miles, D (ed), 1982 *The Romano British countryside*, Brit Archaeol Rep (Brit Ser), 103, (Parts i and ii).
Clack, P, and Haselgrove, S (eds), 1982 *Rural settlement in the Roman north*, CBA Group 3, Durham.
Selected accounts of particular areas and localities:

Cornwall
Brisbane, M and Clews, S, 1979 The East Moors systems, Altarnun and North Hill, Bodmin Moor, *Cornish Archaeol*, 9, 17–46.
Mercer, R, 1970 The excavation of the Bronze Age hut circle settlement, Shannon Down, St Breward, Cornwall, 1968, *Cornish Archaeol*, 9, 17–46.

Dartmoor
Collis, J R, Gilbertson, D D, Hayes, P P, and Samson, C S, 1984 The prehistoric and medieval field archaeology of Crownhill Down, Dartmoor, England, *J Field Archaeol*, 11, 1–12.
Collis, J R, 1983 Field systems and boundaries on Shaugh Moor and at Wotter, Dartmoor, *Proc Devon Archaeol Soc*, 41, 47–61.
Fox, A, 1957 Excavations on Dean Moor in the Avon Valley, *Rep Trans Devonshire Ass*, 89, 18–77 (Bronze Age).

Dorset
RCHME 1970a, 508–12 (section on settlements); 622–33 (ancient fields).

Sussex
Drewett, P, 1982 Late Bronze Age downland economy and excavations at Black Patch, East Sussex, *Proc Prehist Soc*, 48, 325–400.
Burstow, G P, and Holleyman, G A, 1957 Late Bronze Age settlement on Itford Hill, Sussex, *Proc Prehist Soc*, 23, 167–212.

Wales
Unenclosed hut settlements
RCAHMW, 1976, 72–9.

Enclosed hut groups
Smith, C A, 1977 Late prehistoric and Romano British
enclosed homesteads in north west Wales, *Archaeol
Cambrensis*, 126, 38—52.

The North
For early narrow rig, see Topping 1983.
Topping, P, 1981 The prehistoric field systems of
College Valley, North Northumberland, *Northern
Archaeol*, 2, 14—33.
Jobey, G, 1960 Some rectilinear settlements of the
Roman period in Northumberland, *Archaeol Aeliana*,
4th ser, 38, 1—38.
Jobey, G, 1962 A note on scooped enclosures, *Archaeol
Aeliana*, 4th ser, 40, 47—58.
Jobey, G, 1966 Excavations on palisaded settlements
and cairnfields at Alnham, Northumberland, *Archaeol
Aeliana*, 4th ser, 44, 5—48.
Jobey, G, 1980 Unenclosed platforms and settlements
in the late second millennium BC in Northern
Britain, *Scot Archaeol Forum*, 10, 12—26.
Coggins, D, and Fairless, K J, 1984 The Bronze Age
settlement of Bracken Rigg, Upper Teesdale, Co
Durham, *Durham Archaeol J*, 1, 5—21.
Webster, R A, 1971 A morphological study of Romano
British settlements in Westmorland, *Trans Cumberland
Westmorland Antiq Archaeol Soc*, 71, 64—74.

MEDIEVAL VILLAGES

Deserted villages
Beresford, M, and Hurst, J G, 1971 *Deserted medieval
villages*, London.
Muir, R, 1982 *The lost villages of Britain*, London.
Bond, C J, 1974 Deserted medieval villages in
Warwickshire: a review of the field evidence, *Trans
Birmingham Warwickshire Archaeol Soc*, 86, 85—112.
Cushion, B, Davison, A, Fenner, G, Goldsmith R,
Knight, J, Virgoe, N, Wade, K, and Wade Martins, P,
1982 Some deserted village sites in Norfolk, *E Anglian
Archaeol*, 14, 40—101.

Shrunken/moved villages
RCHME, 1975a 25 (Bulwick), 50—1 (Harringworth), 112
(Woodford); 1979a, 31 (Cransley), 141 (Strixton), 147
(Walgrave), all in Northamptonshire.

MEDIEVAL AND LATER HAMLETS AND FARMS
Austin, D, 1978 Excavations in Okehampton deer park,
Devon, 1976—78, *Proc Devon Archaeol Soc*, 36, 191—240.
Linehan, C D, 1966 Deserted sites and rabbit warrens
on Dartmoor, Devon, *Medieval Archaeol*, 10, 113—44.
Taylor, C C, 1968 Three deserted medieval settlements
in Whiteparish, *Wiltshire Archaeol Natur Hist Mag*, 63,
39—45.

Aston, M, 1977 Deserted settlements in Mudford
Parish, Yeovil, *Somerset Archaeol Natur Hist*, 121, 41—53.
In Dorset, RCHME 1970b, 72 (Charlton in Charminster
parish); in Northamptonshire, Brown and Taylor, 1974
(Cotton in Gretton Parish).
Hillelson, D, 1984 Barney Byre: a farmstead in Upper
Teesdale, *Durham Archaeol J*, 1, 51—61.
Lowndes, R A C, 1967 A medieval site at Millhouse in
the Lune valley, *Trans Cumberland Westmorland Antiq
Archaeol Soc*, 67, 35—50.
Gresham, C A, 1954 Platform houses in north west
Wales, *Archaeol Cambrensis*, 103, 18—53.

Shielings
Richardson, G G S, 1979 Kings Stables — an early
shieling on Black Lyne Common, Bewcastle, *Trans
Cumberland Westmorland Antiq Archaeol Soc*, 79, 19—27.
Davies, E, 1980 Hafod, hafoty and lluest: their
distribution, features and purpose, *Ceredigion*, 9, 1—41.

MEDIEVAL AND LATER FIELDS
Fowler, P J, and Thomas, A C, 1962 Arable fields of the
pre-Norman period at Gwithian, *Cornish Archaeol*, 1,
61—84.
Hall, D N, 1982 *Medieval fields*, Shire Archaeology,
Princes Risborough.
Hall, D N, 1978 Elm, a field survey, *Proc Cambridge Antiq
Soc*, 68, 21—40 (ditched strips grouped into fields).
Taylor, C C, 1966 Strip lynchets, *Antiquity*, 40, 277—84.
Robinson, D J, Salt, J, and Phillips, A D M, 1969 Strip
lynchets in the Peak District, *N Staffordshire J Fld Stud*, 9,
92—103.

Water meadows
Whitehead, B J, 1967 The management and land use of
water meadows in the Frome Valley, Dorset, *Proc
Dorset Natur Hist Archaeol Soc*, 89, 257—81.
Kerridge, E, 1953 The floating of the Wiltshire water
meadows, *Wiltshire Archaeol Natur Hist Mag*, 55, 105—18.

LINEAR EARTHWORKS

Prehistoric boundaries

Reaves
Fleming, A, 1978 and 1983 The prehistoric landscape of
Dartmoor, Part 1: south Dartmoor, *Proc Prehist Soc*, 44,
97—123; Part 2, north and east Dartmoor, ibid. 49,
195—241.

Linear boundary earthworks
RCHME, 1970a 515—19 (in Dorset); Spratt 1982 (b), 172—82
(Yorkshire).
Ford, S, 1981—2 Linear earthworks on the Berkshire
Downs, *Berkshire Archaeol J*, 71, 1—20.

Multiple dykes
In Dorset, RCHME 1975(b), 24, Gussage St. Michael; in Yorkshire, Spratt 1984; in Northamptonshire, RCHME, 1981 *An inventory of historical monuments in the county of Northampton. Vol 3. Archaeological sites in NW Northamptonshire*, 182 (Stowe Nine Churches).

Cross ridge dykes
In addition to Fowler 1964 (Wiltshire) and RCHME 1970a, 515–19 (Dorset), see Dyer, J F, 1961 Drays Ditches, Bedfordshire, and early Iron Age territorial boundaries in the eastern Chilterns, *Antiq J*, 41, 32–43.

Usually thought of as prehistoric (p75), but for a probable Romano-British one, Bedwin, O, 1980 Excavations at Chanctonbury Ring, *Britannia*, 11, 173–222; and for Dark Age ones, RCAHMW, 1976 *An inventory of the ancient monuments of Glamorgan. Vol 1, Part 3. The Early Christian period*, 5–11.

Dark Age linear earthworks
Fox, C and A, 1958 Wansdyke reconsidered, *Archaeol J*, 115, 1–48.
RCHME, 1972, 139–44 (Devil's Dyke, Cambridgeshire). Offa's Dyke: Fox 1955; but see Hill, D, 1977 Offa's and Wat's Dykes: some aspects of recent work, 1972–6, *Trans Lancashire Cheshire Antiq Soc*, 79, 21–33.

Parish boundary banks
Cornwall: Thomas, A C, 1967 *Christian antiquities of Camborne*, St. Austell, 12; Northamptonshire: Brown, A E et al 1977.

Town rings (earthworks enclosing village fields)
Hart, 1981, 132.

Belgic oppida
Rodwell, W, 1976 A gazetteer of major Belgic sites and oppida, in *Oppida in barbarian Europe* (eds B Cunliffe and T Rowley), Brit Archaeol Rep (Supp Ser), 11, 325–66.

Medieval deer park pales
Series of articles by Cantor, L M, and Wilson, J D, 1961–78, The medieval deer parks of Dorset 1–17, *Proc Dorset Natur Hist Archaeol Soc*, 83–100.

Sea banks
Taylor, A and Hall, D N, 1977 Roman bank, a medieval sea wall, *Proc Cambridge Antiq Soc*, 64, 63–8.

MEGALITHIC AND RELATED STONE MONUMENTS

Stone circles
Burl, H A W, 1976 *The stone circles of the British Isles*, London.
Burl, H A W, 1979 *Prehistoric stone circles*, Shire Archaeology, Princes Risborough.

Chambered tombs
Fairman, H W (ed), 1969 *Megalithic enquiries in the west of Britain*, Liverpool.
Daniel, G E, 1950 *The prehistoric chamber tombs of England and Wales*, Cambridge.
RCAHMW, 1976 *An inventory of the ancient monuments in Glamorgan. Vol 1. Pre-Norman. Part 1. The Stone and Bronze Ages*, 24–41.

Standing stones
Ibid. 121–4; James, D J, 1978–9 The prehistoric standing stones of Breconshire, *Brycheiniog*, 18, 9–30.

Cup marked stones
Raistrick, A, 1936 Cup and ring marked rocks of west Yorkshire, *Yorkshire Archaeol J*, 32, 33–42.
Barnatt, J and Reeder, P, 1982 Prehistoric rock art in the Peak District, *Derbyshire Archaeol J*, 102, 33–44.

Stone rows
Eogan, G, and Simmons, I G, 1964 The excavation of a stone alignment and a circle at Cholwichtown, Lee Moor, Devonshire, England, *Proc Prehist Soc*, 30, 25–38.

INDUSTRIAL SITES

This book cannot provide a comprehensive guide to the vast numbers and variety of industrial sites of all periods to be found in England and Wales; see the series *The industrial archaeology of the British Isles*, published by David and Charles, Newton Abbot. For fieldwork techniques, Pannell, J P M, 1974, *The techniques of industrial archaeology*, Newton Abbot; and Major, J K, 1975 *Fieldwork in industrial archaeology*, London; for medieval remains generally (quarries, mines etc.), Beresford and St. Joseph, 1979, 251–72. The following is a select list of mainly earthwork sites for which the techniques of recording described in this book would be appropriate.

Neolithic flint mines
Sieveking, G de G, 1979 Grimes Graves and prehistoric European flint mining, in *Subterranean Britain* (ed H Crawford), London, 1–43.

Neolithic stone axe factories
Bunch, B, and Fell, C I, 1949 A stone axe factory at Pike of Stickle, Great Langdale, Westmorland, *Proc Prehist Soc*, 15, 1–20.
RCAHMW, 1956 *Inventory of ancient monuments in Caernarvonshire. Vol 1. East*, London, xlii (Graig Lewyd).

Mining, general
Osborne, B S, 1976 Patching, scouring and commoners: the development of an early industrial landscape, *Ind Archaeol Rev*, 1 (1), 37–42 (eighteenth-century mining in south Wales).

Roman mines
Jones, G D B, 1979 The Roman evidence, in *Subterranean Britain* (ed H Crawford), London, 85–99.
Lewis, P R, and Jones, G D B, 1969 The Dolaucothi gold mines 1; the surface evidence, *Antiq J*, 49, 244–72.

Copper, zinc, lead mines, mostly post-medieval
Hughes, S J S, 1981 *The Cwmystwyth mines*, British Mining No. 17, Northern Mine Research Society, Sheffield.

Tin
Greeves, T A P, 1978 Wheal Cumpston tin mine, Holme, Devon: an historical and archaeological survey, *Rep Trans Devonshire Ass*, 110, 161–71.

Chalk
Le Gear, R F, 1983 Three agricultural chalk mines in north west Kent, *Archaeol Cantiana*, 99, 67–72 (? nineteenth century).

Quarries
Tucker, G D, 1985 Millstone making in the quarries in the Peak District of Derbyshire: the quarries and their technology, *Ind Archaeol Rev*, 8 (1), 42–58.
Stanier, P, 1985 The granite quarrying industry in Devon and Cornwall. *Ind Archaeol Rev*, 7 (2), 171–89.
Cooper, R G, 1977 Quarrying in the Hambleton Hills, North Yorkshire; the problem of identifying disused workings, *Ind Archaeol Rev*, 1 (2), 164–70.
Tucker, G and M, 1979 The slate industry of Pembrokeshire and its borders, *Ind Archaeol Rev*, 3 (2), 203–27.

The iron industry
Much about the field evidence in Cleere, H, and Crossley, D 1985 *The iron industry of the Weald*, Leicester.

Tramways
Riden, P J, 1970 Tramroads in north east Derbyshire, *Ind Archaeol Rev*, 7 (4), 373–96.

Medieval wharves, basins and canals
RCHME, 1972, 42–3 (Burwell); 89–90 (Reach).

Brick works
RCHME 1972, 74 (Horningsea), 84 (Lode), 96 (Stow cum Quy).

Salt workings
Series of articles on Iron Age, Roman and medieval salt workings in Lincolnshire Fenland, *Rep Pap Lincolnshire Architect Archaeol Soc*, 8, 1959/60, 35–112.
Thompson, M W, 1956 A group of mounds on Seasalter Level, near Whitstable, and the medieval imbanking in this area, *Archaeol Cantiana*, 70, 44–67.
de Brisay, K, 1978 The excavation of a Red Hill at Peldon, Essex, with notes on some other sites, *Antiq J*, 58, 31–60 (Iron Age).

Multi-period and multi-type industrial remains (coal mines, quarries, tramways, railways)
Everson, P E, and Welfare, H G, 1984 Surveys of industrial landscapes: Clee Hill, Shropshire and Cockfield Fell, County Durham, *RCHME Annual Review 1983–84*, 18–21.

OTHER SITES

Ponds and earthworks connected with water management

Fishponds
Roberts, B K, 1966 Medieval fishponds, *Amateur Hist*, 119–26.
Aston, M A, 1982 Aspects of fishpond construction and maintenance in the 16th and 17th centuries with particular reference to Worcestershire, in *Field and forest. An historical geography of Warwickshire and Worcestershire* (eds T R Slater and P J Jarvis), Norwich, 257–80.
For surveyed examples of medieval ponds see RCHME, 1972, *Inventory of historical monuments in the County of Dorset. Vol 4. North Dorset*, 70 (Shaftesbury); RCHME 1972, 79–80 (Anglesey Abbey, Cambridgeshire); RCHME 1975a, 31 (Collyweston); 1979a, lvii–lix (Northamptonshire generally).

Dams
RCHME 1979a, 35 (Dingley), 115 (Newton), both in Northamptonshire.

Earthworks connected with fen drainage (drains, pump sites)
RCHME, 1972, liv–lxiv and entries under Burwell, Lode, Swaffham Prior.

Dew ponds
Martin, C A, 1930 Dew ponds, *Antiquity*, 4, 347–51.
Pugsley, A J, 1939 *Dewponds in fable and fact*, London.

Duck decoys
Payne-Gallwey, R, 1886 *The book of duck decoys*, London.

Earthworks connected with woodland management
Hendry, G, Bannister, N, and Toms, J, 1984 The earthworks of an ancient woodland, *Bristol Avon Archaeol*, 3, 47–53 (wood boundary banks, 'trenches' (i.e. embanked roadways for woodland management), sawpits, charcoal hearths (p69), drains, rides, tracks).
    Also for wood banks, Fasham 1983.

Roads and tracks
General description, Taylor, C C, 1979 *Roads and tracks of Britain*, London.

Roman roads
Margary, I D, 1973 *Roman roads in Britain*, London; idem, 1948 *Roman ways in the Weald*, London.

Ordnance Survey, 1978 *Map of Roman Britain*

Fortifications (see also Enclosures and Mounds, p149).

Castles
For good earthwork plans of major castles, RCHME 1970a, 57–78 (Corfe, Dorset); RCHME, 1931 *Inventory of historical monuments in Herefordshire. Vol 3. North East*, 205–8 (Wigmore); Spurgeon, C J, 1978–9 Builth castle, *Brycheiniog*, 18, 47–59; for minor castles, RCHME 1975a, 18 (Benefield), 100 (Titchmarsh), both in Northamptonshire; Baker, D, 1982 Cainhoe castle (Bedfordshire), *Archaeol J*, 139, 32–4.

Seventeenth-century Civil War fortifications
RCHME, 1964 *Newark on Trent: the Civil War siegeworks*, London.
Kenyon, J R, 1982 The Civil War earthworks around Raglan Castle, Gwent: an aerial view, *Archaeol Cambrensis*, 131, 139–42.

Monastic sites
Knowles, D M, and St. Joseph, J K S, 1952 *Monastic sites from the air*, Cambridge.
For examples of earthwork plans: Brown and Taylor 1981 (Sawtry Abbey, Cambridgeshire); Aston, M, 1972 The earthworks of Bordesley Abbey, Redditch, Worcestershire, *Medieval Archaeol*, 16, 133–30; Taylor, C C, 1980 The surrounding earthworks, in Christie, P M, and Coad, J G, 1980 Excavations at Denny Abbey (Cambridgeshire), *Archaeol J*, 137, 142–4; Baker, E, 1982 Warden Abbey (Bedfordshire), ibid. 139, 49–51; Butler, R, 1984, Meaux Abbey (Yorkshire), ibid. 141, 46–8.

Gardens
Taylor, 1983b; Aston, M, 1978 Gardens and earthworks at Hardington and Low Ham, Somerset, *Somerset Archaeol Natur Hist*, 122, 11–28.

Index